POLLY: SEX CULTURE REVOLUTIONARY

Polly

Sex Culture Revolutionary

a memoir

Polly Whittaker

Moral Minority Press
San Francisco, California

Contents

PART TWO

Foreword

Robert Lawrence, Ed.D.

THE PRECEPT that "sex is art, and art is sex" has long colored San Francisco's tumultuous history. I'm glad to say that this concept has played a central role in my life as well. For generations, I have boldly shared with other San Franciscans a love for a city where expression is the rule.

My grandfather, a Texas-born drag queen, came to San Francisco in the 1950s to pick up movies for his "events" in the Central Valley. I wasn't aware of how cool my grandfather was or how hot San Francisco was...I just knew that sailors loved it. And, I knew sailors. It made sense, therefore, that in the late '60s I began sneaking off to Polk Street to visit The Haven or The Swallow. I won't say how old I was, but they would let me in. I would slink into the Tenderloin wearing Fredrick's Little Lies and a Jon Kloss bra. Later on when I was in the US Army on the Presidio, I lived in the Tenderloin and occasionally wore the same lingerie. Except for the loss of so many gay bars, the Tenderloin hasn't changed much in 40 years.

Herb Caen called San Francisco the "Baghdad by the Bay" for a reason. From the Devil's Triangle to the furred interior of a Pacific Heights mansion (which I petted), the draw for sailors and heartland expatriates alike was etched in the streets named after whores like Grace and Minna. It was 1975 when I heard about John Wickett's house from a friend. It was the kind of place that you had to hear about from someone. His home, the ultimate buffet flat, was the staging ground for parties that were truly legendary, including that room with furry walls. (How did he clean it? He must have vacuumed it. I never did figure out how he washed the fur sink.) Wickett collected erotic objects from around the world. He also had two stuffed tigers. (I'm sure they had an erotic function, but I never asked.) And up on top of it all was a giant marionette called "Laughing Sal" who scared the hell out of me. Needless to say, I was getting my first real introduction to life as performance, sex as art.

Then, in 1979, there was a rumor of Hep B hitting the bathhouses. I backed out of the scene and played with a close circle of friends in the East Bay, keeping sex and art alive in my enclave. By 1980, Dr. Maggie Rubinstein had pressed the big red button: there was something going on, and we didn't know how it was passed. The AIDS crisis had begun. I was suddenly afraid of kissing. Did it pass through sweat? We didn't know. The word from local health educators was that it passed through blood. But nobody knew for sure. We were all worried.... Do we have it? Do I have it? We formed chains of support taking food to friends' houses. Doing dishes. Vacuuming. Changing sheets over and over. The hospital finally formed "Ward 5-B," a euphemism for goodbye. There were countless funerals. A sign at the Rose Garden in Golden Gate Park read, "Please Do Not Dump Ashes in the Flowers."

Finally in 1984, Dianne Feinstein et al shut sex down in San Francisco. The bathhouses were closed. Any publicly advertised party, any backroom of any bar—the health department shut them all down. Sex was outlawed in San Francisco.

But you can't keep a good cock down. Sex and art in San Francisco will not be stopped. The outlaws—we simply went underground. In 1989, the underground safer-sex education program I created with my partner Carol Queen found a home in the sex clubs at 890 Folsom. These clubs were also public venues with open doors...so of course, the cops busted us. Our protest became the Coalition for Healthy Sex. We reminded the City that we were promoting safer sex, and that this little thing called the Constitution guaranteed us the right to assemble. Perhaps more importantly (from the point of view of politico egos), we simply asked them what we had to do to stay open. After all, performance art and consensual sex between adults is truly a common interest.

The result: new rules. We began to design parties where guests were met, greeted, given a guide who explained the boundaries, and taken through the space. There were endless bowls of condoms, lube, and dental dams. Hundreds of people at a time in various stages and styles of dress and undress, enjoyed quiet space to chill, loud space to spank, music (sometimes live and sometimes canned), and always a moment when the host would bring everyone together. The Queen of Heaven parties were a panoply of lust. By 1993 we moved into 848 Community Space. It was the only open-gender, pansexual, safer-sex art orgy in town.

Into this rich, sometimes contentious world came Polly Pandemonium. I was standing on Folsom Street in my booth one bright and sweaty Folsom Fair day in 1999 when down the street came what I thought was a delicious, latex-covered drag queen. It took a moment for my gender sense to realize that this towering piece of wonder had natural boobs the size of Kansas.

The other queens were looking at her with a respect that they rarely give to outsiders. Polly was charisma personified, bravado with an innocent smile. I was transfixed. In my heels, I was easily six foot nine. In chains, corset, and skirt, I strolled over to make her acquaintance. She said, "Hello, I'm Polly." And this was my first glimmer of the new San Francisco, and its new underground boss.

Polly made latex fashion outfits. She made Carol an outfit when she was Grand Marshal of the Pride Parade. We fell in love with Polly's art. Most of the latex fashion in SF at the time was black. Polly's introduction of color and costume was a radical shift—mourning was broken. And it wasn't just a color here and there. Polly threw in the whole fuckin' rainbow. She threw out the rigid noir concept and created looks that simply can't be described. A cow with functional udders? Why not! If you could think of it, Polly could and would make it. We giggled as she persuaded the community to accept whatever latex or spandex or fur covered creature walked out her door.

She was (and is) Polly Chromatic. When she went to bars, there was suddenly a bright tableau full of promising sexy joy. People at Polly's events performed as characters just by attending. Sex in her world was not a single intention, but a part of the lovely menu. Carol and I have always been proud to carry the San Francisco sex/art banner…and when Polly took it up, we cheered. She charged into San Francisco, and San Francisco followed.

Polly is a hero in one of the biggest, most beautiful art and erotic scenes in the new century. Reader, beware: your heart will open. And you will follow, too.

Introduction
Polly Whittaker

I REMEMBER the sting of my father's hand on my face. We stood for a moment, defiant, each equally appalled by the other's behavior. My hand fluttered to my cheek in disbelief. I stormed out of the room and locked myself in the bathroom, screaming the angry sobs of a defeated twelve-year-old. I smashed the cup of toothbrushes against the wall. My boot left a dent in the side of the plastic bathtub.

I eventually came out of the bathroom to a quiet house. I found my father in my room, sitting on my bed in the dark. I could see his black silhouette framed by the streetlights outside the window. He clutched my teddy bear, contemplating its chipped, black plastic eyes. When he looked up there were tears in his eyes. I had only ever seen him cry once before. His friend had died in an accident. I had seen him through the crack in my parents' bedroom door. He kicked it closed when he saw me. But this time he wasn't trying to hide. I sat down on the bed by his side and cried with him.

When I first started this book I didn't know I would write about my father. I thought I was writing the story of Kinky Salon—that quirky, erotic party I've been throwing for the last decade or so in San Francisco. I wrote the fun stories, the sexy stories. I didn't want to look at my past; I told myself it was irrelevant. I wrote for a whole year before I understood that I couldn't leave out the painful stories. I realize now that I didn't really know what this book was about until I finished it.

Would my father have approved of what I do? My guess is that it would have challenged him, but he would have tried to be supportive. I don't expect everyone to understand what I do. There are times that even I have questioned its value.

It's true: I throw parties where people have sex. We fuck all together in a big room with lots of beds. There are dark corners for shy people, and exposed areas for exhibitionists. One of the rooms is a dungeon, where we tie each other up to specially designed furniture. We call it the Fun-geon. Some people like to spank each other, or use crops and floggers. Some prefer a softer touch, with feathers or silk.

But *sex culture* isn't just about sex.

It's about art, community, spirituality, relationships, gender, family, self-expression, and—most importantly—love. Sex is a normal and healthy part of life, and sometimes it can also be difficult. Sex culture isn't going to tell you what's right or wrong, or put you in a box. It just acknowledges that human beings are *designed* to be sexual. We have a spectrum of self-expression available to us, and sexuality is part of it, whether that's exploring the smorgasbord of sexual opportunities like an adventurer, or choosing to stay celibate until you meet someone who makes your knees wobble. Sex culture supports all choices and orientations between consenting adults, and sees them as part of a complex, crosscultural, sensual, and aesthetic exploration. Sex is something to sing songs about, and write poetry to.

The superficial story of Kinky Salon would be a fun read. A sordid tell-all exposé of the interpersonal drama that inevitably comes from so many people fucking would be riveting, no doubt. A chronology of my sexual exploits might satisfy some prying curiosity seekers. Apologies in advance if that's what you were looking for. Although much of this story is set in a modern world of open relationships, sexy parties, and alternative lifestyle, that's not what it's about.

You might be surprised to hear that the majority of people who come to Kinky Salon don't come to get laid. They are *deep* hedonists. They come for the community, connection, and sense of family. Wait, now it sounds like a weird sex cult.

Fuck it; maybe it *is* a weird sex cult.

But it's *my* weird sex cult.

PART ONE

My Three Lives

I'VE BEEN born three times in this lifetime so far. The first was pretty standard. Pink and screaming I entered the world, confused, bald, and cross-eyed in Queen Charlotte's Hospital, London, England. I still have the hospital wristband they wrapped around my tiny wrist when I emerged from my mother's womb. It fits around two of my fingers. I keep it because it reminds me of where I came from. It says "Whittaker, Girl."

The only notable difference with my delivery was that my father flirted with the pretty midwife. She slipped her hand under the blankets between contractions, to feel the bump in my mother's belly. My father saw his opportunity, and his hand went up the other side, meeting hers in the middle at the top of the bump. "We must stop meeting like this," he said, with a charming smile. My mother laughed.

When I was a child, my parents recounted this story of my birth repeatedly. That might give you a little insight into my upbringing. "Daddy, Daddy, tell me the story again of how you flirted with the midwife when I was born."

BIRTH ONE. POLLY WHITTAKER. JULY 31, 1974.

Polly Whittaker is a Londoner. She says she's a nihilist, but really she's just unhappy. She grew up too fast. She gives the impression that she knows what she wants to do with her life. She's an expert at pretending she's okay. She knows how to use her sexuality to get what she wants. She knows how to use her sexuality to get in trouble. She knows how to use her sexuality to numb the pain. She dreams about being an artist, a singer, a writer, a poet, but she knows she's not good enough. She's pretty sure she's broken. She had a perfect childhood until it ended. She was a daddy's girl.

My second birth happened when I moved to San Francisco. I left behind my family name and became Polly Pandemonium. Renaming myself was a rite of passage. It felt empowering to be in charge of my identity, to create a name for myself. I took control of who I wanted to be, and in one bold gesture I wrote my own future, and left all the baggage of my past behind. I became a new person.

BIRTH TWO. POLLY PANDEMONIUM. SEPTEMBER 23, 1999.

Polly Pandemonium is a hellion and a rabble-rouser. She loves to dance on tables. She wants to collaborate. She likes to make an entrance. She forgets to listen. She throws fetish parties and makes latex clothes. San Francisco isn't just her hometown; it's her religion. She wants to talk about the sexual revolution. She's quite passionate about it. Sometimes she gets angry about the injustices of culture. She's a feminist. She writes manifestos. She doesn't want to talk about her past.

My third birth happened when I got an arc of rainbow stars tattooed on my belly. I readied myself to heal the wounds from my painful history, and stopped burying them. The stars helped. They marked the beginning of a mythic adventure of self-discovery. A spiritual awakening, I guess. I sought out mystical allies and learned about synchronicity. I met a unicorn and a guru, and I thought I could change the world.

BIRTH THREE. POLLY SUPERSTAR. SOMETIME IN 2005.

Polly Superstar is infinitely optimistic. She's intensely empathic. She believes in the power of positive thinking. She practices yoga and mindfulness. She loves deeply. She's got her eye on the big picture. She perceives patterns and meaning in everything. She sends messages back to her previous incarnations, reassuring them the future is amazing. She loves her life. She believes that humanity is on the edge of an evolutionary leap.

Four Hundred Thousand Perverts

Polly Pandemonium

I ARRIVED IN San Francisco on September 23, 1999, which by happy coincidence was the weekend of Folsom Street Fair.[i] Unlike the unfortunate tourists who stumble across this San Francisco tradition unawares, I was prepared. At the tender age of twenty-five I had already been working in the fetish industry for eight years. I'd had a string of jobs in shops and clubs in London, and designed latex clothes.

My friend Zari was the one who convinced me to come to San Francisco. We went to school together in London, and hung out in the fetish scene before she relocated to the West Coast a couple of years earlier. She's a buxom Persian princess with long, dark, but slightly disheveled hair. Her powerful maternal urge can sometimes come across as pushy, but most of the time I'm grateful for it. She knew I needed to get out of London. I had been lonely and depressed for years, and Zari suggested that making bold changes in my life might help. She had called me on my birthday, when I was wallowing in self-pity.

"Polly, *you need to get out of there,*" she had urged. "Why are you so stubborn? What's keeping you in London?" Her voice was full of concern but my chest welled in indignation at her suggestion.

"It's not like I have a choice, Zari. Who's gonna wave a magic wand for me? You think I'm choosing this?"

"Things are going really well for me here," she persisted. "Why don't you come? Take a long break? I will take care of you. You can sleep on my couch. I would love to have you here for a bit. It would be fun."

I sniffed.

"Come on, this place is amazing. I know you will love it here. You don't have to be miserable, you know. You just need to get the hell out of London. You've got some savings. *What's stopping you?*"

So I quit my job and left London. At first it was just a vacation. It didn't take me long to realize I had found my new home. I had been in San Francisco for just two days when I found myself standing in Zari's cute little apartment perched on the top of Liberty Hill, wearing a handmade, custom, silver latex minidress. Cut like something from *The Jetsons*, it had a short hoop skirt sticking out sideways, matching silver shorts, and a sculpted hood reminiscent of a '50s swimming hat. Outside the window the San Francisco skyline stretched out in front of us. I could see the Bay Bridge peeking out from a glowing downtown skyscraper.

"*Really*, Zari? This is okay?" Although my years of experience in the fetish scene meant I'd worn some outrageous outfits in unlikely situations, on this occasion I was tired, jet-lagged, and not sure I wanted to be so conspicuous.

"It's perfect. You look great," Zari nodded approvingly as she rearranged her boobs in her corset.

"But it's the middle of the day. I don't think I've ever worn latex before sunset. It's hot outside. I'm gonna sweat!" I complained.

"Just trust me. You look great. Come on, we don't want to be late." She picked up her spiked collar and fixed it around her neck.

"Late for what?"

"I signed you up for a volunteer shift. You can't go to Folsom Street Fair without volunteering," she said, and smiled. "This is how it's done in San Francisco. Trust me." I was wary.

On the way to the fair, we drove past a building with couches, lamps, and chairs exploding out of the windows. It looked like the furniture was escaping and running down the walls. I stuck my head out the window, trying to figure out what I was looking at. Then I realized it was art—a kind of art I'd never encountered.

"I know the guy who made that," Zari said nonchalantly as she sipped whisky from her flask in the back seat of the cab. She'd been telling me about the art scene in San Francisco since she first arrived here, sending me photos from the Burning Man festival,[ii] which appeared to be somewhat like Woodstock, but in the desert: naked, body-painted people dancing in the dust. She proudly showed me a photo of a long-haired hippie wearing a diaper shooting a flamethrower off the back of a pickup truck. I didn't get it.

As we got closer to Folsom Street, the population around us began to change. In front of the cab, two men with bushy beards, dressed in leather harnesses and big boots, walked confidently across the street holding hands. A gaggle of drag queens tottered by in high heels, feather boas flying. By the time we turned the corner to be dropped off, the streets jostled with thousands of colorful, sexy, outrageously dressed people. I'd seen crowds like this before, in the fetish clubs of London, but this was *outside,* in broad daylight, and it went on for *miles.*

There were spanking areas set up with people strung up on medieval-looking bondage devices, pink asses exposed to the warm sun. A tall, naked, muscular man with a dark tan and an enormous cock was masturbating on the sidewalk with an audience of people cheering him on and taking photographs.

A tall drag queen met us when we reached our destination. She wore a red PVC nurse's uniform, and a huge, white headdress, which stuck out on either side of her head like something from a classic Flemish oil painting. Her painted white face, and exaggerated eye makeup, indicated that she was one of the Sisters of Perpetual Indulgence.[iii] These nuns are a common sight in San Francisco. They do outreach, raising money for AIDS awareness and other charity organizations in the LGBTQ community. This particular Sister was leading the station where Zari had signed us up, collecting donations from people as they entered the fair.

"Oh my goddess, look at your fabulous dress. I love it!" exclaimed the Sister.

"Thanks," I answered a little sheepishly. "I made it."

"Shut up. Really? Oh, honey, it's *fabulous*." She grabbed the arm of a woman who was passing by, "Lily, check out this *amazing* dress. She made it *herself*."

The woman nodded approvingly. "Really, you made that?"

"Yeah. I'm a latex fashion designer. I just arrived here from London," I answered, a little self-conscious at suddenly being the center of attention.

"Do you have a card? I would *love* to buy a latex dress from you."

I didn't have any cards made yet, or even a phone number, but I wrote my email address on a piece of paper at least a dozen times that day.

An hour later, I skipped down the street, sweating in my latex dress, beaming a genuinely happy smile for the first time in as long as I could remember. People were so friendly and supportive. I met the buyer from the local fetish shop, and a man who wanted me to throw a party in his bar. I reeled from all the opportunities, encouraging conversations, and a sense of community I had never experienced before.

As I turned the corner, I saw a huge crowd swelling around a sound system. The beat was pounding, and an expanse of sweaty male torsos was gyrating in time to the music. Dangling from a crane above the crowd was a cage with a go-go dancer perched inside. I elbowed my way to its base.

"What do I have to do to dance up there?" I asked the operator.

"*You,*" he said, pausing to look me up and down, "just have to ask." He brought the crane back to street level and a skinny boy in black leather shorts stepped out, beaming. He held the door open for me.

"It's so fun up there!" he gushed enthusiastically as I stepped inside. The door swung closed behind me, and I lurched into the air. I sucked in a breath as vertigo swooped in and then subsided. I marveled at the extent of the street fair, seeing it stretched out into the distance: An ocean of leather boys, drag queens, and dominatrixes. I peered through the bars underneath me at the smiling faces of thousands of men cheering. It was their day to be out, open, and free. I gripped the edges of the cage and started to dance.

My love affair with San Francisco had begun.

My Unconventional Upbringing

Polly Whittaker

I T WASN'T just the lure of an exciting new city that enticed me to move to San Francisco. There was a dual action of being drawn into a new life while actively rejecting another. When I left London I called the local thrift store and asked if they had a truck. They took away everything I owned—all my books, plants, and furniture—and left two suitcases standing by the door. I wanted a clean break. To get away from the memories. Maybe I was searching for the family I'd lost. It had all been so perfect when I was young.

I was a true child of the '70s. My parents hosted fondue parties with all their swingin' friends, where they had a rule: if you lost your bread from the end of your little pronged fork while dunking it into the hot pan of sweaty melted cheese, then you had to kiss everyone at the table. At my young age this seemed innocent enough, watching as the grown-ups gave each other drunken, lingering kisses. I had a simple understanding of human relationships when I was five.

I was a weird-looking kid. I had a lazy eye, always pointing in the wrong direction. I got teased a lot. I had an operation to fix it, and had to wear an eye patch over my good eye while

I was reading, to train my bad eye to work properly. It would have been okay, kind of pirate-y, if my mum hadn't glued a piece of flowery fabric to it, to make it pretty. The patch hung from the end of the bookshelf at school for everyone to see. Kids picked it up and tried it on, laughing as they ran around while I begged to have it back.

One day at break time, when I was around seven years old, I looked out of the door to see the playground was empty. There were no fancy games to play in our playground—it was a simple yard surrounded by a high wall, made secure by jagged pieces of glass stuck into the concrete on top. A government-run institution in a dilapidated corner of London.

"Go on, Polly," muttered my teacher, impatiently. "Go out and play."

"But where is everyone?" I asked nervously as I peeked out the window.

"They're probably round the corner. Now go on. Scoot!"

The L-shaped playground meant that it was easy for kids to hide. They waited for me round the corner. The entire school, all 60 or so kids, quiet with breath held, giggled as they anticipated my arrival. I looked uneasily around. As I turned the corner the crowd descended on me, out of sight of the teachers, laughing, poking, and punching—gray, fur-trimmed parka hoods pulled up around their faces, sensible Clarks shoes making bruises in my ribs. I screamed, and ran back inside, crying, back to the teachers with the knowledge that it would probably happen again on the way home.

It didn't help that I looked like a boy. I had short hair because of my neurotic compulsion to pull it out, which started when I was a baby. My mother had long hair when she breast-fed, and I twirled it around my tiny fingers as I suckled. When she cut her hair short, she left me without my comforting habit. I remember when they took me to the hair salon. I felt grown up sitting in the big chair in front of the mirror, looking at my squinty face staring back at me. The stylist cut my hair short, to try to even out the bald patches, and gave me a wad of hair tied in a braid for me to keep.

I caught the brunt of some serious bullying before I learned to fight back. Nine years old, in a frustrated frenzy of childhood violence, I lost my sanity and my fear, and attacked my attacker, biting into his neck. My classmates looked on in horror at my bloodstained teeth, and my schoolyard status shifted.

I'm the youngest of four children. There are my two half-brothers (although we all hate that term), more than a decade older, and my sister, who arrived a year and a half before I did. My father did a terrible job of separating from his first wife, and my brothers were pretty traumatized by the divorce, but in the years following, our parents all worked hard to get along. Marjorie, my father's first wife, became like an aunt to me. My brothers moved in with us and gave my mother the affectionate nickname "Wicked." As in "Wicked Stepmother."

As the youngest child I think it's pretty common to believe your brothers and sisters are the most amazing people in the world. That's how it was for me. The pure bliss of being the baby: No responsibility, and love lavished from every direction.

My sister is incredibly talented—she can pick up a musical instrument and play it like a virtuoso after a few weeks—and she's so smart she skipped a grade in school. When I was eleven years old, and about to start a new school, I enlisted my sister to teach me how to be cool. She made homemade textbooks about how to be a rebel by not pulling up your socks, and choosing the right trousers—in 1985 she supported the wearing of drain-pipe jeans. She created mantras for me to chant while I ran around the garden and did high kicks, and she wrote poetry about being cool with little illustrations in the margins.

"Your sister is a brilliant student, so we have high hopes for you, Polly," my teacher told me when I started at the school.

"How can two such different daughters come from the same family?" she complained, once I had been at the school for a few months. My grades were always above average, but I tended to daydream. I wasn't the conscientious worker my sister was, and I only tried in classes I enjoyed. By the time I was a teenager those subjects were reduced to just one—art. I would hide in the art room at school, drawing and painting on my own.

"Why can't you be more like your sister?" was the inevitable conclusion the school came to.

Our home was modern in every sense of the word—from the bold, geometric wallpaper to the noisy, late-night parties. My parents went to discos, where my mother sported the latest trend of showing her breasts, wearing a pair of skintight blue spandex pants and a sheer fishnet top. They had a penchant for nudity, and enjoyed relaxing around the house without clothes. I made up a poem for those brisk British mornings: "Daddy has a chilly willy, which he waggles willy nilly."

My father, Rodney Whittaker, was a hot air balloon pilot, and his balloon, Serendipity, was the love of his life. He loved to fly on overcast days, exploring above the clouds in the cotton candy landscapes, alone with his gorgeous, round, majestic friend. My mother wasn't the jealous type, but everyone knew her feelings about Serendipity. She hated my father's dangerous obsession.

Before I was born there had been an accident. The balloon touched down after a short flight, and my father climbed out of the basket onto land, when a gust of warm air suddenly lifted the balloon back into the sky. Mum didn't make it out in time, and as she tried to escape, her leg got caught on a rope. Lifted with the balloon, she rose into the sky, dangling beneath the basket. By the time she struggled her foot free she had risen twenty feet in the air. She fell on her head and fractured her collarbone. She never flew again. And, as you would expect from a protective mother, she wouldn't let her children fly either.

In an attempt to encourage my mother to join him, Dad planned his balloon outings with an all-female crew.

"So, are you sure you don't want to come flying this weekend, Ros? Have you seen who's crewing for me?"

"Yes, I have, darling. You go have fun with the ladies."

"But we only have one tent."

"Well, that'll be a squeeze, won't it, Rodney?"

Assisted by this gorgeous bevy of women, he tried in vain to make Mum jealous enough to insist on coming with him. But she didn't fall for his tricks, and turned a blind eye to his philandering, knowing with confidence that he loved her, and that as long as Serendipity didn't take him, he would return home.

My mother, Rosamond Whittaker, worked as a *marriage guidance counselor*—these days she would be called a sex therapist. She was one of the best. Though it was the early days of sex therapy, her work was controversial even by today's standards. Many of the programs she put in place are still operating today, but some of her more risqué methods—like talking dirty to her clients to get them to loosen up—didn't catch on. She was a trailblazer, and she raised me to believe that sex is a natural part of being a grown-up.

I never had the "birds and the bees" talk. I didn't need to go through that awkward moment when parents consider a child old enough: "Polly, it's time to let you know that there is no Santa Claus, and penises go in vaginas to make babies." I didn't need it, because I knew it already. Not only the basics—I understood about homosexuality, two men or two women loving each other was completely normal and natural. I understood what oral sex was, but the prospect of it horrified me. I knew that sometimes men liked to dress as ladies, that some men even *were* ladies, and vice versa. The information flowed freely. The idea that sex could be dirty or bad never even crossed my mind.

At age five, I took a trip to the National Gallery in London, accompanied by my father's first wife, Marjorie—a very traditional woman, the total opposite to my mother. In the quiet whispering rooms of this classic museum of art, I faced a huge canvas of a naked woman surrounded by nymphs and satyrs, giving herself over in communion with Bacchus. I looked up and asked in a very loud voice, completely inappropriate for the surrounding volume of the gallery, but totally innocent in its tone: "IS THAT WOMAN A SEXUAL MANIAC?" Marjorie had no reply for me. She looked down, mumbled something about not wanting to miss the Constables, and pulled me quickly through to a room filled with landscapes. I went home that day and drew anatomically correct pubic hair and nipples on all my dolls, aghast at their lack of accuracy.

When I reached puberty I realized my little familial bubble was completely out of sync the rest of the world. That's when my vocation first appeared to me. Pulling our culture out of the sexual dark ages felt important, and I wanted to be part of it.

Toasters

Polly Pandemonium

SOMETIME in the first few weeks of my arrival in San Francisco, I wandered off the tourist path. With delight I explored this new city, and got lost somewhere in North Beach. Walking down the foreign street, I noticed a *toaster* glued to the wall. I stopped and looked at it for a moment, confused. Then I smiled. I took out my camera and captured it in a photograph. Questions flooded my mind. Who did this? Why? What did it mean? This small but intentional act created a ripple in my reality. An otherwise normal street suddenly became filled with the unknown. People passed by unaware. It was a *glitch in the matrix.* This toaster did not belong there. Toasters live in kitchens, not glued to the wall on bustling city streets.

If this had been in London, where viral advertising campaigns were gaining in popularity, a toaster glued to the wall would be explained in a series of ads on bus stops in the coming weeks. A hip, Scandinavian designer would be releasing a new line of toasters. Wanting to grab the public's imagination and get on the news, they enlisted a marketing company to dream up a racy, modern approach that involved some minor vandalism. When the strategy revealed itself, I would be disappointed.

I told Zari about the toaster, and in her characteristically nonchalant tone she said, "Oh yeah, that's a *Cacophony* thing." It turned out that gluing toasters to walls was not an unusual activity in San Francisco, and that the Cacophony Society, who were responsible for the toasters, were also among the founders of Burning Man.

Those toasters and the simplicity of that playful gesture moved me. In London I had spent three years studying for an art degree. I was told that if I didn't have a gallery show with people buying my paintings, then I was a failure. My teachers scoffed at my interest in fashion. This depressing perspective sapped me of all my will to create art.

In San Francisco, art was something to be lived—not a commodity with value assigned by a dollar. I started to think about what artistic gestures I could integrate into my life. I wanted to make people stop and question their reality. I was inspired.

House of Harlot Fashion Show

Polly Whittaker

IN LONDON I had become jaded. I had been a fetish scene devotee for many years, but its appeal had waned. To walk into a club and find a person suspended above the dance floor by piercing hooks through their back flesh seemed run-of-the-mill. Industrial dance music was the predictable soundscape for tedious shows where strobe lighting and lasers lit bald women wearing latex, dripping wax on each other's heads, or pressing axle grinders onto metal plates on their crotches to release a shower of sparks, arcing into the audience in fountains of light. To me it was dullsville.

I got my first job in the fetish fashion industry when I was seventeen—I worked for a classy little latex boutique in Hammersmith near my school. I loved to dress in sexy cat suits and six-inch spike heels, and to do it all day long. Most of the time the shop was quiet, but about three times a day the bell would ring, and I would put down my magazine and help elderly gentlemen squeeze into latex dresses. I would make them tea and we would try on shoes and talk about sex toys. One time I found a man old enough to be my grandfather attempting to violate a mannequin. I caught him with his hand up her latex skirt, frantically rubbing at her Barbie bump. I was titillated by his desperate display of perversion. I chastised him for his behavior and kicked him out of the store, laughing.

When I was a teenager the fetish scene felt like home to me. It was my niche, a subversive little corner where I was accepted. London is such a huge town, and meeting people can be difficult. Being part of a subculture meant that I could avoid the anonymity of normal London life.

I loved the sleek, shiny, modern clothes that were the uniform for the fetish scene. When I wore them, I became powerful and embodied. Long before *The Matrix* and its black-clad heroes, back when Lady Gaga was just a little girl, latex was a taboo fabric. Creative and rebellious, kinky fashion oozed with sex appeal.

In 1995 I saw a latex fashion show by a designer called House of Harlot.[iv] It broke all the rules—showcasing colorful, whimsical, and beautifully fitted clothes, totally different from the boring black that seemed so popular at the time. It inspired me. I yearned to be part of it.

I asked around my friends at the fetish clubs and got myself a job, working for a small latex design house. For the first time in my life I labored intensively at something to succeed. Initially I was the intern, making cups of tea for the seamstresses and sweeping the floor. Every chance I got I would practice, picking out scraps of latex from the trashcan and gluing them together, trying to perfect my technique. By the end of my first year, the designer enlisted my help to make patterns for the new collection. Sadly, the job ended suddenly when my boss's bad business practices caught up with her, but the timing was perfect. A position opened at House of Harlot, and I had the opportunity to apprentice to a master craftsman for two years before I moved to America and started my own label.

As well as making the clothes, I would often volunteer to model in House of Harlot fashion shows, just to see things from a different angle. The last show I performed in before I moved to San Francisco took place at a huge fetish club in North London called Submission. I wanted to leave on a high—to make people smile.

I wore a latex bee outfit made from stripes of yellow and black, all the way from the top of my head to the tips of my toes, complete with transparent bee wings and antennae. The slick, shiny fabric stretched over every inch of my body. A hood covered my head with three holes, one for each eye and one for my mouth, and they were my only contact with the outside world. A strategically placed window arched across my breasts, squeezed up high and held steady in a magnificent presentation of cleavage. I sweated in the hot club, and the warm layer of moisture between the costume and my skin held me tight in its amniotic bubble. I watched as the backstage area emptied, and performers strutted out onto the stage, lights flashing and strobing.

My partner that night was Katie, a coworker from House of Harlot. Her outfit was a flower, with giant inflatable yellow petals framing her face. Under the petals there were restraints for her arms. Her face looked out from a latex mask with a bouncing flower stamen dancing above her head. She looked utterly ridiculous. I giggled as I twanged her stamen back and forth. With her arms bound, she couldn't stop me.

Our musical cue came over the sound system, and Katie leaped into action. Going out on stage first, she did her best to convey an air of sweet innocence as she shuffled cutely to center stage, and although her acting was impeded by the mask, she still managed to get the emotion across with her big, dramatic eyes.

Then my cue, the sound of a buzzing bee—I buzzed back and forth across the stage, looking menacing, and zoning in on the innocent flower. She spotted me and looked nervous and vulnerable with her arms bound. I buzzed up behind her and began caressing her, grinding against her leg, touching her petals suggestively. I reached lewdly for her crotch, and then I turned her sideways and bent her over, pulling a bunch of flowers from between her legs like a magician. I sniffed the flowers and threw them into the audience. Shocked, the innocent flower had been defiled, but she excitedly came back for more.

I turned her back around to face the audience and stood behind her, caressing her petals seductively. As the music reached a climax she suddenly exploded in a shower of pink Ping-Pong balls that bounced all over the stage and into the audience. We had filled some hidden pockets in the inflatable petals with balls before the show, and then blown up the flower with air so that the petals were under pressure. When I caressed her, I sneakily unzipped them, sending the bright balls flying into the air.

"Goodbye, London," I thought to myself as I watched smiles spread across the audience. "Goodbye, you miserable hell hole."

The Moral Minority

Polly Pandemonium

MY VACATION in San Francisco officially became permanent when I set myself up making latex clothes in a studio in the Dogpatch neighborhood. These days it's becoming gentrified like every corner of San Francisco, but back in 2000 it was a desolate wasteland between Downtown and Hunters Point where the crack slingers would come to do their deals. In the dead of night I would hear cars pull into my parking lot. I'd peek through the curtains to see mysterious, dangerous looking men checking the contents of suitcases, opening them a crack on the roof of the car. This hub for crime was perilous once night fell, but during the daytime the neighborhood was bright and sunny, and the rent was cheap.

I created a glamorous storefront with big windows, pink curtains, and an entire wall of mirrors, where my clients could admire themselves in my latex creations. I slept in the back of my studio on a futon mattress on the floor, in the storage room. You wouldn't have guessed that I lived in the back, bathing with a camp shower over a bucket and eating ramen noodles. I created an air of success. I faked it. I put everything I had into the illusion that I was a successful British fashion designer. I would drink coffee and smoke cigarettes because it made me feel like a grown-up. I didn't need anyone. At twenty-six years old I thought I knew everything.

Over the years I've had some pretty weird encounters as a result of my career in latex, and I have made some people very happy. I transformed a man into a latex pony for his wedding day, so that he could pull his bride down the aisle in a carriage. I created a toe bondage system that prevented a particularly fidgety client from wriggling his toes, by connecting his feet to his genitals with a spike-lined cock ring. Moving would lacerate him, so he stayed still. A middle-aged doctor came to me wanting to be a rubber doll. Using a complex configuration of undergarments with the appropriate padding, support, and cinching, I feminized his body. Over it, I slipped a flesh-colored latex bodysuit, complete with pink nipples, red toenails, and a sculpted pussy. With his cock strapped back under layers of latex, this pussy had a hole that (to his delight) could actually be penetrated. I have fulfilled people's deepest, most secret fantasies and done so with relish.

I'm not a latex fetishist. I love the way it looks, but I'm not turned on by how it feels. Some people take their love of latex to extremes: it is so compelling they live double lives, indulging in their latex-driven fantasies in secret. Most of these fetishists are men. Women like it too, but men tend to be the ones that get weird about it. They love the way it smells and feels—given half a chance they will rub their face in it, huffing its powdery scent like a drug. I'm not an expert on psychoanalysis, but I'm sure Freud would have something to say on the matter.

I must admit I enjoyed the depravity of it all. I loved watching people come alive when given a chance to explore their fantasies, and I had a particular fondness for making bizarre inflatables, accentuating shoulders or breasts with cartoonish silhouettes or encasing people, depriving them of their senses.

I named my business The Moral Minority. Not content to simply make clothes, I wanted to promote a lifestyle of fun, playful sexuality. I filled my publicity materials with absurdist manifestos about the sexual revolution. My shows included a speech about reclaiming the word *pervert* as an act of activism, and ended with me being carried off the stage naked and screaming. I mocked everything in sight with irreverent glee. The sexual revolution was, for me at the time, an abstract concept, a gimmick. I didn't know much about the work that had gone on before me, paving the way for increasingly liberal sexual freedom in Western culture. I wasn't aware of the people who had dedicated their lives in far more culturally oppressive times to bring us to this moment.

I understand it's a pretty common folly of youth to think what you are doing is totally new, and the work of your predecessors is irrelevant. I'm ashamed to admit that I arrived in San Francisco without even realizing it had been a central hub for the sexual revolution and the gay rights movement. I lacked the critical intelligence to see myself as a product of history.

In all my naïveté, I just wanted to sell more latex clothes. I released my first collection with a fanfare and a bubblegum-pink, glossy catalog. An illustrated fairytale, with a whimsical storyline chock-full of innuendo, double entendres, and references to revolution. I starred in it as the hero who traveled across the world and overthrew a corporate monarchy to rescue a princess. With it I took a stance on morality, culture, consumerism, and the military-industrial complex. *But I was joking.* I thought it was funny.

As the years went by, my quirky promotional shtick developed into a real passion. It's a common occurrence in San Francisco to watch people superficially engage, and then develop a consuming vocation. This town has the opposite of the jaded narrative I experienced in London. People aren't afraid to get enthusiastic about their interests here.

I had found myself in the city of erotic possibility, and once I started learning its history, I couldn't help but be inspired. Even a hundred years ago during the Gold Rush, this place had a progressive outlook on sexuality, and the Barbary Coast boomed with its diverse sexual commerce.[v] It was the first city in modern America to allow the exhibition and sale of hardcore pornography, it's been a battleground for LGBTQ rights, and it was home to the sexual revolution and the free love movement. The North Beach clubs boasted a vibrant burlesque scene, and the Condor was home to another first—topless dancing. It all happened right here in this little town nestled on a tiny outcrop of land only seven miles across.

The more I learned, the more I wanted to become part of that history.

The Sexual Revolution Keeps Turning

Polly Pandemonium

W HILE WE'RE on the topic of the sexual revolution, perhaps we ought to get some perspective. Let's pull back to look at the bigger cultural picture, and put this story in context.

Did the sexual revolution begin with the counterculture of the '60s where hippies declared the right to free love, the Pill gave women control over their reproductive choices, and premarital sex became socially acceptable? Or was it earlier?

After the First World War, intellectuals and scientists in Germany started making daring statements about their discoveries in the realm of sexuality. Physician and sexologist Magnus Hirschfeld founded the Institut für Sexualwissenschaft (Institute for Sexology), where he championed gay rights, and psychoanalyst Wilhelm Reich[vi] penned *Die Sexualität im Kulturkampf (The Sexual Revolution)* where he analyzed "the crisis of the bourgeois sexual morality."

It's difficult to imagine the lives of people like Ida Craddock,[vii] the sexual activist who died for free love in 1902. The famous puritan Anthony Comstock imprisoned her for writing educational pamphlets giving instruction to couples on their wedding night. Her advice sounds quaint by today's standards:

"When you are performing your movements, do not indulge in the thought of how much you are enjoying them; rather dwell, in thought, upon how much pleasure you are giving your bride." These ideas, only suggested in the context of marriage, and never with the idea that sex should be enjoyed between *unmarried* people, were so shocking—that *married* women should actually *enjoy* sex, and not simply tolerate it for the purpose of procreation—that they depicted Ida as the devil incarnate. The judge deemed her writing so *obscene, lewd, lascivious, and dirty,* that the jurors weren't even allowed to read it. They sentenced her to hard labor—so hard, in fact, that she took her own life.

But we can go back even further—during the Age of Reason in the seventeenth century, London was a hub for social, political, and intellectual transformation, and with it came a more permissive attitude toward sexuality. Europe hadn't seen anything like it since the dawn of Christianity.[viii]

There's no doubt that since the '60s we've witnessed a rise in the cultural acceptance of more promiscuous sexual practices. The swinging sex clubs of the '70s followed the "free love" of the '60s. Then tragedy struck in the '80s with the AIDS epidemic, but the sexual revolution didn't disappear—it transformed into kink and fetish. Perhaps this was a way for us to process the immense grief and fear generated by this tragic illness.

Since the dawn of the internet, millions of couples have used hookup websites to seek out playmates. More recently, there has been a surge of interest in polyamory—the idea that you can have multiple, loving relationships at the same time—with TV shows and newspaper articles[ix] favorably depicting its utopian potential.

The reality is that the sexual revolution has already made a few rounds, and it keeps spiraling into new territory with each spin. When it comes around it's inevitably countered with a powerful puritanical backlash—with new laws to control people's behavior, or pressure exerted from religious leaders. Well-meaning, God-fearing crowds have burned books deemed inappropriate, and cheered as adulterers met their fate in flames.

Culture itself is experiencing a moral dilemma, and it's such a complicated issue that figuring it out is taking centuries. Sexuality has been our cultural blind spot, and as we evolve as a species, our relationship to it becomes clearer.

When I was at school I was taught that the mechanics of our evolutionary drive could explain why men are more promiscuous than women. Men's seed is plentiful, and they can easily deny paternity and leave a woman with the responsibility of parenting a child. Women have limited numbers of eggs, must carry the child, *and* must prove their fidelity to ensure paternal support. In other words, men can happily spray their seed like a farmer in a field, knowing that wherever it lands their genetic legacy will live on, but women need to select a man who will take care of her, so she trades her sexual fidelity for financial and material stability, thus explaining men's preoccupation with sex, and women's caution toward it.

As a young teenager obsessed with sex, this struck me as bullshit. A neat explanation designed to justify a fucked-up part of our culture. In biology class that day my young mind silently screamed: *"Men love sex because our culture gives them permission to, and women are cautious because we've been burned at the stake, stoned, shamed, and raped into submission!"*

This rather Victorian image of chaste women protecting their precious eggs is an idea that's been questioned recently. A new scientific theory suggests that in our prehistory as hunter-gatherers, we shared everything. That includes spoils from the hunt, and berries gathered from the bushes, raising children, and our choice of sexual partners. When hunter-gatherers became farmers, the concept of "ownership" was applied to all the resources we previously shared.

According to this theory, the concept of sexual control only came about 10,000 years ago, when the more complex social structures that evolved from the development of agriculture shifted our relationship to sex. That's a brief moment, in evolutionary terms. Perhaps this drastic behavioral shift from hunter-gatherer to farmer, and the change in sexual behavior that happened alongside it, explains why our culture is so confused about sex.

It could be that making sex "bad" was a necessary part of the evolution of our species. Before our brains had evolved to comprehend the philosophical, emotional, and spiritual questions that sex can trigger when it's not constrained by the natural structure of the tribe, it might have been true that we needed simple answers or there would have been chaos.

Although our attitudes in general seem to be progressing away from our prudish, sex-negative past, there's no doubt we still live in a pretty fucked-up world when it comes to sex. Even the fact that I use the word "fucked" to talk about something bad, well, that's pretty *fucked*.

One issue that seems to be a particular challenge to our generation is the idea that if a woman is promiscuous she's a slut, but if a man acts the same way, then he is revered. Many women are still held to blame when they're raped. They wore the wrong shoes, or walked down the wrong street at the wrong time. Women are still temptresses, while men try their best to control themselves in the face of such lustful seduction. This conservative attitude toward gender is a sexual double standard that harks from a bygone era of sex negativity.

In my journey as a sexually exploratory woman this is an attitude I have encountered firsthand many times. I remember a one-night stand that turned sour after I consented to anal sex. I got the lube from my side table. He was a little rough, but I liked it. Then afterward he said he was going to the bathroom, but I heard him leaving my apartment. I ran out, confused. "Where are you going?" I asked. He laughed.

"Why would I want to stay, *slut?*" he said as he slammed the door in my face.

His behavior upset me, but he didn't convince me I'd done something wrong. Is it the way my parents raised me, or is it just evolution? I did not feel ashamed.

Shame exists for a reason. It helps us identify wrong or foolish behavior. When we are raised, our parents are the litmus test we use to ascertain the things we should be ashamed of. Mine raised me without the laundry list most people carry.

We live in a shame-driven culture, and it's used as a means of social control. People stick within the limits of our preassigned moral structures because they feel bad about it if they don't. In some situations this is appropriate. You should feel bad if you kick a puppy. But experiencing shame because you ate too much chocolate, have a strong opinion, or fantasize about threesomes? Time to let that go.

Perhaps there are some people who think that shame is a good thing, that it's society's way of keeping people in check, or even God's way of communicating the wrongness of things.

Temptation is the devil causing us to stray from the path of righteousness, and shame is the signpost that leads us back to God.

Humans are adept at creating mythic structures to reinforce cultural standards. The development of religion and belief systems is a universal human trait. I'm not knocking people's beliefs—I support religious freedom—but I am fascinated that the development of these ideas fit so neatly with the cultural history of our morality. Hunter-gatherers worshipped a goddess of abundance as they grazed their way across a plentiful planet, and sexual promiscuity was socially acceptable. Farmers rejected that goddess. Instead, they worshipped a righteous God who "told" them that coveting their neighbor's property (which included their wives) was sinful, and sexual infidelity was punishable by an eternity in hell.

I don't believe in the idea of the "noble savage"—that our prehistory was some kind of perfect utopia—but when you look at these two belief systems it seems pretty clear that one is using shame to impose control over people's behavior. Is it God stepping in to save us from ourselves? Or a complex means of cultural control developed over generations to protect farmers from leaving their land to someone else's son? That's a debate that's tough to reconcile.

My First
San Francisco Parties

Polly Pandemonium

T THE VERY first party I produced in San Francisco I celebrated the best way I knew how—by dancing on the bar. I put one knee on the barstool and lifted myself up, moving drinks to either side so I could step up without kicking anything over. The bartender smiled and clapped. Neon signs for various beer brands blinked behind him. I always liked to dance at least head and shoulders above people, so dancing on the bar seemed logical. For a moment I caught my reflection in the mirror behind the bar and smiled. I had created an outfit especially. I wanted to make people laugh. So I dressed as a cow— a skintight, latex, black-and-white cow complete with oversized cartoon hooves and squirting pink nipples that projected arcs of liquid at the push of a button. I filled the pumps with White Russian cocktails and shot them directly into people's mouths.

The crowd dancing below me hooted and cheered as I danced. Maybe I'd had a little too much to drink, but I had every right to celebrate. This was the first event I had ever produced, and it rocked. I packed the bar with happy guests, and downstairs in the basement dungeon things were getting frisky. In the past I had helped out with other people's events, handed out fliers, produced fashion shows, performed, and worked the door, but this was my very first event—all mine from start to finish.

I named the party Rubbish, and I held it at a bar called Jezebel's Joint. The notorious Mike Powers, who ran a gigantic and rather seedy sex club called Power Exchange, owned the bar. That meant a green light to our kinky escapades in the basement.

I promoted the party with a spoof line of personal hygiene products called Moral Minority Facial Cum Removers. I used stickers to transform the packaging on individually wrapped wet wipes. The front featured a hilariously nasty-looking photo, showing my face covered in what looked like jizz, but was really ranch dressing. On the back it said, "Moral Minority facial cum removers are the convenient way to get rid of excess cum after sucking cock and/or muff diving." I stapled them to the flier and distributed them all over town. The flier showed a picture of a woman tied up with pink tape, in a chair looking scared, with a teddy bear holding a gun to her head. But the gun was actually a dildo. A pink teddy bear with a dildo gun and a menacing look on his face, and the word RUBBISH in big, bold, flowery pink letters.

I created latex barnyard outfits for my key members of staff. The hostess dressed as a pink pony, and the door girl was a pig, with a set of six pacifier nipples. A sign by the door read, *"For your safety please do not harass the pig."* I reveled in the absurdity of it all.

It was selfish, really; this was the kind of event I wanted to go to. I grasped at ideas, without really understanding the deeper rationale behind it, but I knew intuitively that humor was the key to making provocative events more accessible.

At the end of the night I stood on stage and made the announcement: "Thank you everyone—we are The Moral Minority, and our club is Rubbish."

Vegas, Baby!

Polly Pandemonium

I HAD BEEN in San Francisco for about nine months, making clothes and throwing parties, when an opportunity crossed my path. I was ready to take it to the next level. I received an invitation to put on a fashion show in Las Vegas. This would be the biggest show I had ever produced. They invited me to be one of the main attractions, alongside a fledgling Dita Von Teese—who has since become the most famous burlesque performer in the world. The opportunity would be huge, but I didn't have the resources I needed to pull it off. I barely managed to pay my rent, but I knew that this show could be the key to my success.

I sat in my studio gluing thousands of tiny spikes onto little squares of latex, preparing a rather intense-looking inflatable bondage device for my favorite client, Gumby the Gimp, when the phone rang.

"Hello, Moral Minority," I answered chirpily.

"Hi, is that Polly?" asked an unfamiliar voice.

"Yes. Who's this?"

"Hi there. My name is Scott. I'm a fan of your work. I was wondering if I could offer my help with anything you're up to."

"Um.... Well.... What kind of stuff can you help with?" I

said with more than a hint of sarcasm. Bear in mind that I am from London. In my world, people didn't call and offer help without an agenda. All my alarm bells went off. *What is this person trying to scam from me? Is he trying to sell me something?*

He launched into his pitch: "I'm an event producer with experience in the fetish scene. I produced an event called Ritual, and I have also done all sorts of corporate events. I can do stage shows and walk-around character troupes. I've worked with designers to create some really great fashion shows and I was wondering if you had anything coming up you needed help with. I can do everything from directing the show to providing the models and creating the lighting design."

"I'm sorry, have we met before?" I asked, confused.

"Well, not really, we met in the line for a club on Halloween. I complimented your latex outfit and asked if House of Harlot had made it. Anyway, I've been watching what you've been up to and I just wanted to introduce myself and offer my help." I recalled the incident—I was impressed that he could spot the influence of House of Harlot on my designs—but I didn't remember his face.

"Actually I've got this thing coming up in Vegas in a couple of months. It's pretty big." My words were hesitant. My mind reeled with questions. *Who is this guy? Is he qualified to help me? Can I afford to pay him?* I desperately needed the help, so I warily went over a few basic details—the party was a hotel takeover, with a big ball on the Saturday night.

"Maybe I should come over so we can talk about it?" he suggested. "It's definitely something I can help you with." We made arrangements for him to visit the next day, and I put down the phone.

"Lori," I called through to the next room. "Do you know a guy called Scott?" Lori was my assistant—I called her my Rent-A-Friend. She's a deeply loving and maternal character all wrapped up in the body of a hot, tattooed lesbian, and she was my greatest ally when I first arrived in San Francisco. She poked her head in the door, a piece of latex dangling from her hand.

"Of course. You know Scott. I'm sure you've met him."

"Where would I have met him?" The name sounded so familiar.

"Oh, I don't know. He's around. Everyone knows Scott."

"He wants to help with the show in Vegas." By the tone of my voice you could tell I wasn't convinced.

"Oh, that would be great. He's done a lot of fashion shows. He's super creative. Yeah, yeah, yeah, he would be perfect for the job," she said excitedly.

"Well, he's coming over tomorrow to talk about it. It would be so great to get help on this one."

The next day I found myself sitting opposite a man who would become the most important person in my life for the next twelve years. He was wearing a garish orange and brown plaid suit, and a straw porkpie hat. His mustache curled up at the ends like Mephistopheles. He arrived on a bicycle with deer antlers on the handlebars that jingled with little Indian bells heralding his presence. He told me his history: He had been to art school, produced club nights, and directed performances at fetish events. He coyly admitted his biggest passion was for traditional British puppetry. Eight years older than I, he seemed confident and experienced.

"So tell me about this show," he asked. I filled him in with the details, but when we got around to talking about the budget, or more accurately the lack of budget, he surprised me. "I don't need to get paid," he said. I was suspicious.

"I don't think I get it," I stammered.

"It just sounds fun. Let's take a trip to Vegas!" he said. Then for a moment he looked a little awkward. *What's his angle? Why is he being so nice to me?* I was wary, but the opportunity was too good to be missed.

We drove from San Francisco to Las Vegas in a rented fifteen-seat bus packed to capacity, with Gumby the Gimp at the wheel. The event was in a swanky hotel just off the Strip. I rented one giant party suite with a wet bar and a hot tub, and Scott decked it out with party lights and decor. The rooms I rented for the models to sleep in were in the cheap motel next door. "Fake it till you make it" was my catchphrase, and this time I had co-conspirators.

The first night we arrived I made a Nipple Patrol sign for my hat, and I went around the ball issuing tickets. *"Hello, Moral Minority Nipple Patrol here. Please can I check your nipples?"* People smiled and pulled up their shirts obligingly. I gave them a tweak. "Everything seems to be in order. Thank you for your cooperation," I said, ripping off a ticket from my book and handing it to them. It was a nipple permit, and an invitation to the afterparty in our suite, which was getting crazier by the minute. A porn star danced naked on the coffee table, and an enormous clown passed out on the floor. Guests packed the suite, and I gained a reputation: The British latex designer with the fabulous friends.

The fashion show we produced for the ball on Saturday night was an extravagant spectacle. I couldn't have done it without Scott—he provided all the models and helped me create the plot—but I was still suspicious of my collaborator, convinced that he had some sort of hidden agenda. I even cast him as a villain in the show, getting him to chase space babes with a giant ray gun. With that curly mustache he had to be a bad guy. My entrance was the grand finale of the show—I rode in on the back of a four-legged stilt walker, wearing a pastel multicolored corset with a matching hood. The crowd at the ball loved my wacky, colorful collection.

This was my audience. Rich perverts with money to burn. I got up early each morning and put on a latex dress to schmooze and measure people for custom outfits. I stayed up late to watch over the party suite, keeping the energy up and cultivating my infamy. By day one I had enough orders to cover the cost of the trip. By day three I had built a regular clientele large enough to support my fledgling business, and I went back to San Francisco with a bulging binder of orders to complete.

Mission Control

Polly Pandemonium

I CAME TO San Francisco to make latex clothes. I thought running my own business would be more fun than working for someone else. Soon after my fashion show in Vegas, I started to realize that being your own boss meant spending less time being creative and more time making spreadsheets. Everything from tracking orders to pricing materials needed a spreadsheet. While I developed a talent for wrangling information, it wasn't how I enjoyed spending my time. I sat at my desk, trying to figure out my strategy for pricing, when the phone rang.

"Happy Birthday, honey!" The person on the end of the line sounded like they had just drunk a bottle of whisky and smoked a pack of cigarettes. I knew that voice.

"Hi, Flash. It's not my birthday today!" As well as being the bartender at my favorite bar, Flash was one of those San Francisco eccentrics who made me fall in love with the place. He taught me how to shoot a gun by blasting teddy bears out of trees with an AK-47.

"Well, I'm celebrating your birthday today. Come on. Let me take you out for an adventure."

"I'm working! I can't!" I always have an intense sense of

responsibility when I'm working. I guess you could call me driven. Or maybe a workaholic.

"What have you got going on today that can't wait till tomorrow? COME ON. I'm going to Kabuki Hot Springs. COME WITH ME. Relax. You need a day off. It's your birthday! You gonna make me celebrate on my own?" We both laughed.

I contemplated this proposal as I looked around my office overflowing with papers and bright little square sticky notes. I hadn't had a day off in months.

"Okay, fine. Sure. I can take a little time today." I paused, grateful for my persuasive friend. "Thank you, Flash."

We made a quick pit stop on the way. A friend of Flash had a building over on Mission Street, which he was trying to rent out. Flash had agreed to help because his friend was stuck in New York on family business. When we arrived we found a group of bohemian-looking people standing in front of a nondescript black iron gate. Flash did some quick introductions and unlocked the gate.

"It'll just take a few minutes," he reassured me as we walked up the stairs. When we stepped into the lobby of a gigantic Victorian apartment excitement began to rise in me. The people checking it out were circus performers, and they needed high ceilings for their aerialists, so they weren't interested. But I could see its potential. It had gorgeous Victorian details: floral wainscoting, picture rails, and panel doors. There were four big rooms that made up the communal areas, and then another seven private rooms of various sizes, and a sun-drenched patio. A tech company had recently inhabited the building. It looked generic, with white walls, gray carpets, and high-speed internet access in every room. I saw it in my mind's eye flooded with

59

color and soft fabrics, and it felt like home.

My mind whirred. I could rent out the rooms to artists, writers, and craftspeople. Host sexy parties to pay the rent. Live in the back. I had no idea how, but a voice came to me, clear and simple. *"Follow your dreams and magic will happen."*

"I didn't know you were in the market for a new place, Polly," Flash said as we drove to Kabuki Hot Springs.

"Neither did I, Flash. Neither did I."

I moved in the day before New Year's Eve. I told the landlord I needed to have a couch delivered, so I got the keys a day before my lease started. Instead, I brought in DJ equipment, black-light art, and beanbags. I put neon duct tape in designs on the walls and projected black-and-white movies at exaggerated angles. I hired Scott to book the performers.

I'd always loved the Mission—its colorful bodegas, mystic murals, and abandoned theaters charmed me, and its bars and coffee shops were the liveliest in town.

It was before the days of massive online social networking, so I promoted my events the old-fashioned way, by handing out fliers wherever I went. I needed to boost attendance, so I came to a deal with a friend who hosted sexy rave parties, and combined their mailing list with mine, blending the perverts with the ravers. I gave the parties a classic funk soundtrack, completely different from the goth industrial music played at most fetish parties. The space was still very bare—I threw pillows on the carpeted floor and lit the white walls with colored bulbs.

I named the place Mission Control, but not just because of its location; the title suggests a central hub for something bigger than itself. Lofty ideals motivated me. I had a vision:

a global network of creative, sexy parties, helping to restore health and balance to culture's relationship with sexuality.

I consciously revised the strict rules of fetish parties, allowing space for more playfulness and creativity. I wanted the events to be fun and accessible, cultivating a livelier vibe than the seriousness of the leather and latex set. I experienced a sense of openness and respect in these little events that made me feel safe, and I started to think about what it all meant for the bigger picture.

I understood that sex could be about pleasure and connection. As I was becoming a woman, I was starting to appreciate its potential as a tool for personal and social transformation. The angry teenager in me, who had seen sex solely as a tool for rebellion and power, was starting to grow up.

Every teenager has a reason to be angry. For me, it was my father.

Daddy Issues

Polly Whittaker

WHEN I WAS a child my father was my hero. I always wanted to be near him. I helped him with his projects. We were always cooking together, or watching photographs develop in his makeshift darkroom, or painting folk art accessories for our canal boat. I went to him when I was hurt or sad.

I remember one time; I was no more than five years old. I stood in the kitchen of our home in London, holding my favorite rag doll. Satisfied with the integrity of the wonky nipples and labia I had drawn onto the pink fabric of her body, I had nonetheless covered them with a pretty blue dress. My hair was short and uneven, I was cross-eyed, and I wore tinted horn-rimmed glasses that protected my oversensitive eyes from the painful glare of sunlight. Absentmindedly, I sucked the index and middle fingers of my left hand. Behind me, big bay windows faced out to the garden where the cherry tree blossomed. My father sat at the kitchen table reading a newspaper. The sound of my sister practicing the piano floated in from the next room.

"Daddy, my leg is hot." I complained. My father reached down to check on my tiny leg.

"It *is* hot." He picked me up and sat me on his knee with a worried expression on his face.

"I feel funny," I complained.

"What kind of funny?" he asked, pressing the back of his hand on my forehead and looking at me with increasing concern.

"My head is funny," I replied, my bottom lip protruding.

"Yes, your head is rather funny," he said, smiling at me and ruffling my tufty hair. "Let's take a proper look at this," he said as he examined my leg again. Roasting hot from my knee downward, he pulled down my sock to discover the cause. A large, waterproof Band-Aid stuck to my shin, ballooned up, stretched out but still sticking firmly around the edges. On it was a picture of my favorite cartoon character, Mr. Bump. Featured in a series of children's books, popular in the '80s, he was one of many characters named for their principal traits. There were dozens—Mr. Messy, Mr. Grumpy, and Mr. Tall. Mr. Bump, named for his clumsiness, was a round blue figure covered in bandages. I loved him because I was clumsy too.

"Polly," said my father, "how long have you had this plaster on?" I wrinkled my forehead and glanced down guiltily.

"I don't know." I could tell I'd done something wrong, but I didn't understand what. "It's Mr. Bump."

"I can see it's Mr. Bump." He went back to my leg and softly touched the back of the Band-Aid. Clearly alarmed by its temperature, his hand pulled back quickly. "Ros! I think you'd better come look at this."

My mother came on the scene, and they inspected my leg together. She fetched some tissues, and my father slowly picked at the edge of the Band-Aid. When the first corner breached it popped a little under the pressure, and a yellowish green liquid spurted out onto my leg. It smelled rotten.

"Jesus Christ," my father said as he covered his nose and carefully peeled back the Band-Aid all the way, revealing a festering wound. Without a doubt, ground zero of my hot leg and woozy head. I don't know how long the Band-Aid was stuck there.

I remember I had been at a friend's house, playing in the garden, and I had tripped on the stone stairs leading up to the pretty spring flowerbeds. It was just a small graze, and my friend's mum went to fetch the first aid kit, returning with something so awesome my crying stopped immediately—a Mr. Bump Band-Aid. She applied it expertly to my little leg and I went back to playing happily in the garden. Not understanding the complexities of how the human body works, I didn't tell my parents about my awesome new leg accessory. And time had passed.

"Come on, we need to get this seen by a doctor," my dad said, as my mum examined me anxiously.

"I'm coming with you," she said, gathering up my sister.

My dad lifted me up onto his shoulders and held firmly onto my feet as I clung to the back of his head. I loved riding on my father's shoulders. I felt like I could be part of him. As we walked down the street, my noxious, vile leg dangled right next to his face, and he watched it with a mixture of concern and repulsion.

Luckily, we live in the age of antibiotics and infected-flesh-healing ointments. If it had been another time perhaps I would have died, or at the very least had my leg amputated. That tiny graze went septic, giving me an infection so severe that I had to treat the wound twice a day for an entire year. In the evenings it was my father's job to apply the ointment. He would lean over me with a look of concentration as he dabbed on the healing salve and redressed the wound. To this day, there is a dent in the flesh of my shin.

My biggest scar isn't on my skin, though. You can't see it like the scar on my leg. But it's there, deep inside me.

When I was nine years old my happy childhood came to an abrupt and brutal close. My father had a tumor in his brain, lodged firmly on his pituitary gland, messing with his hormones. He had been misdiagnosed for years. The doctors assumed his health problems stemmed from overindulgence in food and alcohol. He altered his lifestyle—he biked to work every day and stopped tippling his signature Glenfiddich Scotch whiskey—but it didn't make any difference. By the time they discovered the tumor he was forty-eight years old, and the prognosis was bad. A radical operation was his only hope, but his chances were decidedly slim. My family prepared for the inevitable.

Shaken apart, I shattered—all understanding of "family" and "stability" torn from me. I cracked open like a spoon hitting the top of perfectly soft-boiled egg.

Before the operation, my parents sat my sister and me down to talk. That was the first time I said goodbye to my dad. Sam wore earrings the shape of zippers, and Dad joked that the doctors would install them on his head, just like my sister had. We laughed because he laughed. He used Sam's head to mime unzipping her skull. He pulled out her brain and dropped it on the floor. Sam furrowed her brow. She'd always been a worrier. I sat on my dad's knee and he held me close, pressing my head against his chest. I said goodbye. How could I show my fear when my dad was so brave?

But he didn't die. Not that time.

From ages nine to sixteen I spent a lot of time in hospitals.

My father received the death sentence more times than I can remember—locked in a succession of operations and recovery. I would go to the hospital and sit in the bed next to him doing my homework on his bedside table. I brought him Chinese takeout to trade for his hospital food. I happily ate his mashed potatoes and gravy while he munched on spring rolls. I drew pictures and put them up on his walls to cheer him up. I would befriend his neighbors and then watch them die. His terminal diagnosis always put him in the most tragic corners of the hospitals. Crying relatives and gray-faced doctors. Death surrounded me.

Then he would recover and come home—hope would return. He had bought himself another six months. We rallied around him, grateful for the reprieve, but with tension growing each time, stretching us thinner and thinner. The latter years of my childhood, as I became a woman, were a never-ending cycle of anger, fear, sadness, grief, bravery, and survival. Defying all odds, my father lived for seven years after his first terminal diagnosis. The doctors said he was a miracle in action.

From the moment the doctors found that tumor in my father's head, my childhood ended. There was no room for me to be a normal kid anymore. There was always another treatment, and another slim hope we shouldn't believe in. My teachers at school knew. My friends' parents knew. A cloud of pity buffered me. It made me angry.

When I was eleven years old I started a new school. I remember looking around the site at the gymnasium and the tennis courts. There was an ancient vaulted assembly hall with the names of honored students from eons past etched on plaques. The library was vast and silent, with students dressed in identical uniforms studiously scribbling in books. As we entered the central courtyard at the heart of the institution I remember asking the teacher who was showing us around, "Excuse me, where is the playground?"

"We don't have a playground," she replied.

"Can we just play here in the courtyard?" I asked, innocently.

"No. The courtyard is a place for quiet conversations only." She paused and looked at me sternly. "Young lady, your time for playing is over."

I was mortified. No playground? No playing? What kind of monstrous place was this? I went home and complained to my mother, but she repeated the crushingly depressing reality the teacher had said: I was a grown up now, going to *big* school. Games and toys were a thing of the past. There would be no more play.

Life Is Just a Game

Polly Pandemonium

ONE EVENING, about one year into my residence at Mission Control, I was showing a prospective tenant around the space. She looked glum. "I don't think it's big enough," she admitted, shaking her head to the empty room.

"Well, I do have another room available," I said, "but there's someone staying in there at the moment." Scott had been staying with me for a few weeks. We had continued to work together since Vegas, producing events and shows together, and I felt like I owed him a favor. I had two rooms open at Mission Control—keeping all seven rooms rented was proving to be a challenge. Artists came and went at an alarmingly fast pace, and most were pretty difficult to deal with. My parties weren't big enough to support the space on their own, so renting out rooms seemed like the only option. But it was silly to let a room lie fallow when a friend needed a place to stay, and he had helped me out so much. I was glad to be able to offer him a room for a month or so while he got himself on his feet.

"I don't want to be any trouble," she said. I was pretty sure that either way she wouldn't take the room. She had a pained expression on her face when I explained the nature of the sexy parties I hosted there—that people dressed up in leather and tied each other to the furniture. She clearly wasn't into the idea. But I was desperate.

"No trouble at all. I'm sure he won't mind us poking our heads in the door. It's really a much nicer room." We walked down the hallway and paused outside the door as I knocked.

"Hello? Scott? Are you in there?" No answer. We walked into the room and tried to ignore the fact that, from floor to ceiling, complex notes and diagrams covered the walls, looking as if a crazy person had drawn them. I showed her the big windows that opened out to the patio and talked about how lovely and light it gets in the summer. She glanced nervously around her.

On the floor a large altar took up half the room. The cloth at the bottom had a geometric mandala painted on it, and laying neatly on top were a wide variety of objects: crystals, blue finger puppets of Hindu deities, busty action figures, Pokemon cards, a bit of bark, wilting flowers, a little plastic alien, feathers, candles, photos from magazines, a plastic devil head, and stickers I recognized from a vending machine outside a dollar store on Mission Street. In its center rested a pyramid, and at the top sat a little round earth made of foam—possibly one of those stress-relieving hand exercisers but repurposed as a centerpiece to the strangest, most colorful altar I had ever seen. In the corner of the room was a very neat sleeping bag laid out with the zipper open enough to see that nestled inside was a little toy chameleon.

"The serial killer will clear out by the time you move in, don't worry," I quipped, trying to make light of the strangeness of the situation. She made her excuses and shuffled out of the room saying she'd call. I knew she wouldn't. I said goodbye, and I watched her walk down the stairs. I stood for a moment outside his room contemplating whether I should go and take a closer look. I was so intrigued. Eventually I stepped back inside sheepishly, hoping that he didn't suddenly return and catch me in the act. I walked up to the wall full of scribblings and notes, images, and formulas. It made no sense to me, but I found something about it compelling.

There were drawings of people standing in infinity symbols. Rainbow-colored images pointing toward a computer screen. Network diagrams with arrows and indecipherable symbols that simultaneously seemed like something a child, a mad scientist, or an occultist might have drawn. Flaming eyes. Flaming hearts. Trees. Butterflies. Apples. In the center of the mass of images and words was a large drawing of a fountain with the words "*So that all may play.*"

When Scott came home later that day I knocked gently on his door.

"Come in."

I opened the door and peeked inside. "Hey, how's it going?" I asked, a little awkwardly.

"Great," his eyes sparkled. I paused, suddenly self-conscious that I was prying into his personal life. But curiosity won. I took a step into the room.

"I wanted to ask you—what is all this stuff you're working on? I was in here earlier showing a new tenant around and I was...curious."

He smiled and waved me over so we were standing shoulder to shoulder in front of the wall.

"I'm mapping the *science of celebration,*" he said cheerily. "Cross-referencing system designs for emergent culture." I had no idea what he was talking about. He noticed my expression, and his tone became emphatic. "There are correlations between all these things," his hand waved across the wall, pointing at diagrams. "Sacred geometry, storytelling, myths, and all kinds of social structures. I'm looking for the *binding narrative.*"

My curiosity deepened. "What's it for? Are you just studying, or are you creating something?"

"Oh no, it's not just academic. I'm mapping a system that'll use technology to facilitate cultural transformation. It's called *Superstar Avatar.*" He paused, seeking the words to explain his vision more clearly. "Think of the internet like the nervous system of the planet. Imagine infecting it with a *happy virus* to shift culture into something more authentic and sustainable. From the outside it'll just look like a game. Harmless. Something that connects people's everyday lives into a kind of mythic reality. Something that helps them to share their stories." I nodded my head; my brow furrowed a little in contemplation. I loved how he talked. He continued, his voice taking on an urgent tone. "But it's not just online; there would be events. We could all be connected via mobile phones, but we could also use customized trading cards. And we could make action figures of ourselves that store all our information, and use bluetooth to connect them together." He gestured toward a diagram on the wall with a slightly manic twinkle in his eye. "People could have showdowns where they face each other off with style, wit, charm, charisma, sex appeal—*whatever they've got.* It's going to be a whole new way of being social. But the key is that it will be embedded with tools. Without even realizing it, people who play will learn about themselves and their friends, have their creativity sparked, learn that the *quality* of play is a

71

direct reflection of *how* they play, and they'll become better human beings as a result."

Superstar Avatar—A Mythic Game with cultural transformation as its goal. The idea inspired me, even if Scott did appear to have a bit of a messiah complex.

If you think about it, life *is* a bit like a game. There are rules and points; you have your character and your power level. You can write out the rules for Western culture in a little rulebook like Monopoly. Some people take this game really seriously, accumulating "points" in their bank accounts and gaining "power," but ultimately it's all just a game.

Every day we are role playing. We play the characters we have created, using the skills and resources we have gathered on our adventure. But, there's a problem. The rules of this game suck. The people who don't play fair win, and it leaves the majority of us feeling cheated and stressed out. Our current cultural game rewards selfish, heartless people, paying them with wealth and power. What if this New Game rewarded passionate sincerity and long-term strategy?

I had been driving at full speed but only seeing the rearview mirror, motivated by this idea that I was an outlier, a rebel, fighting against a system that stifled people's freedom. I saw my story and laughed. It seemed so childish. *It's just a game.*

My obsession with sexuality as the tipping point for transforming people's lives suddenly seemed immature. What if these concepts of freedom, creativity, and self-expression weren't just limited to the realm of sex, but were available on *all* levels? What would that kind of freedom look like?

Fuck the old game! Let's throw out the rulebook and create a new culture!

My First Burn

Polly Pandemonium

O N MY FIRST adventure to Burning Man—that dusty athanor in the Black Rock Desert—I discovered that this fantasy of living in the realm of pure play had already been born.

I watched San Francisco fill with dirty cars and listened to excited stories of this apocalyptic party *twice* before I succumbed to making the pilgrimage myself. It turned out that my friend Flash, who had found Mission Control for me, was also one of the cofounders of the festival, and his offer of a free ticket finally persuaded me to go.

We have a lot of festivals in England, and I had seen my share of dirty tents and drug-fueled partying. Could this really be that different?

I packed my tent and a few outfits into a backpack and hitched a ride with a friend. When we stopped in Reno to buy food and water, my credit card didn't work. It was an English card, and the phone number on the back wouldn't connect from my American cellphone. I watched my friend pack her supplies into her car. She lent me enough money to buy a couple of jugs of water and some energy bars.

There was no going back now.

I had arranged to meet Flash in a bar in Gerlach, the town closest to the desert where the festival is held. As we pulled in, the morning sun made the landscape wobble. I pulled on my backpack and waved goodbye as my friend drove away.

"BRUNO'S COUNTRY CLUB: MOTEL–CAFÉ–CASI-NO–SALOON," the sign read in tall, red letters in a decidedly Western font. A tumbleweed rolled past, and the wind blew in my face like a hairdryer. A little Ennio Morricone played on my internal Walkman.

When I opened the door and stepped inside it took a moment for my eyes to adjust. I squinted, hunched my shoulders self-consciously, and made my way to the bar. All eyes followed me as the crowd of dusty people judged my arrival.

"Hi there," I said brightly, not allowing myself to be intimidated by the atmosphere, "Do you know Flash?" A man snort-laughed behind me. I turned around as the whole room sniggered into their coffee.

"Yes honey," said the friendly waitress. "Have a seat." She gestured to the stool in front of me. I pulled off my backpack and sat down.

"Have you seen him today? He's supposed to be meeting me here." My British accent was incongruous in this place, and the titters of the crowd made me self-conscious.

"Not today. He's around though." She leaned in, "Don't worry about those guys; they're just playin' with you. What can I get for you while you wait?"

"Well…I don't have a lot of money." I opened my hand and looked at the pile of change and crumpled ones. "How much is a coffee?"

A couple of hours later, the dusty people were buying me

drinks and laughing at my jokes. They were astounded at the boldness of this perky blond Brit who rolled up to Bruno's with no money.

"You don't have a ticket? You don't have any food or water?"

"Nope. I'm supposed to meet Flash. He said he would get me in. I've got Clif bars." I said weakly.

Hours passed. People came and went from Bruno's. I started to panic. I didn't have a lot of options. I sat there for a total of six hours before the dusty people decided I needed their help. One guy stepped forward. He had a long beard that ended in a braid, and his eyebrows were gray with dust.

"I'll get you in. Come on, come with me," he said.

"Really? Wow, that would be so great. I don't know where Flash could have got to. He said he would be here. Oh my god, I would be so grateful."

"Do you know where you're camping?"

"Yeah, wait a second," I pulled out a piece of paper with an address scrawled on it in a strange language I didn't understand. "*Ill Ville. Seven-thirty Esplanade.*" Zari had handed it to me with instructions I hadn't listened to when she left hurriedly a few days earlier. Luckily, my dusty hero knew his stuff.

"Illumination Village? Oh yeah, these guys'll take care of you." I picked up my backpack and my water jugs and made my way outside. If I thought it was hot before, I had been kidding myself. The afternoon sun baked the road as dusty gusts swirled around my ankles. Immediately I became drenched with sweat and then dried again. The scorching air sucked moisture from my body with every breath.

Following my hero's instructions, I climbed into the back of his pickup truck and he pulled a blue tarp over me. "How long do you think I'll be in here?" I asked, trying not to sound like a pussy.

"Don't worry. I'm DPW. I have a pass so I don't have to sit in line. We'll be there in about fifteen minutes. Just keep your head down, and don't get me in trouble." I didn't know what DPW was, but I did understand that this kind man was taking a risk for me, the stupid blond Brit who showed up with no cash, no ticket, no water, and no food. I felt like an idiot. I didn't have a choice but to accept his offer. I thanked him again as he pulled the tarp over me and attached it to the sides of the truck.

There were dusty blankets on the bed of the truck, and the breeze coming in through the tarp made the trip bearable. We shot past the long line that stretched out to the road and rumbled onto the desert floor. Dust kicked up and blew into my face. It had an unusual scent. Clean and ancient, like a fossil. My hero exchanged a few words at the gate. I heard a voice outside in the distance:

"Have you got any virgins in there? Come on out and ring the bell. Wooo! Welcome to Burning Man! Welcome home!" I laid still in the back of the truck, breath held, heart pounding. We lurched forward, and a few minutes later came to a stop.

"Come on out," he said, lifting the tarp. Sweat and dust caked my face. I sat up, trying to brush the dirt from my T-shirt. He laughed, picked up a handful of dust, and threw it at me. Suddenly I realized I looked like them now. I had become one of the dusty people. He hugged me and whispered, "Welcome home" in my ear.

Zari emerged from a structure that looked like a shantytown made from scaffolding, cardboard, and a patchwork of fabric. "Polly! You're here!" She sat me down in the shade and fed me a watermelon and mint salad. It was cool and fresh. *Where did she get this?* I didn't even ask as I gratefully munched down the ambrosial feast. My eyes hurt from the bright sun, the sweat made them sting, and I didn't have any sunglasses. *What am I doing here? I'm an English rose. I am not designed for these kinds of conditions.* It seemed to be getting hotter, even though it was late in the day. I stripped down to my underwear and dozed half-naked in the shade.

Then I awakened to a loud, familiar sound.

Memories of my childhood flooded back....

Camping, waking early, hearing shouts outside the tent, then...that sound...propane. Poking my head out of the tent, cold moist misty morning air in my face, I saw hot air balloons being inflated, momentarily lit inside by flame as they billow into fullness.

KSHHHHHHH.

That past I was trying to forget pressed through a crack in this dusty desert floor, and my heart filled with melancholy and yearning. I opened my eyes. The heat had subsided and the sky was a whimsical shade of violet. The purple-gray mountains on either side held us in a gentle embrace. People rode by on bicycles, each one unique, jangling with bells and flapping with flags, some pulling utilitarian baskets behind them, some powering kinetic sculptures that moved with each pedal push.

KSHHHHHHH.

Out in front of the camp, a gaggle of women gathered around a propane tank with what looked like a huge lotus flower blossoming from its connectors. Zari stood with them. They laughed and jumped up and down. It looked like a victory. K-K-K-KSHHHHHHH. A huge flame spurted into the air, accompanied by a black smoke ring that rose gently, widening and dissolving. The girls hugged each other excitedly. Zari was part of a small collective of women who had learned to create fire art, and this was their first creation. They called themselves the Flaming Lotus Girls.

"WOOOO!" they yelled in chorus as the flame breached the sky. Zari saw me, and ran over happily.

"You want to come press the button?" she asked. Her enthusiasm was infectious.

"Sure."

I staggered out into the clearing and they handed me a controller. Just a red button on a box. I pressed it. KSHHHHHHH. A flame shot into the air.

As the sky went dark, a dust storm blew through as I tried to pitch my tent. Zari gave me goggles, and a scarf to put around my mouth and nose. I had waited until sunset because attempting to do anything in the day seemed impossible. In the half-light of near darkness, I struggled with my little tent, which was blown around violently by high winds. As I wrestled with the flimsy fabric, I felt hopeless. Tired and thirsty, I just wanted to be inside. The vastness of the desert was overwhelming, and I had nowhere to escape to. Just as I was about to give up and sob in the dust alone, a truck pulled up, their headlights perfectly illuminating my tragic little scene. A woman stepped out and handed me an icy cocktail.

"I saw you struggling over here. You looked like you needed a drink," she said, smiling.

"Oh, yeah. Thank you so much," I said as I sucked down the cool beverage. The hefty measure of vodka made me gratefully woozy. Another guy joined us and started looking at the pieces of the tent.

"Yeah, this is easy. We'll have it up in no time." In the light of the truck they bustled around my pile of camping equipment, and within a few minutes I had a home.

"Thank you! Oh my god, you guys rescued me!" I said as they got back into their truck and drove away.

"That's our job!" They said, smiling and waving as they left. I was so accustomed to struggling alone; I hadn't even thought to ask for help.

I unzipped my tent and pulled my bag inside. The loud rustling of the fabric in the wind made me anxious. Being in my tiny tent didn't help the overwhelmed feeling, even though it was good to have a home.

"Polly, are you in there?" It was Zari's voice.

"Yes, hang on." I put my goggles back on and stepped outside.

"Come on, are you ready for an adventure?" She said.

"I don't know, Zari. I'm feeling pretty tired. I might just settle in."

She laughed. "Nonsense. You're at Burning Man. Sleep when you're dead. Come on, you haven't even seen the city yet."

I didn't have the energy to put up a fight. She piled me into the back of a pickup truck and put a cold beer in my hand. As we drove, the storm got thicker. We couldn't see anything. People on the truck laughed and chatted while we choked on the powdery alkaline dust swirling in the air.

We slowed down as the storm cleared to reveal a huge, ornate structure looming over the desert. The full moon shone through a baroque looking spire, and clouds of billowing dust settled as we stepped down from the truck. Suddenly I could see stars in the sky. The desert floor was lit silvery blue by the cosmic display. Eerie and haunting, towering before us was a temple. A structure so massive and beautiful I couldn't believe it was there.

"Glad you came?" asked Zari as she put her arm around me.

"I'm not sure," I replied truthfully as I looked up in awe. "That's pretty amazing though." I tipped my beer bottle toward the temple.

"You just wait till we burn it!" she said, gleefully.

To be honest, that first Burning Man wasn't easy. I couldn't adjust to the heat, and I was totally unprepared. Most of the time I was hungry, thirsty, and tired. But something magical was happening around me, and the struggle seemed like it was part of the spell. There was a sense of playfulness, freedom, openness, and generosity I had never experienced before. In the car on the way home, I excitedly made plans for next year.

Unlike the festivals I knew, there was no vending area, no sponsored stages. The people who attended were the ones who made it happen, collaborating to build the massive sculptures and throw the enormous parties. They hosted bars and glee-fully gave away drinks. They invited strangers into their camps for bacon and Bloody Marys. It felt like a family. I understood why they called it "home," but from the start, my mind whirred with questions. *What's stopping this sense of community from happening all year round? How do we harness this and bring it home?*

At Burning Man, the rules are changed. Collaboration, creativity, and generosity are rewarded. That's why there's that sense of freedom. There are clearly articulated tenets like "radical self expression," encouraging people to be creative. The amorphous "gift economy" simply encourages generosity. It makes it cool and fun to give. People leap out of nowhere to help, like the couple that fixed my tent.

I thought about Scott's project, Superstar Avatar, and I got excited about its potential. We don't need to go out to the desert; we just need to bring the new rules home with us, and Superstar Avatar could be the magic ingredient to make it happen.

My Diamond Superpower

Polly Pandemonium

MY WORK relationship with Scott became a comfortable give and take of favors and mutual inspiration. He helped me with my events, and I helped him with Superstar Avatar.

We traveled to Los Angeles together. I went to pitch my new collection to fetish shops, and Scott went to produce a promotional event for Superstar Avatar in an art gallery. He needed support to develop his idea into a fully fledged product, so the goal for the evening was to attract investors and potential business partners with a wild, colorful show.

I had a free evening, so I crossed town to help him set up the space, and afterward we started talking. Things got personal. I started to open up. Just a little.

"I have so much anger," I confided in him. "I don't know what to do with it." We sat perched on the edge of the balcony, overlooking the cavernous event space below. I took a deep breath and stared at my beer bottle, tears welling in my eyes, but blinking fast to make sure they didn't fall. "Sometimes I feel broken, like there's been so much pain, and so much pressure, over so many years, that the core of my being is like a diamond." I peeked at him out of the corner of my eye. He looked straight ahead in contemplation.

I might have moved to a new town and given myself a new name, but underneath all the boldness, I still defined myself by my pain. The anger that appeared during my teen years while my father was dying had etched itself into my consciousness.

"I just don't know what to do about it. It feels so immovable, so entrenched inside me. It's sharp and hard and painful, and when I have a quiet moment it's all I feel." I paused, filled with angst. "Do you know what I mean?"

He took a moment before he replied, sipping at his beer thoughtfully. "But, diamonds are beautiful, right? The pressure is what creates that beauty. Without the pressure it's just a piece of coal." I nodded. "Your diamond, which has taken so many years to create, is now your lens. You can hold it up to the light and it can give you a new perspective. Without that lens you wouldn't be able to see the things you see." He smiled a little encouraging smile. "You're a powerful woman, Polly, and you have a big effect on people. This diamond you've worked so hard to create isn't just for you. You can hold it up for other people too." He lifted up his shirtsleeve and showed me the tattoo on his left shoulder of a seated figure with blue skin and multiple arms. It sat in a skyline of domed roofs at sunset, and looked like a Hindu god, but with comic book styling. I'd seen it many times before but never asked who it was or what it meant. "This is Rogan Gosh," he said smiling. "He's a karmanaut, just like you."

"What's a *karmanaut?*" I asked, curious and stepping forward to inspect his arm more closely.

"It's like a superhero, who helps people move through heavy karma, stuff they can't do on their own. Your diamond is like your Karmanaut superpower." I was a little dumbfounded. Nobody had ever talked to me like that before. It made me want to kiss him.

That night we slept at the venue together in a corner under a blanket. We had nowhere else to stay in LA, and the owner of the gallery had said it would be okay. We lay down next to each other and said goodnight, the closeness of our bodies glaringly awkward as we drifted off to sleep.

In the morning as the sun streamed in on our cozy little nest, I woke up to find Scott's arm around me. I am usually a very touchy-feely person with my friends, but Scott and I had a strangely hands-off relationship. Our physical interactions had never gone further than a pat on the shoulder or a brief awkward hug.

I lay there frozen with his arm draped over me. I tried to make subtle movements to wake him up so that he would move, but he slept heavily. I felt so shy and embarrassed. Had he meant to put his arm around me? Or had it happened as he turned in his sleep? Would he wake up feeling as awkward as I did? Eventually I plucked up the courage and wriggled out from under his sleepy embrace. *"Good morning,"* I said perkily as his eyes opened in little slits, assaulted by the brightness of the sunlight. "Did you sleep well?"

"I was having a dream," he replied in a slurry morning voice. He looked confused for a moment as he recalled his nocturnal story. "We were in a strange land filled with giant flowers, and we were exploring. We were small enough to actually fit inside the flowers, and they were so beautiful and colorful." He paused and smiled shyly as he continued. "They were weirdly fleshy. The whole thing was kind of erotic." He laughed and scratched his head.

"Weird," I said. "We were humping flowers?"

"More like..." He paused, seeking the appropriate word, "*communing...*" He laughed again. "Okay, maybe there was some humping."

Later that day I sat on a stool in the gallery, taking a break from setting up. It was one of those hot spring days in LA and my "English rose" constitution melted. The venue buzzed with people bringing in the last minute pieces of equipment and art, and performers stood around waiting to sound check. I watched Scott come down the stairs from the mezzanine level, fielding questions from various people as he added final touches to the decor. Earlier in the day he had been wearing a T-shirt, but in the heat he had taken it off and put it on his head, like an Arab headdress. On top of it he perched his straw pork-pie hat. His colorful plaid pants hung off his slender hips, held up by a single suspender—the other dangled at his side. I could see the extent of his tattooing—a large Indonesian-looking piece stretched across his entire upper back, and more covered his upper arms too. At his chest blazed a flaming hand with an eye at its center. As he stood there barking answers to various questions I suddenly realized that I found him incredibly sexy.

I fantasized for a moment about what it would be like to touch him, allowing my eyes to wander over his body as he talked. Then I froze and recoiled. What was I doing? This was *Scott*. Did I want to jeopardize our work relationship? I thought about what it might mean. We were clearly excellent collaborators, and had been through all sorts of stresses together already, moving gracefully through drama. We both wanted nontraditional relationships. Last night we had connected on a very spiritual level, and I felt closer to him than ever before. I stood up suddenly as he walked over to ask me a question. He paused, noticing my startled expression. "Are you okay?"

"Yes, I'm fine, it's just a bit hot in here." I fanned my face with a flier, trying to look normal.

"Right. Well, do you have any idea where we should put that ball?" He gestured toward an inflatable ball, fifteen feet high, designed so that people could get inside and hang out in the padded interior. The cells at one end were transparent, so you could see in, and there was a hole to climb inside. It made a comfy place to chill in an otherwise stark gallery space.

A couple of hours into the party I found myself in that ball with a penis puppeteer. Scott had booked him to walk around the gallery with a mini theater around his crotch. His penis, complete with little arms and legs, starred in the show, jumping around and coming to life. He was taking a break and had found me alone in the ball escaping for a moment from the chaos. We decided to roll the ball so that the entrance faced upward, to stop other people from coming in. I think we made out for a minute, but we were mainly chatting and laughing. Suddenly I had an idea. "If we threw our clothes out of that hole it would look really funny from outside." I suggested, excitedly. I always know how to liven up a party.

He was game. We took off our clothes and threw them out. The guests squealed with laughter as our garments landed in the middle of people's conversations. "Do you think if we ran in this thing like a hamster ball we could move it?" he asked, panting, naked, and a little sweaty in the enclosed space.

"We could try!" We picked a direction and started running, the ball lurched forward and the people outside squealed again, moving out of our way. We rolled back and forward a few times, landing in a heap on top of each other. We laughed, out of breath, and made a new plan.

"The door to get in here is a double door, right? Maybe if we go fast enough we can pop right through the door and end up on the street." We checked to see the path between the door and us, and aiming carefully we started running with all our strength, pushing the ball forward on its course. When we reached the door, we didn't make it through. The idea was ridiculous. We fell back laughing and panting on top of each other, thrown back by the force of the sudden stop. When we regained our composure I noticed a woman staring at us through the entrance; we landed at the perfect angle for her to get a clear view of the situation. Her face was stern and angry. It was his wife.

He suddenly stopped laughing and stood up, moving toward her. *"This is not okay,"* she hissed. *"Get out of there NOW."*

He leaped out of the ball, apologizing and trying to placate her.

"Put your clothes on; *we're leaving,"* her voice bubbled over with anger. He looked around at me with a face that said *I'm sorry,* and in a moment they left, and I was alone, still a little out of breath, and naked. I sat for a moment not sure what to do. I had no idea where that thunderstorm of anger came from. I peeked out of the ball to find my clothes. Thankfully my panties were just a few feet away, so I reached out and grabbed them. The room had gone back to its chatter after the rather dramatic end to our entertaining scene. I sat for a moment with my legs dangling out of the side of the ball, contemplating what happened.

Why was she so angry? He was walking around with his cock on display all night and she worried about nudity? Even her dress had been see-through, proudly displaying her totally shaved pussy. They seemed like a modern sort of couple.

I left the ball, collected the rest of my clothes, and went outside to get a breath of air. The wife of the penis puppeteer approached the building as I stepped outside. "Ah, *there you are,*" she said in a tense voice. "I was just coming back to find you. I just wanted to let you know that whatever that *thing* is you're doing"—she emphasized the word "thing" and waved her hand in my general direction—"you just end up looking like a *cheap slut.* You're disgusting." She turned around and stormed off. *A cheap slut?* How was I supposed to know what their agreements were? Surely it was up to her husband to communicate to me what was cool with his wife. To blame *me* seemed totally unfair.

I went to the bar, figuring a shot of tequila would be good medicine for my ills. As I stood there, Scott came up beside me. "I'll take one of those," he said, holding out his glass. I sloshed the potent liquid into the glasses and stood for a moment before downing the shot. "*To a successful night,*" he said as our glasses chinked.

"The strangest thing just happened to me," I said, and told him my story. "Do you think I look like a cheap slut?" I giggled, pressing my body toward him and looking up at him doe eyed, wriggling suggestively.

"Mmmm," he said, looking down at me with a wry little smile, "*cheap slut.*" When our lips met it was electric. Our arms reached around each other as we kissed and held each other closely. We kissed for a long time, and when it finally ended he looked at me very tenderly and said, "I've been waiting a long time to do that."

For the next few days we couldn't be together without

touching. If we were in the same room the compulsion to touch was too strong. Our arms constantly wrapped around each other, hands reaching for hands, heads resting on shoulders, legs intertwined under tables. The spell broke and reversed; the polarity of the magnet shifted.

Having sex with someone you're falling in love with is magical. The deeper connection, beyond the physical, creates a powerful bond. I remember the excitement of our kisses and the lingering seduction of his touch. I wanted to lose myself in the tender moments of intimate affection.

But something held me back. I was afraid to tell him, because underneath all the bravado I felt like a failure. I was twenty-seven years old, and I had been sexually active since I was fifteen. I had experienced more than most people do in their lifetime. I had fooled around with threesomes and orgies. I had fucked men and women. I had traveled far across the vast expanse of sexual possibilities like an adventurer. But my orgasm had always been elusive to me. I was so embarrassed and ashamed by my failure. I stayed silent.

I'd talked to my mother about it. She claimed it was normal. She told me some unbelievable statistics. One in three women have difficulty reaching orgasm? Eighty percent of women don't orgasm from intercourse alone? How could these statistics be true? From where I stood it looked like bullshit. Everyone but me had orgasms. I felt ashamed, and blamed myself—I was incapable of intimacy. I secretly read magazine articles—they told me that learning to relax and not be uptight about sex would be the key to reaching orgasm, but *I wasn't uptight about sex.* Everything I read on the subject seemed to be written for someone else, not for me. So what was wrong with me?

My teenage masturbation always ended with frustration. My young sexuality became tinged with anxiety. My friends all came of age, one at a time, victorious. One even told the story of her first orgasm when she was ten years old. She had brushed her nipple by accident and suddenly exploded in a full-on preteen orgasm. Eventually it was just my sister and me who seemed to experience the same block. When she finally reached the goal I comforted myself that she was almost two years older. My time would come. As the years clicked by I stopped talking about it.

I had my first orgasm on my own when I was twenty-four. I drunkenly confessed my predicament to a friend, and she bought me a deluxe vibrator. One of those rabbit vibes with the swirly dildo that looks like a candy machine, and tickly rabbit ears to stimulate the clit. "Here you go, love—problem solved. This'd get an orgasm out of a stone," she quipped when she gave it to me.

"Maybe I'm more frigid than a stone," I thought to myself when I still couldn't orgasm.

It took months of solo experimentation with this new toy before it finally happened. I was alone in my house. My bedroom was a cozy nest of mismatched pillows. Bubblegum-pink walls. Shiny black floors and trim. A fake fur leopard print bedspread thrown across the bed, which took up most of the room.

My hands traced my body, touching the contours of my hips and the softness of my breasts. I felt conflicted. I knew this path led to pleasure for a while, but it always ended in frustration and fear.

I plugged in my headphones and lay back on my bed,

closing my eyes. *Forget the voices, forget the fear, no goal, just...sensation.* My hands explored my body. They became the hands of my lovers. The candlelight flickered on the ceiling, dancing with the shadows of my imaginary helpers. Feather-light kisses, lips, and tongues. My body reacted with a tingling, a flush, a wetness. I reached for the vibrator.

Alone in the house with music on my headphones, the candlelight, the door closed. I was no less depressed, no less stressed out. I didn't breathe differently, or alter my routine in any way. Half an hour later, my wrist sore, sweat on my brow, the familiar path took me all the way to the edge. I knew this place. Frantic, frustrated, face contorted. But then suddenly *something new.* Sweet honey-dripping ecstasy. A rush of completion. A moment of dissolution. Transported, and returned, back to my bed, panting. *That was it.*

Stunned and confused I lay there breathless. Sure, I was glad it finally happened, but it was such a fleeting moment. Was it even real? Had I imagined it? I knew I hadn't. I still sensed its energy rippling through my body. I wanted it back. I waited so long. Would I have to wait another decade? My hands reached again, greedy for more, wanting confirmation. This time it only took a few seconds. My body quivered, alive with a flickering flame of sensation.

Once I learned how to orgasm with a vibrator, I became a little addicted. I was making up for lost time. Practicing. But having lived the first nine years of my sex life without ever having an orgasm, I couldn't shake off that all-consuming feeling of brokenness. I was a sexual cripple. A failure. A fraud.

Meeting Scott and falling in love meant I couldn't hide anymore. One-night stands and short affairs were easy. Most men didn't even notice I focused all the attention on them when we reached that climactic moment. Since leaving London I hadn't been in a relationship where I felt comfortable enough to talk about my orgasm, so I pretended. Camped it up a little so they didn't ask questions. I never lied outright, but I did anything possible to prevent them from asking. I didn't want to do that with Scott though.

We're all wired differently. The complexities of the human brain and physiology make it difficult to know exactly why my body reacted the way it did. But I wonder—was it because of the stress of my father's death? My body awakened into adulthood during this painful time. Perhaps I internalized the trauma and somehow blocked my own path with impenetrable psychic barriers I would never understand. The overload of anxiety I experienced during puberty constricted my vital energy, gripping tightly, preventing me from developing the spaciousness I needed to experience that release. It wound its way around me like a boa constrictor, smothering me, and severing connections to my ecstatic consiousness.

Sex Is Simple;
Culture Is Complicated

Polly Pandemonium

IN MANY WAYS, sex is simple, natural—yet it's the cause of so much anxiety and stress for humans. Our culture has given us some impossibly conflicting ambitions: Be sexy, but don't be afraid if you don't feel sexy, because that's really *not sexy.* But don't be *too* sexy. But *don't* be a prude. We're tied up in knots with the contradictions. But it's not just personal—culture itself is as confused as we are about the role of sexuality.

Centuries ago, the complexities of sex culture became simplified. The only acceptable model was one man and one woman, sanctioned by the church, for life. These days sex culture can spin out in many directions, with the basic tenet of *consenting adults* being the only limitation. We are currently in a learning phase, figuring out how this new, more liberated sex culture works.

Wilhelm Reich, the Austrian American mid-twentieth-century psychoanalyst, was responsible for coining the phrases "sex positive" and "sex negative." In his own words, "some societies accept the inherent value of sexual expression and indeed insist on it as a prerequisite of mental health, while other human groups despise sexuality and are ceaselessly inventive in devising austerities and prohibitions as a means of social control."

Our culture used to be sex negative. For most of Western history, fornication out of wedlock was a crime, punishable by the courts and subject to the death sentence. Society widely accepted that sex was disruptive to social order, and made God angry. The veneration of sexual discipline meant seeing celibacy as the ultimate ambition in purity. Sex was dirty, bad, and wrong and should be avoided at all costs. These days it's not so simple. We no longer have neat answers.

I am not a free love idealist. I don't believe we should all fuck each other like bonobos. The human heart can be a complicated playground, and everyone has a different comfort level, so creating standards and boundaries is important. There are no black-and-white answers anymore. Questions that used to be simple have new dimensions. This new sex culture needs sliders instead of checkboxes.

If there's a scale with abstinence at one end and promiscuousness at the other, we can explore all the points on it without being *right* or *wrong*. As long as all parties are consenting, it's up to each of us to make or own choices, changing or adapting to new circumstances. Even I choose to occasionally have periods of abstinence.

It is true; sex can bring up some scary stuff. We store a lot of pent-up frustrations, phobias, and hang-ups in our sexuality. Like a supercharged microcosm of our personality, if approached with awareness, sex can be a button we can push for a fast track of personal growth. I think it's healthy to experiment, to try out styles and personalities, and I don't think that this opportunity for personal growth has to end when you fall in love.

Polyamory is a word I learned when I arrived in San Francisco. I found a copy of *The Ethical Slut*,[xi] which is the primer on the practice of polyamory, or *ethical nonmonogamy*. It teaches you how to build trust and communicate better.

People sometimes ask if I named myself *Polly* because of polyamory, but I didn't. Polly was the name my parents gave me, and I don't label myself as polyamorous. It's not that simple. Relationships are as unique as the people in them, and convenient labels are often inadequate.

Just like with promiscuity, relationship styles need a slider. At one end, there's total monogamy, where one person meets all your emotional needs, and even deep platonic friendships aren't allowed. At the other end there's relationship anarchy, where boundaries are flexible, and multiple relationships are navigated without fixed rules. Between those two things there's a whole world of possibilities. My slider goes back and forth, but I wouldn't be happy at the extreme ends of that spectrum. I'm not a dedicated polyamorist, and I'm not ever going to be totally monogamous.

Ideally I'd like to be somewhere in the middle. But that's just me.

Sex, Power, and Pain

Polly Whittaker

I LOST my virginity to a punk boy on a mattress in a squat on the eve of my fifteenth birthday. He stopped his grunting to ask, "Are you gonna come?"

"I don't think so." I replied self-consciously.

"Why not?" he said.

"I don't know."

The act itself was disappointing, but even worse was the boy I had to deal with. He was stupid and immature, and then he left me for a friend of my sister. It was not a momentous moment in my sexual history.

The following week, a friend wrote an account of my sexual exploits in her journal. Her mother found it and read it. Appalled at what she discovered, she took it upon herself to call my mother, telling her that I was a slut and banning me from hanging out with her daughter. When she put down the phone my mother confronted me about the news.

"Is this true, Polly?"

"Yes, it's true." I said, feeling like a little kid who got caught stealing. She paused and looked at me, brow furrowed with concern.

"Did you use protection?"

"Of course I did, Mum!"

"Good." She struggled to deal with the news. Her gut instincts screamed out to punish me, to lock me up in my room and throw away the key, and ban me from hanging out with boys ever again. That's what her father would have done. But she wanted to be a different parent. She shifted in her seat and took a deep breath as she tuned into a more empathic, compassionate mindset. "Well, I didn't realize you had lost your virginity to that boy. No wonder you were so upset when he started hanging out with Sam's friend. I understand now. You poor thing."

"Yeah, whatever, he was dumb."

"It's a big deal to lose your virginity, sweetheart. Don't underestimate it. You're becoming a grown-up now. My baby's becoming a woman." She reached out to hold my hand.

"Mum, don't be weird," I said, holding her hand awkwardly as she looked searchingly into my eyes.

"I love you, precious. That's all. Don't listen to this ridiculous woman calling you names. Don't ever let anyone make you feel bad about your sexuality. It's completely normal and natural to have those kinds of urges at your age. You're a bit young to be having sex, but you're very mature for your age. Just be careful, take care of your body, and respect yourself, okay? Make sure you use protection, and let me know if anything ever happens that you aren't happy about."

"I will…. Thanks, Mum."

I realize that this isn't the normal way such conversations usually go down. My mother supported my young sexuality, gave me the tools to stay safe, and created an open invitation for more conversations if I needed them.

Soon I discovered that the hidden mysteries of adulthood,

shrouded from my curious young eyes for so long, were trickier to master than I had anticipated. I found it difficult to meet boys—my intensity intimidated them, and my sexual forwardness terrified them. I remember pretending to be stupid so that they would be less afraid to talk to me. There isn't a lot of cultural support for intelligent, sexually empowered young women, and my attempts to connect with the opposite sex often ended with humiliation. After all the effort and potential pitfalls, the smushing together of body parts seemed decidedly anticlimactic.

Everything changed when my friend Abby discovered a magazine called *Skin Two*. I don't remember where she found it, but she showed it to me at school and it captivated us with its stylish images of leather, latex, and bondage. A slick and modern publication, it showcased fashion and stories from a world we wanted to explore. With the '90s about to be born, we felt like grown-ups. We had discovered the secret. The hidden truth even my mother kept from me. Sex wasn't just about procreation—it wasn't even simply about pleasure. In those glossy pages we discovered that sex could be a way to express power and pain, and its potential turned us on.

Let's backtrack for a moment so I can tell you about Abby: When I met her she was a pale-skinned bookworm with long, tangled, auburn hair, thick glasses, and a nasty case of bulimia. She grew into one of the most beautiful women I have ever known. She was the daughter of two American expats. Her father had been a reporter during the Vietnam War, and the horrific atrocities he had witnessed left him traumatized. One night I was staying at her house, and we were sneakily watching TV when we knew we should have been in bed. Thirteen years old, we were testing her parents' boundaries. Her dad came in, swaying with a glass of bourbon in his hand, and locked the door behind him.

"You want to watch TV, girls? Then you're gonna watch what I wanna watch." He put in a video and sat down heavily in the armchair. He showed us uncut footage of his reporting in Vietnam. Fresh-faced, young soldiers being interviewed, beaming proud smiles, sending messages back to loved ones. Then panic, bombs, screams; as the shaky camera followed their steps, the soldiers ran into the trees and to their deaths. Violent and bloody. We had watched, wide-eyed, until he let us leave the room. We never tried to watch TV late again.

Abby and I became friends at Secondary School in the Lower Fourth. That's about twelve years old. A group of "popular" girls turned on me during one lunch break. They were relentlessly teasing me, following me around the classroom with a pair of scissors trying to cut my hair.

"Come on, Polly. You need a haircut," one girl said while snipping the scissors dramatically in the air. The others crowded behind me, giggling and pushing me forward.

"Leave me alone, you guys. I'm really not in the mood." I slipped past them and sat down at another desk.

"*Snip, snip!*" the ringleader said, coming up behind me and grabbing my hair.

"Get off me!" I yelled, "What the fuck is your problem?"

"What's my problem? What's your problem? Are you gonna cry?"

I pushed her away and grabbed hold of the desk with my hands, standing, teary-eyed and frustrated. In a moment of insanity I shoved the desk in their direction with all my strength, and then I collapsed in tears. Wide-eyed, they laughed at my extreme reaction, following me across the room chanting *"Cry baby, cry baby."* Abby stood up for me. She blocked their way, standing between me and my tormentors

"Do you even know who she is?" Abby shouted. *"Do you care?* You're not her friends, you're *horrible* people." They laughed at both of us, but after that we became inseparable.

I remember a conversation we had soon after we met, discussing how the cultural attitude toward sexuality had changed over the centuries.

"It's weird though, right?" said Abby as she leafed through a book with photographs of antiquated fashion: bustles, corsets, and towering wigs. "In Victorian times, things were different. They weren't even allowed to show their ankles."

"It *is* weird." I nodded in agreement. "I wonder what they'd have made of your skirt." I pointed at the skirt ruched up around her hips as she sat cross-legged. She self-consciously pulled at it and laughed.

"If we were young Victorian ladies, we would get in trouble," she said as she grabbed the book and held it up to her face, fluttering it like a fan. "They couldn't even get a peck on the cheek without *outrage* and *disgrace*."

"I can't imagine. What a weird life. I prefer miniskirts and snogging at the bus stop." We both laughed. My young mind grappled with the idea. "Do you think it'll be just as different in the future?"

"Like how?"

"I dunno. Like people just having sex everywhere?" I suggested.

"That's probably a bit unhygienic." Abby replied. "Ew. Can

you imagine? People just doing it everywhere?" We imagined that reality for a moment, noses slightly wrinkled.

"Well, maybe they'll have sex at parties."

"Maybe." We pondered the idea. Why not? It seemed reasonable.

As Abby and I both turned sweet sixteen she found a listing in the back pages of *Skin Two* for a party scheduled to happen in a bar in the East End of London. Our young minds filled with shiny, salacious possibilities. We looked older than our age, and had no problem getting into nightclubs. We dressed the part, to the best of our abilities, donning fishnet stockings and black lace underwear from Marks and Spencer, slicking on thick, black eyeliner, greasing our lips with red lipstick, and swooshing our hair into fashionable up dos.

When we arrived at the door of the club, we found people loitering outside in black plastic raincoats and military uniforms. We flashed them smiles filled with counterfeit confidence. It worked like magic. They opened the door and ushered us inside.

The interior was not what we expected. Far from the slick, modern ambiance we anticipated, we found ourselves in a classic British pub with brown floral carpets, maroon leather seats, and signage extolling the virtues of drinking more Guinness. We hurriedly ordered some cocktails—already familiar with the etiquette of drinking in bars, we squeezed our lemon slices, stirred our drinks with our straws, and sat in a corner trying to look inconspicuous.

Our entrance had unavoidably garnered some interest, and before long the men at the next table asked if they could join us.

Sliding over, they engaged in some polite conversation while we awkwardly sipped our Bacardi and Cokes. They seemed like gentlemanly types, and we settled into some innocent flirting. The guy next to me had a classic look, slicked-back black hair and a chiseled jawline. His rather manly black leather jacket hinted at experience. He leaned over as I nervously sucked down the last of my cocktail and asked if he could buy me a drink.

"Sure," I said, giving him a coquettish side glance. I looked over at Abby, giving a little wink to my adventurous partner in crime. But instead of returning my wink, her eyes widened as she stared back at me in disbelief. I turned around to see that my flirting partner stood up to reveal that below his leather jacket he wore nothing but patent stiletto thigh boots and a leather thong, revealing his hairy, masculine butt cheeks as he swaggered to the bar in his six-inch heels. Abby and I tried not to laugh as he returned to the table with drinks.

"Do you two feel like checking out downstairs?" he asked as he handed me my cocktail. I didn't know what we might find downstairs, and the revelation of his outfit from the waist down caused me to reassess his suitability as a suitor.

"*No thanks, we're okay,*" I replied casually. Tugging on Abby's arm I planned our getaway. "Excuse us, gentlemen, we need to go powder our noses." We grabbed our purses and our cocktails and headed to the ladies room, giggling excitedly as we reapplied our lipstick.

"What do you think is downstairs?" Abby asked.

"I dunno. Shall we check it out?"

Our curiosity got the better of us, and we headed down the dark staircase to the basement. We could hear the sound of spanking mingled with whimpers and groans. From halfway up the stairs we stood frozen, watching with a jumble of horror and compulsion as we saw our very first real, live dungeon.

Strange-looking devices and furniture filled the room. An X-shaped crucifix stood in the center with bolts and rings on each extremity, designed to splay a person in every direction. Tethered to its crossbeams was a woman. A man flogged her ass mercilessly. Her skin became red, raw, and bruised from the beating.

A man sat close by, watching the scene with his cock bobbing up and down in his hand, flushed purple with the intensity of his masturbation. I'd never seen a man jack off before. All over the room scenes of this style repeated in various configurations. A naked man licked the boots of a woman who sat in a throne barking orders at him, forcing him to suck the heel.

The activities were pretty standard fare for *Skin Two* magazine, but they seemed so exposed, and the intimacy of being in the room with them was overwhelming. They weren't posing for photos, trying to look scared, pouting their lips like models—this was the real thing.

The heady smell of sex suffocated me. I suddenly became aware of my own body, my skin scratching the fabric of the cheap lace, beads of sweat collecting on the small of my back. I was as real and fleshy as they were, connected to them in our animal skins desperately looking for a way to feel alive.

The man on the couch ejaculated with a guttural cry, spurting cum all over his leather gloved hand, and leaned back in relief. He massaged the last few drops from his softening cock as he looked up to catch my eye.

The shock of connecting in that intimate moment propelled me away. I pushed Abby up the stairs, and we managed to maintain ourselves for long enough to gather our coats and rush out the exit. Out in the cool air of the city night, we clacked down the cobbled street in our stilettos. We turned a corner and were out of sight of the club before we looked at each other in disbelief. We didn't know what it meant.

Disgusted and shocked, we retreated. Compelled and enthralled, we returned. The experience was so real and so visceral—body and soul a slap in the face. We saw the shadowy underbelly of erotic possibilities and were deliriously scandalized.

Ironically, the brazenly sexual world I inhabited as a teenager was the safest place I could be. I never had to face sexual violence, which for so many teenage girls is commonplace. The explicit etiquette of the fetish scene protected me. Men are schooled to be polite or risk being ejected. I could wear provocative clothes, and I ventured out wearing thigh-high stiletto boots and little else, knowing that once I was in the club I wouldn't just be safe, I would be *respected*.

In the fetish scene, a place of such boundless sexual possibility, it's understood that the golden ticket comes with a caveat: Respect women; value their sexuality as a precious gift; honor their boundaries; don't be an asshole. I'm not saying harassment doesn't happen at fetish clubs, but it's nothing like the epidemic of ass grabbing that is taken for granted in regular bars and nightclubs.

This was where I first experienced the power of my sexuality, the sense of liberation that accompanies it, and a brand of feminism that allowed me to express my sexuality on my terms.

Be Brave and Bold

Polly Pandemonium

I GUESS I've always been a sucker for novelty. I love new experiences. That's what I found so exciting about Scott's work with Superstar Avatar. I wanted to be part of something new, and I was captivated by his idea of combining technology and counterculture to create a game that could transform culture. After the event in Los Angeles, and amid the newness of our budding romance, I threw myself into helping him, and as I did, my own projects seemed less important.

The urge to collaborate with Scott was so powerful; I think I lost myself a little. The work was inspiring, but I also had an intense desire to become so intertwined that he couldn't do his work without me. I wanted to make myself irreplaceable. Afraid to love, to be vulnerable, I engineered a few guarantees in order to make my heart safe.

Scott had a plan to return to Los Angeles, and I would stay in San Francisco and earn some money. Throw a party. Make some latex. Join him down there in a few weeks. It seemed like a sensible plan.

My day started with a trip to a quaint little country club in the Oakland Hills, which doesn't have a front desk. If you know how, you can breeze straight in the front door and out to the pool before anyone even realizes you're not supposed to be there. From the hot tub you can see the bay, the whole of San Francisco, and the road from Oakland snaking across the Bay Bridge. I wanted to paint that road yellow to make it look like the Emerald City. Something about the skyline, with the point of the Transamerica building jutting into the clouds and the sun setting behind it, makes the view look fantastical from that angle.

I sat there, giddy with optimism and terror. Neither emotion took hold. As the warm water caressed my body I found myself gently vacillating back and forth. *Giddy optimism.* Terror. *Giddy optimism.* Terror.

Later that day Scott would be leaving town, taking the red-eye Greyhound to Los Angeles. He had plans to launch Superstar Avatar with a big party at a glamorous Hollywood club. I glanced at the clock and realized I should hustle if I wanted to get to our meeting on time. I pulled myself out of the hot tub and reached for a towel. As I dabbed myself dry I walked across the warm concrete to my friend Cara, who lounged in a chair, hiding her pale skin under a huge hat. Cara had been living at Mission Control, running an art gallery in the lobby and the large front room. We'd been friends since I arrived in San Francisco, but she didn't approve of my new relationship with Scott. The truth is that many of my friends complained about being neglected since my new romance began. Scott and his project took up all my time.

"Hey, Cara, we have to leave soon if I'm going to make that meeting." She glanced up at me and nodded.

"Mmmhmmm, I'll be there in a second," she said, nonchalantly looking back down to her magazine. I went inside and got changed. I was excited to see Scott. I would miss him when he was down in LA. I checked my phone and found a message.

"Hi Polly. It's Scott. Can we meet at Trader Vic's in Emeryville at seven? We've got lots to talk about. Call me and let me know your plan."

I checked the clock. 6 PM. It would take half an hour tops to get to Emeryville—plenty of time. I called him to confirm and headed back out to find Cara. She swam lazily in the pool, enjoying the sunset.

"Hey, Cara. Can we leave soon? I need to make it to Emeryville by seven."

"Yeah, no problem," she said as she turned to swim another lap. I didn't want to be pushy. It had been my idea to come out here, and she had driven. I went back to the changing room and packed up my stuff. By the time she finally came in the clock said 6:20 PM.

"*Come on, Cara. Can we get moving?*" My stuff sat in a neat pile ready to go. I had dried and styled my hair. I passed the last ten minutes reading trashy health magazines.

"*What is your problem?*" she said irritably, "It only takes twenty minutes to get to Emeryville. I'm going to take a shower."

I sat on the little wooden bench outside the changing area chewing my fingernails as I listened to the sound of the shower. I didn't want to be late. We didn't have long before Scott's bus left.

The following hour was a catalog of frustrations that left us stuck in an empty parking lot under the freeway. There seemed to be no way out from this labyrinth of on ramps and parking lots.

"Try that way," I suggested, pointing toward a dark corner we hadn't explored yet, "There must be a way through somehow."

"Let's get back to the main road and look for signs." She ignored my advice and swung the car back around the way we came, heading for the street. The road veered off to the right, taking us even further away from our destination.

"We need to be going that way," I whined.

"Let's get back on the freeway. There'll be a sign," I didn't like this plan.

"But how do we get back on? Fly?" The road soared overhead, with no visible on ramp that we could see.

The phone rang.

"*Where are you?*" Scott sounded tense.

"I'm trying to get there. Sorry, we're a bit lost."

"I need to see you before I leave." His voice cracked a little.

"I know, I know, I'm coming. Just hang tight. I'll be there in five minutes."

Cara annoyed me by taking so long, and driving us round in circles. I'd been calm the whole time, I hadn't raised my voice or made a scene, but the anger and frustration took over.

As we circled the parking lot again, coming to yet *another* dead end, something in me broke. I suddenly laughed, seeing the perfection of the situation.

If I stopped and paid attention I suddenly realized—I didn't need to hurry to meet Scott. *I needed to go to LA with him.* Why was I holding on so tight? If I wanted so badly to be with him, then I should just go. The last half an hour spent driving around in circles wasn't just a frustrating waste of time—*it was a sign.* I cracked through the veneer, and the important things became clear.

By the time Cara dropped me off at the bar my mind was completely calm. Scott looked frazzled and nerve racked.

"*Where have you been?* I wanted to spend some time with you." He sounded pained. I smiled and reached for his hands.

"It's okay. I'm coming with you." He looked at me for a moment, confused.

"You're coming to LA?"

"Yes. I need to come with you. Let's go to Mission Control and pack. I'm coming with you tonight, on the bus."

I took a leap of faith and followed the inspiring voice of a man I was falling in love with, abandoning my fledgling business and my life in San Francisco to follow a crazy dream to change the world. I didn't think that giddy optimism I felt earlier in the day sitting in the hot tub could get more extreme, but it had. I soared with hope for the future. In equal measure, the terror deepened too. A clawing, dark, profound fear that I was making a terrible mistake. That I was fooling myself. *How will I survive? Where will I stay? What if it goes wrong?* I ignored the voice of fear in my head, begging me to forget this absurd fantasy: "*Stay on the plan. San Francisco, latex clothes, play parties, sexual revolution. Remember? That's why you came here.*" I pretended the voice wasn't there as I packed my bags and went to the bus station. Instead I focused on the voice that said: "*This is what you really came here for. Follow your dreams. Grasp the opportunity. Be brave and bold, and magic will happen.*"

Looking back now, I can see what a thorny little tangle it was. I told myself I was being brave and letting the river carry me onward to unknown lands. In reality, it was a mask of bravado. I clung on to Scott with sheer will, terrified I would lose him. I fashioned a story that justified my actions, and made them seem romantic and heroic. But deep down, I was afraid that if I let Scott leave he would launch into a new life without me. Leave me behind.

We sat on the Greyhound bus and watched the streetlights whiz by the window. My head rested on Scott's shoulder, and my arm linked around his. In the six hours that passed since the tiki bar I made some calls and formulated a plan. Everything seemed guided, predestined. A friend offered me a place to stay in LA, and Cara was excited to expand the gallery at Mission Control. We were going to be flat broke, but we would survive. The terror subsided to a quiet but incessant buzz.

We couldn't stop talking. From the bar to Mission Control, all the way to the bus station, then onto the bus. We talked about the future, about culture, about Superstar Avatar. By 2 AM, exhausted and still only halfway to Los Angeles, our conversation had finally petered out. We sat quietly. My mind wandered, and I started to think about our future. An important issue surfaced in my mind. It wasn't something I particularly wanted to talk about, but I couldn't avoid it anymore. "There's something I want to tell you," I said, breaking our silence. I paused for a moment. "Something I've never told anyone." He shifted in his seat and looked at me, curious.

"Okay." He waited. I took a deep breath. I needed to say it. I needed him to know. I wanted to be honest. I lied to lovers. I pretended that if nobody else knew, then it wasn't happening. Suddenly I became racked with so much shame, so much self-doubt. But I couldn't turn back now.

"I don't orgasm." There. I said it. Finally. It was out in the open. I wanted to apologize. I wanted to say: "I'm sorry for being half a person. I'm sorry for making you think I was sexually evolved when I am clearly just faking it. I'm so sorry. You probably don't want to fuck me anymore, and I don't blame you. I am broken. It's my fault."

He looked at me calmly. *"Really?* You've never had an orgasm?"

"Well, I have. I can. I do. I mean…I can when I'm on my own. But it takes a really long time. I can't do it just from sex." I blushed furiously. "Look, I'm sorry. I shouldn't have said anything. I just wanted you to know."

"It's okay. Don't apologize. Thank you for telling me," he said, tenderly. "We can work on it together." He smoothed my hair away from my face and kissed me. Gently at first, then passionately. By the time his hand reached into my pants I was already wet. His fingers were gentle, but persuasive. We kissed as I writhed on his hand. No pressure, no destination, no goal.

"This is it," I thought to myself. "This is the one. I can go there with Scott. We can do this *together."*

As the sun rose, the landscape changed from flat nothingness to buildings and palm trees. That landscape would become familiar to us; the Greyhound route into downtown Los Angeles was a trip we would take a dozen times in the next six months. It seemed romantic, until we arrived at the bus stop. As anyone who has taken the Greyhound bus to Los Angeles is aware, it drops you off in an ugly building in a desolate part of town, teeming with crazy homeless crack heads. Hungry and tired, we needed to find food before we started the long trek all the way across town to the blue skies and sandy beaches of Santa Monica, where we would be staying.

We stood on the sidewalk with our wheeled suitcases, delirious with sleep deprivation, and realized that our quest for food might to be harder than we thought. We searched for a city bus. Any bus, we didn't care. Just take us to breakfast. After inquiring at the information desk we found ourselves standing on a street corner with twenty or so people also waiting for the bus from nowhere to somewhere. It was rush hour. The bus arrived, packed full of people. We dragged our heavy suitcases on board and stood next to them, crammed in with the commuters and holding on tight as the bus lurched forward. After a dozen or so blocks we spotted a diner and pushed our way off the bus back onto the street.

There were signs outside showing plates of food with prices. *Clifton's Brookdale, eggs and bacon only $2.99.* Maybe not the highest-quality food, but the price was right. We stepped through the doors and, to our surprise, came face-to-face with an animatronic beaver. We were *not* expecting that.

The beaver moved slowly, turning its head from side to side before disappearing back into its tree stump. We stared at each other in disbelief. Inside, the restaurant looked like a rundown Disneyland ride. Mechanical animals grazed on fake grass, a river trickled its way past us, and giant fake rocks emulated a mountainous terrain. A thick layer of dust coated everything—time had forgotten this place. They served the food from a buffet, and most of the clientele looked like they were homeless. We picked up a tray and served ourselves from the steaming piles of egg, bacon, and toast. Like wide-eyed tourists just landed in a foreign land, we found a table on the second-floor balcony overlooking the restaurant. From where we sat we could see that fur on the back of the beaver's head had worn thin, the giant painting of a redwood forest on the wall had started to peel, and dust covered the huge, fake redwood trees.

As we sat there laughing at the absurdity of the situation an old black man approached us and introduced himself. Silver duct tape patched the elbow of his jacket, and he wore pants held up with a piece of rope. He spoke in a thick Southern drawl, and although I tried hard to understand what he said, I lost half of it. We sat forward, rapt, trying to decipher what mysteries he might be revealing. Clearly unused to the level of attention his introduction had garnered, he continued to speak. A rambling monologue that I barely followed. He talked about his travels. He talked about jazz. He recalled the day he arrived on the bus from San Francisco twenty years before full of big dreams. He wished us luck, and then he left.

"Was he just talking about getting off the bus from San Francisco?" I asked Scott, disoriented and a little stunned.

"Yeah, he was."

"How the fuck did he know where we came from?" I asked.

Scott shrugged. "I have no idea."

Deliriously tired, we wondered if we heard him right. Was it a sign? A coincidence? Did he see us get off the bus? *How could he have?* We were blocks away from the bus station.

Just when we thought things couldn't get any stranger, we noticed a little building with a neon crucifix over a tiny door, perched on the edge of a fake cliff above the buffet. We finished our eggs, and left our bags tucked next to a fake redwood to explore.

We peered into the tiny doorway, and found a dark interior of a small cave. It took a moment for my eyes to adjust. There was a seat inside just big enough for two. I sat down and pulled Scott inside. There was barely enough room for both of us, and we giggled as we shuffled to get comfortable. Straight ahead was a window onto a miniature forest scene. A diorama that looked as old and dusty as the larger version outside. On the wall I found a button. I pushed it, and the scene lit up. Suddenly, music drowned out the clattering of the dining room below. It sounded tinny and mournful. Then a voice started to speak—a radio voice from the past with a fatherly tone. The recording crackled.

> *"If you stand very still in the heart of a wood,*
> *You will hear many wonderful things.*
> *The snap of a twig, and the wind in the trees,*
> *And the whir of invisible wings.*
> *If you stand very still in the turmoil of life*
> *And you wait for the voice from within,*
> *You'll be led down the quiet ways of wisdom and peace*
> *In a mad world of chaos and din.*
> *If you stand very still and you hold to your faith,*
> *You will get all the help that you ask—*
> *You will draw from the silence the things that you need:*
> *Hope, and courage, and strength for your task."*

The universe reached out to deliver this message, and we listened. All my fears about working so closely together, about taking this leap, faded away. A romantic notion swept me up: fate brought us together, and divine forces we couldn't understand directed our work on Superstar Avatar. We watched for signs and saw them everywhere. When the recording ended and the light in the miniature forest clicked off, we stared at each other open-mouthed for a moment and then collapsed in exhausted laughter.

This had to be the right path—the path to love, success, and changing the world. It was destiny.

It Looked Like Hollywood

Polly Pandemonium

THREE MONTHS into our Los Angeles adventure we were ready for the big time. High on ambition, we partnered with a gaming company led by a woman called Chenoa. We were the creative team, and she took care of the business side of things. We prepared for our big Superstar Avatar launch party, hoping that there would be a big wig in the crowd with money to invest in The Next Big Thing. That's how it works in Los Angeles. Or that's what Chenoa told us.

We rented a gorgeous but slightly ramshackle club—an art deco Hollywood classic with brick walls painted cherry red and thick, velvet drapes covering the windows. The ret-ro-glam backstage area had big shiny mirrors surrounded by bright round bulbs. We set up two stages with burlesque back-drops, giant gold vases, and red velvet furniture. Dangling from the exposed rafters of the cavernous ceiling, a giant disco ball lazily spun twinkles of light around the room. In the center stood a raised dais, surrounded by gold railings. It *looked* like Hollywood.

We signed up local actors to play roles in our interactive script, designed to demonstrate the potential of Superstar Av-atar. The guests could participate by using cards we created.

Each one contained a snippet of information, so that they could use their imagination and creativity to collaboratively build the story together. We envisioned the evening as the beginning of an ongoing experience, with a website, board game, and live events to follow. We planned to invite people to make their own cards, joining the story by creating customized decks for their characters, using them to inspire storylines and connect with other players in our mythic world.

I wore a latex outfit I designed for the occasion, with asymmetrical lines and a high collar on one side. Made in slippery blues and whites, it featured spiraling curls of glowing orange, and corset lacing stretching from my left hip to my right collarbone. As I waited for the doors to open, exhilaration gripped me, so extreme I felt like a junkie. As I looked up at Scott standing on the stage, sound checking the microphone, waves of optimism flooded over me. "One two. One two." The sound of it bellowed around the vast room. I was so proud of us, and excited for our future. I wanted to live in this world, where we were successful entrepreneurs blazing the trail with our pioneering project.

As the evening progressed, everything seemed to be going according to plan; the venue we spent the last three days sweating over looked perfect, the actors all knew their roles, and the cards were ready. But there was a problem. Nobody came. Our business partner, in charge of the promotion, promised us crowds, but in the end we put on the show of a lifetime to an empty room.

"Hold up the star to see the game live!" Scott yelled into the microphone, which squealed with feedback. The audience, made up of a few of our friends, some confused curiosity

seekers, and the actors we had hired, all looked baffled by our efforts to rally them for a heartfelt moment.

"What's happening?" I saw one person ask another.

"I'm not sure. I think there's a card we're supposed to hold up."

"HOLD UP THE STAR CARD," yelled Scott, sweat pouring down his face. *"Hold up the star card and let the game begin!"* Another screech of feedback caused some of the audience to put their fingers in their ears, with pained expressions on their faces.

"Which card are we supposed to hold up?" They looked through their cards, trying to understand. I stepped off the stage and pushed cards into people's hands.

"IF YOU WANT THE GAME TO LIVE, HOLD UP THE STAR CARD!!" Scott gave up on the microphone, and just yelled at the audience.

This was the moment we scripted. The culmination of the evening, when the players invoked the game, the music played a rousing upbeat song, and we all became part of something. When we planned it, I imagined a packed venue of people screaming "YES, LET THE GAME LIVE." Instead we got a confusing anticlimax, which left us *all* feeling inadequate.

Once we got over the initial disappointment, we managed to maintain a positive attitude about moving forward. It was a learning process, and we were ready to take the lessons and move on.

We continued to work with Chenoa. I had my doubts about her abilities, but I wanted to support Scott. My sacrifices seemed insignificant in the face of our imminent success.

She had our egos in a vice grip, and fed us bogus stories

of investment money that was always just around the corner. Confident that the project would be financed soon, I freed up the last of the small inheritance my father left me when he died. One of the conditions of the bequest was that it be invested in either property or business. I couldn't just fritter it away on myself. I had already put half of it into launching my latex business, and now I put the rest into Superstar Avatar. Excited to be part of something bigger than myself, I wanted to prove my worth in the world. I gleefully wrote proposal after proposal. I drew maps and detailed schematics. I put everything I had into it. I wanted my father to be proud of me. I fantasized about my success, and the thought of his approval from the clouds made me giddy with pride.

It was a blow when we realized Chenoa was a con artist. If you look her up now, Google will send you to sites like Ripoffreport.com, scumoftheworld.com, and complaintsboard.com, where you can see a litany of accusations from people telling similar tales of promises, delays, lies, and scams. She was a small-time hustler, and the intensity of our ambition fueled her con. I have a court order for the $10,000 she owed me, but we could never track her down to pay it. Apparently she changed her name to Marie.

We tried to keep a positive outlook, gave up on Los Angeles and the pipe dream of suddenly being flush with investment money, and came back to San Francisco, humbled.

We realized that if we wanted to create a game that hacked reality to initiate a new culture of creativity, we needed to do our homework. The cards we created for the launch party were showpieces, designed to demonstrate the potential of the game. They looked great, but they came across as cryptic.

We became researchers, studying the dynamics of social

interactions to create a more solid structure for the cards. Scott's original vision was inspiring, but rather vague. We had to figure out how it worked. The cards needed a self-explanatory structure that made them self-contained and intuitive to use.

Willpower squashed any drifting moments of doubt. We had gone too far to turn back. We were living, working, and playing together twenty-four hours a day, seven days a week. Like having a child together, we were committed to the work, and to each other. This wasn't just a side project for me anymore—it became my life. I believed with every cell in my body that we would change the world.

The First Kinky Salons

Polly Pandemonium

MONEY was one reason we threw the first Kinky Salon. We needed a regular income and sexy parties seemed like the obvious thing to do. We also wanted to generate a community that could be the Petri dish for our social experiments. We joked that the guests played two roles—unwitting angel investors in our business and guinea pigs in our laboratory.

It felt right to be working on parties again.

The first events were simple—arty, themed fetish parties with a comical cabaret. Back to that formula I had been trying to perfect before I started working on Superstar Avatar. We no longer categorized our work as "mine" and "yours." It was all "ours."

Over the years Mission Control would transform into a colorful labyrinth of themed rooms, with richly painted walls, soft fabric swathed on the ceiling, thrift-store artwork, and expansive lounging areas. But in the beginning the early Kinky Salons had to be stand-and-pose parties because we had nowhere to sit down.

People didn't have sex at those first parties, but the events had a sexually enlightened vibe. We allowed nudity, and people were playfully sensual. There was bondage and spanking.

Occasionally things went further if daring guests decided to be exhibitionists, with blowjobs on the dance floor and cunnilingus on the couch, but people weren't actually fucking yet.

The original white walls and gray carpets of Mission Control slowly transformed, but without a budget it took time. Before we had any furniture, we created colorful altars in every corner. They overflowed with fake flowers, twinkly lights, and statues we picked up at yard sales.

Both Scott and I love to build altars. I'd done it since my teen years. Not because I followed a religion or a specific tradition, but because I had an intuitive urge to put precious things, which held memories or meaning, on display. These displays remind me of concepts like love, community, and gratitude, and they keep me on track with my goals. We had a goddess statue in the hallway of Mission Control, which I painstakingly covered in tiny plastic rhinestones, perched within folds of fabric and flowers. A huge carved tiki, on permanent loan from a friendly art collector, stood guard in the bar, teeth exposed in a wide smile.

On the night of the first Kinky Salon, we lit the white walls with red clamp lights in a valiant attempt to give the space a seductive ambiance. A small stage took up the center of the main room, with a fabric proscenium draping down from the ceiling. Guests stepped up onto the stage to be photographed—a conveyor belt of fetish fashion. Leather, latex, corsets, and straps.

In the corner a woman teetered on unfeasibly high heels and leaned against the wall to be spanked. Her waist cinched in tight to a latex corset and her pale ass bulged out from under her girdle. Her lover slapped her gently at first, rubbing affectionately between spanks, teasing her and whispering inaudible taunts in her ear. She giggled. Then, gradually, he came back with more and more force until finally she squealed and writhed at the onslaught, as her cheeks turned pink. People standing nearby paused their conversations to watch, and smiled encouragingly.

On stage, two girls posed for a camera. I had started teaching a latex fashion design class, and these were two of my students. They wore colorful, shiny latex—blocks of primary colors re-creating the Hot Dog on a Stick uniform you see at the mall.

We gathered the crowd together for the cabaret. A girl in a pink Afro wig sang a whimsical song accompanied by an accordion, and a clown gave us a lesson on safer sex.

As months passed, the crowd shifted away from the classic fetish crowd. The parties weren't just about kink. They had a sense of humor and a relaxed vibe. The stilted rules of the fetish scene didn't fit. As long as people were aware and respectful toward each other, we could create a more lenient atmosphere than the strict vibe of the fetish clubs.

Some traditional fetishists hated the flirtatiousness, the unsolicited hugs, and the casual attitude toward chattiness. They preferred the safety of structured etiquette. But we wanted to explore a different territory. We ditched the traditional dress code of leather and latex, and went for something more creative, giving people themes to inspire costumes.

Those first few Kinky Salons were fun, but things really started to get interesting about nine months into throwing the parties, when the event took an unexpected turn. Someone forwarded the invitation to an email list of people we didn't know, and an unusually rowdy crowd of unfamiliar faces packed

Mission Control. It seemed like I had spent the entire evening with a mop in my hand trying to keep up with the drinks being spilled all over the floor.

"What's up with this crowd?" Scott asked, when I found him bagging up the trash by the bar, looking tired. The Voodoo Lounge sign blinked lazily behind him.

"I don't know anyone here. They seem to be having a good time." I tried to see the positive side of things. He stopped what he was doing and looked at me tenderly.

"But are you having a good time? That's what's important," he emphasized. I shrugged.

"I'm okay."

He picked up the trash bag and flashed me a smile. "Tell you what—I'll take these out, and let's turn this evening around. Have some fun."

As I stood waiting for Scott to return, I went over things in my head. What made this night different? From the perspective of a guest, it was exactly as advertised—colorful and costumed, with a crowd of sexy folks having a good time dancing, socializing, and flirting. The problem only became apparent from our perspective. Previously, the party had a delicate balance between respectfulness and playfulness. It happened naturally. Guests stepped up to help out, like friends at a house party. But tonight, they weren't even being polite—they were bratty and entitled, and treated us like servants. The place slowly got trashed, while they partied. The disrespect wasn't intentional— they just didn't notice.

As I stood there pondering these thoughts I looked down and noticed a puddle of water collecting at my feet. My eye followed the stream down the hallway to a torrent of water gushing out of the bathroom door. Horrified, I sprang into action. The bathroom stalls were empty. Scattered fragments of porcelain lay on the floor, and water poured from the pipe where the toilet should have been. I didn't stop to think about what mysterious assault our toilet had undergone. I teetered around on my stiletto heels, bent over the broken plumbing trying to find the shut-off. My face was hot from exertion and rising fury. "WHAT THE HELL JUST HAPPENED?" I yelled to the hallway. "Seriously people, *how the fuck did this happen?*"

A couple of guests tried to help, but nobody had answers. I shook with anger. I felt stupid and vulnerable, and took it personally, like the attack on the toilet had been an attack on me.

The rest of the evening continued to be disappointing. Scott had to kick out two people for being too drunk, and someone vomited all over the one toilet that worked.

"*Goodbye Kinky Salon*" said the subject line of the email we wrote the next day. Maybe we were being a little dramatic, but we wanted to get people's attention. We said: "*Kinky Salon is an evening dedicated to sex positive self-expression, co-created by a community of intelligent, conscious, fun loving freaks,*" and we invited people to join in the conversation about how they were going to participate. We didn't want to become a product, where people arrived with expectations of being entertained—just another case of consumer culture. Pay your money at the door and expect to be served. We wanted Kinky Salon to be a shining example of *creator culture*. It wasn't just for the sake of Superstar Avatar—we craved the deeper connection that comes from creating community together.

Social networking wasn't popular yet, so we set up an online discussion board. We worked with the community to create a charter—our own take on those classic fetish club rules. Like the party, the rules were playful. We developed the volunteer system, and people stepped into the roles. We used monitors to keep an eye on the guests, and called them *hosts*. We weren't the first people to figure out this configuration. The format of using volunteers, monitors, and house rules was pretty standard in fetish parties. But we crowdsourced the details, giving the entire community a voice and a say. The structure morphed for years until we hit the magic formula we use today:

DO
Be creative about how you dress
Contribute when and where you can
State your boundaries
Play safely and consensually
Have sensible safe sex practices
Respect our space and each other
Clean up after yourself

DON'T
Linger unaccompanied in play spaces
Cruise aggressively (even if they are really cute)
Get too intoxicated
Take photographs
Use your cellphone
Gossip about what goes on here

We asked for help, and were awash with volunteers. They painted walls, refinished furniture, and sewed curtains. All of a sudden the people in the community became invested, and we honored their contribution, no matter how small. It was a barn raising. We said: "If you take out the trash you're a VIP at Kinky Salon," and something magic happened.

The true meaning of the word community is "to give among one another." Sharing is built into the etymology of the word. Through sharing, Kinky Salon moved from being a party to being a community. We rallied teams of volunteers to help out, and in just one month the membership of our little online forum grew to the hundreds.

People started to come to me with stories of their experiences. One time a topless girl took me aside in the hallway and hugged me. She had tears in her eyes. She told me that she had struggled with body image and eating disorders for years, and she had never felt comfortable being topless in public before. Another time a cute young guy gushingly admitted his attraction to men. He had his first boy-on-boy kiss, and he was glowing with pride to tell the story. Some stories weren't as happy. One partygoer, on seeing someone suck cock for the first time, had a flashback to child abuse. We held her in the office as she cried.

I fell in love with Kinky Salon, head over heels, like a Hallmark romance with the whole community. It pressed itself into my most intimate places, making me gasp and want it more. I wrote poetry to it, and I wooed it like a lover. I felt supported and valued. It was the family I had always yearned for.

Phoenix

Polly Whittaker

I GUESS I've been trying to create a family since I was a teenager. Not in the traditional sense of the word with a husband and 2.4 children, but a family on my own terms. My ovaries have never twinged for a baby, and I can't imagine children ever becoming a priority for me, but I do have an atavistic urge to gather a tribe.

My first attempt to create a family was with my first love, Phoenix. I met him just before my seventeenth birthday. A couple of years older than me, he wore a black leather jacket with band logos hand painted in white. When he let me wear it I felt protected. I loved him like a teenager who just lost her father—jealous, clingy, and fearful. I didn't know how to articulate these feelings, so I cried a lot.

With Phoenix and my best friend, Abby, I moved into a two-bedroom Georgian cottage in Camden Town. Our unique little home stood just outside the entrance to the local council estate. You might be thinking an estate is a fancy place with a big posh house, but actually it's completely the opposite—it's blocks of flats the government provides for low-income families. What you might call the projects. I called this little house The Fort, because it was on the edge of a war zone.

I didn't want any of my friends to feel alone and abandoned like me, so I had a vision: I wanted to turn this squalid, decrepit, 160-year-old house into a home for me and my friends. We were kids, building a fort together. My father wasn't around to take care of me anymore, so I took on the role myself.

The experiment started well—we patched plaster and painted the walls. It didn't matter that there were no stairs and we needed a ladder to get to the upper floor. It was an adventure.

I salvaged the furniture from my family home, and brought it all to The Fort. The brown couch from the living room. The kitchen table my dad had built. The print of a Montgolfier balloon in a frame, which had hung in the living room. The lamp from my father's bedside table. The family portrait from happier days—a black-and-white photo mounted on a burgundy background with a gold frame. My brothers wearing huge collars. My mum in a dress that looked like a tablecloth, her legs draped casually over my dad. My sister biting her lip while looking out from under her hair with impossibly cute eyes. Me, cross-eyed, looking like a boy, clutching my teddy bear. Like trying to put together a jigsaw puzzle when half the pieces were missing, I tried to replicate that feeling of home, but never even came close.

It didn't end well.

The downhill spiral began when Phoenix moved out. We were together for nearly five years. I was pretty much a wreck the entire time. If you do the math you'll realize that in that whole five-year relationship I never had an orgasm. We met just before I turned seventeen, and had moved in together immediately. He had been my only sexual partner during that time. We had been pretty kinky and explorative, and we tried to communicate openly, but I was too young and fucked up to have the language to talk about it. By the time I hit twenty-one, I was desperate to explore.

The day Phoenix packed his bags and moved out of The Fort was the first time I realized that traditional relationships would not work for me. Breaking up with someone I loved because I wanted to fuck someone else felt like the stupidest thing in the world. But I didn't know any other option was possible.

To Love Unquestionably

Polly Pandemonium

A LOT HAPPENED between leaving Phoenix and meeting Scott. By the time I moved to San Francisco I was resolute in my desire for an open relationship. I had grown in confidence, and wasn't a clingy, jealous teenager anymore. I was an adult—independent and self-assured—ready for a relationship that gave me the freedom to grow. Or that's what I told myself.

"I can't imagine limiting myself to one sexual partner for the rest of my life," I confided in Scott when our relationship began. "Sexual monogamy is an unrealistic model for me. It's not going to make me happy." The idea seemed crazy. It still does.

There are tons of sensible ways you can approach opening up your relationship. You can make agreements and create boundaries that work for both of you and help you feel safe. You can start with a foundation of honesty, building slowly over time. Or, if you're like Scott—scared, freaking out, trapped, and not knowing where to begin, you can start seeing someone without telling your partner, and wait for them to figure it out. I don't recommend the latter but that's how it started with us.

A year went by before it happened. We expected that one of us would meet someone, and we would open things up, but we hadn't communicated much about how it would work. I don't think either of us really knew. It began with a laptop lying carelessly open.

I stared at the computer screen open mouthed. I couldn't believe what I was reading. *Did he leave that open for me to find? Was it intentional? Or was I prying?* Either way, I couldn't unread it. Here's a lesson—never glance at your partner's email unless you're prepared for what you might see.

"I got a strange vibe from you the other day when Polly was around, and I wanted to double-check. You guys have an open relationship, right? I want to make sure we're cool and that she knows what's going on between us." When I read the words my heart froze.

Erin was a friend of both of ours. We met her at a meditation retreat. She was cute hippie girl with short, blond hair and a breezy attitude—I liked her. He had gone to a couple of parties with her, which I knew. But he hadn't mentioned that their friendship had developed into something sexual.

He wasn't *actually* breaking any agreements because we didn't have any. We were free floating, with a vague understanding that we didn't want to be exclusive. I thought that when it came up, our ability to communicate and the strength of our connection would be enough. When he came home I confronted him.

"Is there something going on with you and Erin?" I asked, straight to the point. "If you're having sex I just want to know."

"I was scared to tell you," he admitted, looking down.

"I don't understand why you would do that without saying something." I started to cry. I couldn't help it. This wasn't how I pictured this happening.

"This is why," he said, sounding exasperated, "because I knew you would be upset."

"But I'm upset because you didn't tell me, not because you had sex." Frustration and fear rose in me. Jealousy reared up in an overpowering bout of nausea. I wanted to run. I wanted to pack my bags and leave. I wanted to sob and scream and kick.

"I'm sorry. You're right. I should have said something," he paused, looking at me, his eyes watery with tears and filled with fear. "We can figure this out. Please. *I love you.*"

Those three words. They were the key. Believing those three words. I had a choice. I knew I loved him; that wasn't in question. If I trusted that he loved me, that he wasn't trying to hurt me, then anything was possible. We were unstoppable.

I didn't know what kind of relationship I wanted. I didn't have a plan. All I knew was that sexual monogamy wasn't for me. I hadn't imagined it beginning this way, but I did want to experiment with new relationship styles. Once the anger and fear subsided, with reassurance from Scott, we started to define what we wanted.

From the perspective of an outside observer, the story of our relationship might seem more like a cautionary morality tale, rather than a glowing account of how open relationships work. We made it up as we went along, flailing around, crashing into each other's hearts in unpleasant ways.

I don't subscribe to the fantasy that people have pretty, perfect relationships—monogamous or not, it gets messy. The trick is to learn from your experiences; admit when you're wrong, and where you're scared, and love each other without condition.

The truth is I had never experienced this depth of connection with another human before. I exposed the tenderest parts of myself to him, and I marveled in turn at the sweetness of the parts he revealed to me. I basked in the surety that we shared a future together, and loved intensely, unbreakably, unquestionably.

Now that we had opened up, the perfect place to find new playmates was in the community we created. We just had to open the doors, and they flooded in. We traded partners with other couples, exploring a diversity of bodies and hearts. Sometimes we brought a single woman into our bed. I was turned on to see him fucking other women, and I loved to watch. A rare treat was when another guy joined Scott, and I was the center of attention. Occasionally I found myself in a Fellini-esque configuration of limbs and costumes as dawn broke over Mission Control, exhausted and half-naked bodies draped over couches and beds in postcoital prostration.

The difference with these new experiences, compared to my previous explorations, was the ever-present *love*. Not just between Scott and me, but also with the people we were playing with. Love was expressed in these group configurations as intimately as it would be for two. Our interactions would slow for a moment to hear one person voice their feelings to the group. Scott would blow kisses at me across the room over the tangle of limbs. I discovered that after all the years of exploring sadomasochism, bondage, and power play, I had finally found my kink. *Love.*

A few months later I started dating too, experiencing for the first time in my life being deeply in love with someone, while still having the freedom to explore sexually and emotionally with other people. This configuration was new for both of us, but with love and communication, I felt like we were getting it right.

My first lover was a musician. He played accordion in the cabaret at one of our events and could eat pussy like he played—with breathtaking skill and a touch of wildness. Then there was the fireman. He would bring the fire engine and park it outside Mission Control during parties, just to tell me he thought I was beautiful. That always scared the doorman, who thought it was an official inspection. Then there were *the boys.* My dream come true. Two bisexual men who had been together for over a decade, they were deeply in love with each other, but wanted a girlfriend too. I couldn't imagine a hotter configuration than being between two men in love.

It was never perfect. Navigating multiple relationships isn't easy. The complexity of managing the emotional rollercoaster can be exhausting. But it's what I wanted at the time, and it gave me the opportunity to learn a lot about myself, and experience many different flavors of love.

Beat Me and Fuck Me

Polly Whittaker

S EX WITHOUT LOVE is another story. I'm not against it. I've certainly had my fair share. I've enjoyed numerous impulsive one-night stands in my lifetime. Some were exciting; some were average; some were downright dangerous. I left a few of them cheap and disrespected, and left others exhilarated and empowered.

One time back in London I fucked a guy in the restroom of a fetish club. He wore black latex, tattoos covered his arms, and his cock jangled with a dozen or more piercings. I invited him home, and he brought a bag of toys with him.

"So what do you like?" he asked as he slowly took off my clothes, savoring each moment.

"I dunno. I like to fuck," I replied, facetiously. I enjoyed the way his eyes lingered on my body.

"You like a little power play?" he asked, looking me directly in the eye.

"Sure," I said, excitement pulsing through my body.

"Well, I like to be in control, so I hope you enjoy submitting." His eyes sparkled.

"Show me," I said, and in an instant he turned me around

and held my hands firmly behind my back. He reached into his toy bag to find his restraints. A few moments later I found myself naked, cuffed, face down on the bed.

"I think it's time to teach you a lesson," he said playfully, and pulled his toys out of the bag one at a time, stinging crops and thudding floggers. He laid them on the bed beside me. "What are your boundaries, honey? Can I beat you and fuck you? Do you like it hard or gentle? I'm asking you now because you won't be able to talk in a moment," he pulled out a ball gag from his bag. A round, pink rubber ball on a strap.

"Yes, yes," I said into the pillow, "beat me and fuck me."

"Good girl," he said as he pushed the ball gag in my mouth and placed the strap around the back of my head. It occurred to me in that moment that this was dangerous—letting this stranger tie me up. Nobody knew he was here with me. I didn't even remember his name. Panic waved through me as he lifted my hips and the first blow hit my buttocks. But then…surrender. Yes. Hit me. I need the pain. I want to feel it. With every blow I let go a little more. He spread my legs wide and hit my pussy with a paddle. Thud, thud, thud. I arched into it. "Good girl," he cooed. "Give me that pussy." He pulled out a flogger with heavy leather straps and beat my legs, my shoulders, my ass. I started to cry. With every blow my grief, heartbreak, and sorrow all disappeared into sensation. No history, no future, just *this moment*. I wanted to be pure, like a newborn baby. I wanted him to beat every memory out of me.

Then he fucked me. With his fingers first, then I heard the snap of latex and felt his cock. With my hands behind my back I couldn't do anything but succumb. My face pushed into the pillow, covered in tears and snot, mouth held wide open with the ball gag. He turned my face toward the mirror. He was still wearing his clothes, his cock pulled out from his latex pants, black ink snaking up the sides of his neck out of his shiny black tank top. "Look at that," he said. "You're being fucked by the devil. How does it feel to be ridden by the devil?" He stuck out his tongue at me and flicked it up and down, laughing, and then he fucked me harder.

Yes, I liked being fucked by the devil. It was real. The most real thing I could do. I sobbed as he fucked me and pushed back onto his cock, greedily filling myself over and over. My numbness was penetrated. I had no place to hide. I was as real and raw as a person could be. Laid open, bare and vulnerable. With my wrists sore from the restraints, and my jaw tired from being held open, I didn't want it to end.

Jealousy

Polly Pandemonium

THERE'S A THEORY that so many anti–open relationship commentators are fond of—*once you've
broken trust you can never go back and it irreparably
damages your relationship.* That might be true for some people,
but not for me.

Can you trust that someone will always do exactly as they
say? No. People will always make bad decisions, fuck up, or
just need to do something different. It's inevitable. Can you
trust that they love you, they're doing their best, and don't
mean you any harm? That's the question.

For some, the idea of an open relationship is terrifying, and
I get it. The common question is: "Don't you get jealous?" The
answer? Sure, I get jealous. People get jealous, whether they're
in an open relationship or not. It's part of being human. Some
people don't want their partner to talk to anyone they might
find sexually attractive. Some heterosexual men find the closeness of their partner's girlfriends threatening. Some are okay
with their partner sharing kisses and cuddles with their friends.
Other people's reasons might seem ridiculous if that's not how
you feel, but we all have different histories. There's no right or
wrong way to love.

When Scott discovered I liked cute Japanese miniatures, he started going to Japantown to buy me tiny plastic desserts. It was his way of telling me he loved me. When I found out he was buying tiny desserts for his lover I will admit I was jealous. I had a moment where the little girl inside me stomped her feet and cried, "that's my thing!" But I would never put a toddler in the driving seat of a car, and I prefer to keep my inner child out of the driving seat of my personality. Instead of freaking out, I let my inner therapist take the wheel. After a little soul searching I realized that, in truth, I just wanted to feel special. "If you need exclusive access to tiny plastic donuts in order to have self-esteem, maybe that's something you should look at," said my inner therapist. She can be a bit harsh sometimes, but she's often right.

Jealousy is a complex and misunderstood emotion, often blamed when it's not really at fault. If you're scared, your jealousy might include fear. If you're annoyed, it might include anger. Jealousy in itself is pretty benign—it's when the other emotions are involved it can get messy. To ask the question, "why am I jealous?" is often missing the point—it's usually pretty obvious. Better to ask, "what am I scared will happen?" The answers often have nothing to do with what's actually happening, and are related to old traumas instead. It's okay to be jealous because it cracks open these Easter eggs of neurosis for you to take an honest look at. I'm not the kind of person who likes to sweep things under the carpet. Jealousy is inevitable; it's how you deal with it that matters.

"Don't you believe in finding a soul mate?" Absolutely I do. But I don't think that level of connection is limited to one person in your lifetime. "Don't you get scared he'll fall in love with someone else and leave you?" No, I think he'll fall in love with someone else and stay with me. "Do you tell the people you're dating that you're in a relationship?" Yes. That conversation is usually how I start a first date. "Do you hang out with his girlfriends?" Not really. I like to give him space. But I usually invite them out for tea after they've been on a few dates so we can chat and I can welcome them to the family. "Does he take your boyfriends out for tea?" In my experience, women seem to want this kind of communication more than men. "What about STDs?" We are human beings, and we catch bugs from each other all the time. Just because I'm afraid of getting a cold doesn't mean I don't get on the bus. Safer sex can protect us from the dangerous stuff. "How do you manage your time seeing multiple people?" Google Calendar.

Strategic Planning

Polly Pandemonium

IT TURNED OUT that Gumby, my favorite latex client, was also a retired business strategist, and he became curious about Superstar Avatar. One day, we met at Mission Control for a marathon planning session.

Scott and I sat on a couch in the middle of the room, and Gumby stood by a whiteboard. The scene could have been normal, except for the fact that Gumby was wearing six-inch spike heels, and a black shiny latex cat suit with a hood covering his face. The mask's large eyeholes made him look like a cross between an insect and an alien, and he spoke through an opening for his mouth. He came out of the bathroom dressed this way five minutes earlier and requested we secure his arms. A metal belt circled his waist, which attached by chains to cuffs on his wrists.

The whiteboard he stood in front of said GAME in big blue letters. He picked up a pen, pulled off the lid, and went to the board to write, but the chain attached to his wrist prevented his hand from reaching the whiteboard. He tugged for a moment, just for dramatic effect, and then looked at us, eyebrows raised.

"Do you see what I'm trying to say here?" he asked in a businesslike voice. I started to giggle. This was the silliest, most awesome business meeting I had ever been to. Gumby remained straight-faced.

"Something about limitations?" Scott said, playing along.

"Yes, exactly," Gumby pointed to Scott with his other hand, and the chain pulled taut.

"Constriction," Scott continued, "being chained to yourself."

"Yes, yes," Gumby licked his lips through the mask, "I am bound. I am chained."

"Does this have anything do to with Superstar Avatar, or are you just being a pervert, Gumby?" I asked, laughing.

"Look at the board, what does it say?" he asked, maintaining his serious tone.

"Game," Scott and I said in unison.

"Game," he repeated. "It's this word that constricts you. You always call Superstar Avatar a game. But it's not a game. If you keep calling it a game, you limit yourselves. You have chained yourselves to a word that doesn't fully express your potential. You need to think bigger than this."

Gumby was right—it wasn't just a game. But what was it? I was giddy with ideas. Was it a playful social design? A framework for creator culture? A language for cultural evolution?

There's a little book called *Finite and Infinite Games* by a religious studies professor named James Carse. Scott gave me a copy when we first met and it blew my mind. It starts, *"A finite game is played for the purpose of winning, an infinite game is played for the purpose of continuing the play."* In this tiny tome he talks about wars, religion, relationships, and sex, all within the context of this simple idea of finite versus infinite games: A infinite player's goal is to expand the game to include *more* people and *more* play, while a finite player plays to win, and, therefore, to end the game.

Calling Superstar Avatar a game made sense to us, because we meant it in the context of the infinite game. But we didn't want it to be misunderstood as something childish or trivial. We were talking about creating a whole new way of being social, and of bringing creativity into everyday life. This wasn't a game in the traditional sense of winners and losers, which you played on your day off.

Gumby helped us identify the first steps: Start with what you know. Throw Superstar Avatar events at Mission Control. Prove the concept and record the results. Leave behind the word *game* and think bigger. Then show the world what we're capable of.

We became obsessed, spending every minute available analyzing and theorizing, writing proposals, and drawing color-coded diagrams. Superstar Avatar prepared for blastoff. We planned the trajectory and laid out a plan, but would the world be ready for us?

The Press

Polly Pandemonium

DREAMS. Hope. That rollercoaster. I'd been working full time on Superstar Avatar for more than two years, finalizing the structure for the cards, creating websites and brochures and testing the system. We didn't earn a penny from it. The events and my latex business supported us financially. Just as my energy was beginning to wane, an unexpected prospect revealed itself.

A journalist from the *SF Weekly* watched our progress. She called us to ask questions, and scheduled an interview. Before we knew it, they called us in for a photo shoot, and to our delight, the story made it to the front cover. Could this be the opportunity we had been waiting for? The headline, printed March 2004, read, "Superstar Avatar, A Game of Life and Lust on the Social Frontier."

We waited with anticipation for the phone to ring. Angel investors with fat checkbooks enamored with our amazing ideas. Maybe TV producers would want to make a reality show about us. Or we would be invited to speak at big conferences about innovation. This would be our big break. All we needed was the chance to be seen, and destiny would take its course. Confident that the right person would read it, we waited for the opportunities to flood in. This would change everything.

For one week, while every street corner newspaper box in town featured our faces, people recognized us wherever we went. Once the week ended, we disappeared back into obscurity. Sure, we got a few inquiries, but it was a fantasy to think Superstar Avatar would suddenly be projected into the big time. We begrudgingly accepted that we would have to keep pushing.

Kinky Salon, on the other hand, steadily grew. Scott started to resent the popularity of the events, frustrated with the community of people who only seemed interested in partying. I felt guilty for enjoying them. My heart and ambition pulled one direction and then another.

Regardless of my needs, Kinky Salon took on a life of its own, and it even won a Best of the Bay award.

"Best Sex Club for Freaks and Geeks." I read aloud to Scott from the newspaper. "What the fuck?" Although my ego fluttered with ambition, I couldn't be happy about it. "This is ridiculous. I don't want that award. I've been to sex clubs, and we are definitely not in the same category. They are sleazy, and the floors are sticky, and they smell of bleach, and single men follow you around trying to jack off on you."

"People *were* having sex here last weekend," Scott reasoned. There had been illicit encounters. Gropes in darkened corners, but it was rare that people had sex. Although one small room, all the way up in the front of the building, had become the exception to this rule. Past the dance floor, painted in dazzlingly Pepto-Bismol pink, with cozy couches and pillows, it became more than just a place to make out. At the previous party I stood in the doorway and witnessed the gently moving

146

outline of bodies in the dim light. This little corner of the party had taken on a new vibe altogether. They weren't naked—they pulled cocks out of pants and slid hands inside dresses, like naughty teenagers in the back seats of cars. They giggled and peeked over shoulders to see if anyone was watching. When they noticed me peering into the room, the grinding paused, or at least slowed, unsure if they were breaking the rules.

I liked the idea of people having sex openly at Kinky Salon; it seemed like a natural step to take. We couldn't turn back from being labeled a *sex party*—like posting a naked photo to the internet; we knew it would always be out there. So that very afternoon I crafted an email making it explicitly clear that sex would be allowed at a special event we called Kinky Salon XXX.

Our First Balls-to-the-Wall Sex Party

Polly Pandemonium

UMANS ARE TRIBAL by nature, and it's surprising how quickly people can shift their behavior given the right conditions. Create an atmosphere that's different enough from normal, everyday life, and then change the social rules. That's what happens at Burning Man—by plucking you out of your life for a week you're shown your potential as a creative human. It's *normal* to be an artist at Burning Man. And at Kinky Salon...*being sexy* became normal.

In preparation for the party, we hauled two California King beds up the back stairs, and laid them side-by-side in an area we gigglingly named the *horizontal socializing space*. We covered all the furniture with clean sheets, and tucked them in neatly and securely. We put out bowls of safe sex supplies, like candy in their shiny wrappers. Piles of towels stacked by the beds with wet wipes, tissues, and an oversize martini glass full of latex gloves with a sign that read, *"No Glove No Love."*

There's no doubt about it, sex is compelling. When it's happening close by you can't ignore it. That sticky-sweet, pungent taste of pheromones swirling in the air. Realizing that a conversation you're having might develop into sex, right here and now, does change how people interact. That coy side glance could mean so much more in a place like this.

At the first Kinky Salon where we explicitly permitted sex, I buzzed with excitement and nerves. Flirting, making out, spanking, and the occasional playful grope all existed within a realm I was comfortable in, but what might happen tonight? Would I have sex with someone? All my friends were here. I'd experienced threesomes and foursomes. I'd self-consciously played the exhibitionist at seedy sex clubs, we had hosted after-parties for a few select people plucked from the crowd, but I'd never had sex in community. Sex surrounded by friends.

My previous experience of sex parties fell into two basic categories. They were overrun with single guys—circles of desperate men jacking off at any opportunity. Or, if the gender balance was even, sex completely took over and the interactions became pure pornography—being present without participating seemed awkward. Kinky Salon was neither.

"What's your name?" asked a cute guy with blond hair and freckles when I went to the bar to refill my champagne.

"I'm Polly," I smiled at him, a little shy.

"You're the Polly who puts on the parties?" He seemed impressed.

"Yep, that's me!" I imagined what it would be like to let this man touch my naked body, and I blushed.

"Thank you for this! It's my first time here. This place is great!" His blond hair flopped in front of one eye, and he coyly tucked the stray lock behind his ear. I noticed the curve of his neck, gracefully feminine, and the broadness of his chest underneath his shirt. He kissed my hand, staring unflinchingly into my eyes, and my body lit up with anticipation.

My leather corset felt amazing. I loved the way it exaggerated my shape and made me stand a little taller. I kept touching my waist and hip. That curve is my favorite part of a woman's body, and to experience it on myself was incredibly sexy. I'd attached fishnet stockings to the garters on the corset, and with knee-high boots and a big, blond wig I looked like a bit of a whore. Sex-fantasy Polly. Red lipstick and perfume on my tits. Ready for action. Proud, feminist, powerful—and a bit of a porn star cliché. My favorite combo. The outfit I wore gave me the confidence to put his hand on my hip as I reached across for my champagne bottle. I dizzied with the swirling energy of desire as he leaned close and paused for a moment, his lips a fraction away from the side of my face. He waited for my lead, but he would have to wait a little longer. I couldn't disappear so early.

"I have to check in with my volunteers," I said, apologetically. "Can I find you again later?"

"I'm not going anywhere," he smiled to reveal dimples, making tearing myself away even harder.

The evening progressed on a trajectory similar to previous parties: preparty tension, volunteers arriving, doors opening, guests arriving, crowd reaching critical mass, flirting, dancing, cabaret. But then...something different. After the cabaret...*people started fucking*. Bodies packed the back-room beds. This was sex happening in a way I'd never witnessed before. No gawkers. No circle jerk. No pressure to participate. Just a room full of adults doing the most natural thing in the world.

I checked in with Scott; I'd found him with a cute girl perched on his knee out on the patio. I gave him a wink and a nod, our secret signal, and he smiled back encouragingly. I found the cute blond guy and let him lead me to the back room.

He lowered me onto the bed with passionate kisses. The room was lit with red lamps, just enough so you could discern the outline of the beds, and the people sprawled across them like seals at Pier 39, playfully nuzzling at each other. Deep red fabric draped down in sumptuous curves from the ceiling. The music played loud enough to complement, but not drown out the giggles, squeals, and moans emanating from the crowd. It all became part of the same soundtrack—the throbbing bass line spliced perfectly with the ambient swoon. Bodies surrounded us. In my peripheral vision, I drank in the dreamlike apparition of their ecstatic intimacy. One of the red lamps backlit a rather handsome foursome on the other side of the room. A man with a shaved head and broad shoulders. A brunette woman on all fours on the bed in front of him. Behind him, a second man wrapped his arms lovingly around his gently muscled and tattooed torso. A redhead tucked herself in underneath, with her slender, pale legs sticking out. The crisp silhouettes of their bodies showed every detail: how the woman on all fours took his cock in her mouth, how the second guy traced his finger around his lover's nipple, how the woman tucked underneath gently explored the body above her.

There were no unwanted wandering hands, no staring eyes making me self-conscious. I became overwhelmed with a sense of pride. *Fuck yes.* This feels right. It feels *good.* These are my tribe—these crazy pleasure seekers. These brave pioneers of love. I can see it in their eyes too. Something magical is happening here.

At the end of the night I curled in Scott's lap on the couch in the lobby, and a few of us chatted as the party wound down, when suddenly a guy came out of the Pink Room seeming distressed and holding a stuffed toy. *"What the fuck is wrong with this tiger?"* he asked us plaintively, turning its face in our direction. "Do you see its expression?" Sure enough, there was something very strange about its face. The cheap toy had been printed badly, and its mouth looked distorted in a weird angle, making it seem rather snooty, as if it looked down its nose at you disapprovingly.

"I think it's *judging you,*" Scott replied.

"Jesus, I can't look at that thing. Can you take it away, please?"

We laughed uncontrollably, trying to stare down the tiger and failing.

"*I feel so judged!*" wailed Scott, throwing the tiger at me. I held him in my hands and turned his face to mine, staring deep into his eyes.

"It's like a test. If at the end of the night after everything you've done you can look into the face of the Judgmental Tiger and experience no remorse or shame, *then you pass.*" I stared into his eyes and paused, contemplating the plush, sneering face. One at a time, we looked into the eyes of the tiger and either squealed and threw it away or nodded and smiled knowingly. His badly printed mass-produced face had unwittingly created a myth: Like the Sphinx of ancient Egypt, he represented a challenge and a gateway. It was totally ridiculous, and yet kind of profound too.

I have to admit looking in his eyes I had a twinge. Although all my instincts were saying yes—this kind of party did have value, and I was happy there—I had a small voice telling me that if I continued down this path then nobody would ever take me seriously; I would always been seen as a party girl, my goals

of cultural change would be laughed at, and I would never succeed. This voice was new. A nagging mosquito buzzing in the
background telling me that the ambitions of my youth were immature—these parties weren't the important work—and I had
to focus on Superstar Avatar.

But these events were paying the bills. And besides, I was
having so much fun that the idea of stopping seemed ludicrous.

Club Kiss and the Lifestyle

Polly Pandemonium

THERE WAS one other sex club in San Francisco at the time, but it catered to a different crowd than Kinky Salon. It was for couples and single women only, and it wasn't queer friendly. When it suddenly closed down one day we were flooded with requests to throw a similar party at Mission Control. So we created Club Kiss.

Forget whatever stereotypical image you have in your head of *swingers;* the *Lifestyle* scene is *hot.* Yes, that's lifestyle with a capital L. You might be shocked to hear how popular it is in America. Google it. You'll find hundreds of websites with thousands of couples, all looking to hook up. The internet mobilized this scene, and it exploded. Even if you don't think you do, you probably know some people living the *Lifestyle.*

We always struggled with money, and we saw this party as a way to earn some fast cash. Scott had given up his puppetry and performance career when we started working on Superstar Avatar together. I still made a living from designing latex clothes, but the chemicals needed for the process started to give me headaches, and I desperately wanted to quit. The path to earning money from Superstar Avatar had not yet revealed itself. We had a choice—to leave Mission Control or to throw more parties. We weren't ready to leave. So we amped up the schedule, and we threw events *every weekend,* alternating between Kinky Salon and our new party, Club Kiss.

For a couple of weeks before our first event we scoured the Lifestyle websites for potential guests and sent them personal invitations. When the evening arrived I sat at the top of the stairs, perched on a tall stool, and doodled on the guest list absentmindedly.

The thin fabric of my glittery red mesh dress revealed my lingerie underneath, and I swept my hair into an updo, and fastened it with a rhinestone pin. The mirror ball in the dance floor sent sparkles of light out into the lobby with every rotation. I checked my lipstick again in the little mirror I stashed in the cashbox.

Scott had trimmed his curly mustache back a little so our new guests didn't think we were a couple of weirdos, and he wore a perfectly tailored suit with a classic fedora hat. A couple came up the stairs looking nervous. They glanced around the lobby with skittish eyes and clutched each other's hands. Our welcome was warm and sweet as hot fudge sauce.

"Don't worry," I reassured them, "it's actually great to be the first to arrive, because it means you can get your bearings before the others get here. Barron will show you round, and if you like you can sit up here on the couch and watch the hotties arrive. It's really the best seat in the house!"

"Come on, let me show you the lay of the land," said Scott as he gestured for them to follow him. "*Thank you, Princess.*"

We had decided that in order to pull off this event we would need to create new personas. It helped us get into the unfamiliar role of throwing a party for *normal* people. Scott chose to go by his birth name, Barron, and I was Princess Polly.

A rush of couples arrived, and by eleven o'clock, the party was lively. Mission Control filled with the kind of couples you usually see at swanky bars. Tall guys wearing dark designer jeans with polished shoes. Slender, well-manicured women. People chatted in little groups.

I peeked in to the dance floor and scanned the crowd. They looked like teenagers at a high school prom, trying not to look awkward as the DJ played to an empty dance floor. I pulled Scott over and we plotted how to get them to relax. There was only one thing for it.

I swanned confidently across the dance floor, feeling all eyes on me as I spoke to the girl in coat check. She was a Kinky Salon regular, and we knew each other *well*. "Hey sweetie, can you do me a favor?" I asked in an angelic tone.

"Sure, what's up?" She was always ready to help out.

"Do you mind jumping out of coat check for a minute and helping me get this party started?" I had a twinkle in my eye. So did she.

"I like the sound of that," she replied as she bobbed under the barrier to join me. I pulled her out to the dance floor and we started to move. My hands ran over her waist and I pulled her closer. She was at least six inches shorter than me; the bangs of her black bob were long and seductive, almost brushing her eyelashes as she looked up at me, smiling. We knew the couples in the room were watching as we whispered in each other's ears. She giggled and squirmed under my touch. Couples started to drift onto the dance floor, watching us out of the corner of their eyes. We smiled at them teasingly.

"Do you want to take my dress off?" I asked, cheekily. My

collaborator was only too happy to oblige. She reached her hand under my dress and caressed my body for a moment before she lifted the whole thing up and over my head. I laughed and threw it aside.

"Shall I take my bra off?" she suggested, helpfully.

"That would be awesome!" I was so grateful for this perky little assistant. She whipped off her bra and stood there for a moment, breasts free. With gleeful approval I pulled her close. It wasn't long before other couples followed our lead. Tops flew off left and right.

A new couple arrived and stood nervously at the coat check, waiting for my friend to return.

"I should go deal with them," she smiled.

"I think our job is done here," I gestured around the dance floor. "Thanks for helping."

"Anytime!" she said emphatically as she ducked back into the coat check.

I didn't expect to, but I loved this new party. It was fun to make people happy. We created a safe, consensual, comfortable space for regular folks to push their sexual boundaries and explore new territory.

Plus it paid the rent.

If you're looking to explore something new in your relationship, sex at parties is a great way to open up. It's a bit gentler than going on dates with other people. There's less pressure. You can start by simply going to a party and checking it out.

People often tell me they're scared to come to my parties because they don't want to be thrown in at the deep end. They're afraid that their partner might go off without them, or they'll be dragged into a situation they're not comfortable with.

They think it's all or nothing, black and white. But the truth is, you to decide what you're comfortable with.

For newbies, I always advise agreeing to take care of each other for your first event. Be solely invested in each other's experience. Don't flirt or get distracted. Build trust slowly, and then go home and talk about it. Don't try to change the rules on the fly. If you meet someone you both like, don't suddenly decide you're ready for a threesome. Take it gently. Build on your experience, and make sure you feel safe every step of the way. If you're single, then the person you're taking care of is yourself.

Once you've had some practice you might reach your capacity and decide you don't want to explore any further. Or you might find that those baby steps were just the beginning, and it feels liberating and fun to meet new people and expand your relationship. And who knows where that might lead you.

PART TWO

Seven Stars

Polly Superstar

POLLY SUPERSTAR was born when I tattooed an arc of seven rainbow-colored stars on my belly. It wasn't an act of vanity; it was a ritual. I wanted to bring color and light to my sacral chakra—the energy center in the body where your sexuality resides—and help myself to heal. I sat in the chair at the tattoo parlor and watched as the ink etched into my skin. I wept at the pain. I had spent so many years believing I was damaged and inadequate; I was ready to flood my sexuality with love, and finally let go of the story that I was broken. The tattoo symbolized my rebirth.

There wasn't a specific incident that triggered this birth. It was a slow realization. I gradually woke up to the ugly neuroses that kept rearing their heads and influencing my life. I felt like a predictable product of my sad history—a bundle of fears and impulses with a trail of breadcrumbs that led neatly back through my past. I didn't want to be ruled by them anymore.

In the same way I had created a new name and a new persona when I arrived in San Francisco, I rewrote my reality once again. I invented a future me: Polly Superstar. She was a balanced, healthy version of me, and she lived in my future. She still does. She's the person I'm becoming. By claiming her name in the present, I connected to that future self and started my road to becoming whole.

Then, Polly Superstar started communicating with me. She would come to me in dreams and meditation, with clear messages. She told me that I was on the right path, and that my future was amazing. I know this might sound weird, but it's as if I created a time loop within my own lifetime, allowing my consciousness to speak to my other selves.

I was just an inchoate version of this future me, but she gave me a mission: to connect to my past selves and comfort them. Fulfilling this directive, I dug out some old photos I hadn't looked at since I moved to San Francisco. I looked at the pictures and felt strangely disconnected, like I was looking at someone else's life. "Don't be sad for this girl," I thought to myself. "No pity, she hates that."

In the background of the photograph I could see a collage of pages from magazines covering the walls of my teenage bedroom. Fashion models with their eyes cut out. Faces scratched with black pen. Heads put on the wrong bodies. The room was filled with clutter and overflowing ashtrays. Books and cassette tapes crammed every surface.

I closed my eyes and sent my consciousness back through history, across oceans. In a mixture of remembering and imagining, I found myself back in that room. Like a ghost in my own past—a shadow from the future—I reached out to comfort the girl that was me.

At first she was closed. Adamant in her pain. She had walls like a prison camp. I persisted, reaching out with my consciousness and flooding her with love. Slowly, gently, I felt her open. Just a crack. Her heart eased. There was a flutter of recognition.

A wary suspicious glance. A tinge of relief.

"Hey, Polly. It's okay to be sad, but you're not alone. You're never alone. I'm always here." She started to cry. A tear in one eye at first, she sniffed and wiped it away, defiantly. Then the floodgates opened. Streaming, silent tears.

Then *I remembered.* I remembered *this moment* when it happened the first time around—that comforting voice coming to me in my sadness when I was young. Shocked at the memory, I blinked my eyes open in the present. I looked at the photo again and this time it was different. I could remember being her, and I distinctly recalled hearing that voice. Was it real? Had I imagined it? Suddenly I realized I was weeping too.

The River Delights to Lift Us Free

Polly Whittaker

I HAVE A PHOTOGRAPH of the last time I was with my dad. He gazes directly into the camera with his one good eye. His other eye closed years earlier—a symptom of the massive tumor pressing against the back of his eyeball. I remember that day—he was coherent for the first time in a couple of months. Being pumped with morphine made him confused, and the pressure of the tumor on his brain affected his thinking in unexpected ways.

In the photo I am sitting next to him, with my arm around his shoulders. He is covered in spots and abrasions, and he's very thin. My eyes are black with thick eyeliner. I'm smiling for the camera, but I don't seem happy or sad—my expression is unreadable. Distant. My long, pink hair extensions drape down in front of one eye. A nurse took the picture for us.

A few days before we took this photograph, I had been walking home from school when our Christmas tree came sailing out of the living room window. I had just turned the corner onto our street—a broad avenue in West London with big trees planted by Victorians. We had lived in this house since my birth. The crisp, cold air blew through the leafless trees. I finished my cigarette and flicked the butt at a lamppost. My eyebrow raised as I saw our Christmas tree, complete with decorations, fly out onto the street. My mother stood at the window, but she didn't see me.

"FUCK CHRISTMAS!" she yelled at the top of her voice to the empty street and slammed the window behind her. The tree lay on the sidewalk, twinkling tinsel fluttering in the cold wind, the lights still connected by an umbilical cord through the window.

I hadn't been to visit my dad in the hospital for a while. My sister, Sam, would get angry with me. She was there all the time, helping him eat and taking care of Mum. But the last time I saw him it freaked me out, and I didn't want to go for a while.

I had been at the hospital in his private cubicle on the terminal ward, sectioned off at one end with a green curtain. Sam puttered around the room, arranging flowers and chatting to Mum. I sat next to Dad while he slept, holding his hand and looking at his peaceful face. He slept most of the time, and when he was awake he didn't make much sense. His hand twitched, and his eyes opened. They were watery and his eyeballs rolled in their sockets as he tried to focus.

"Hi Dad," I said, smiling at him. He took a moment to recognize me.

"Polly, I-I'm so glad you're here," he said. His mouth was dry and I fed him some water through a straw. He strained toward me, urgently, with a weak, raspy voice, "There's something happening here I have to tell you about." I leaned in so I could hear what he was saying.

"You have to help me." His eyes looked at me, but I couldn't decipher his expression. Had I heard him right? "Please, Polly. Please help me," he croaked. Panic waved over me.

"What's going on, Dad?" He started to mumble. I strained to listen.

"I don't understand, I'm sorry." My heart filled with pity and love for this husk of a man. I wanted to understand, to be there for him. His other hand reached for me suddenly, and he rose up out of bed. He clutched at me with both hands, terrified.

"You have to help me," he whispered again. "They have me trapped here."

"What do you mean you're trapped, Dad?" I held his hands and looked into his frightened eyes.

"They have me trapped!" he said, this time more loudly, gesturing toward Sam and Mum. He leaned in and in a desperate tone he whispered, *They have me in a medical trap, Polly; you have to help me get out of here. They are trying to kill me.* I started to pull back, but he drew me close. "Don't let them kill me. Polly, please, you have to save me."

By the time Sam and Mum joined me by the side of the bed, Dad was clinging on to me, sobbing. As the nurse put an extra dose of morphine into his drip, which fed directly into the back of his hand, I watched as his expression shifted from desperate terror to sleep in just a few seconds. He was hallucinating, paranoid, and frightened. Brain tumors can do that to you.

I didn't tell Sam that story until I wrote it down. I thought she would be upset by it. When she finally read it she said, "Oh yeah, the medical trap. He used to say shit like that all the time." I looked at her and realized how strong she had been, to be by his bedside, and how much she had gone through when I ran away.

A month later, succumbing to pressure from my sister, I visited one last time. "Happy Christmas," I said as I walked in the door, nervous but hiding it. He sat up in his chair and smiled broadly when I walked in.

"Hello. Look at you. I like your hair. You look like a princess." His voice slurred from the morphine.

"Thanks, Dad." I smiled and touched my long bright pink hair, a little self-conscious. He hadn't talked sense in many weeks, and to see him so perky caught me off guard.

"Turn around; let me see it," he said, and I spun around to give him the whole effect. It reached the backs of my knees. "Cor blimey, look at that. What is that? A wig?"

"No, Dad, it's extensions. They're in there all the time."

"You'll never get a job looking like that."

"I've got a job." I replied defensively as I pulled off my coat and sat down next to him.

My dad was never that distant British stereotype who didn't know how to talk to his children. My brothers might disagree, but I always had an easy rapport with him. Overcoming death for so many years, facing fears, and having such an opportunity to realize what's important made him emotionally available in a way many fathers are not.

We chatted for a while. He asked me about school. I told him about the art college I applied for. Then I told him I wanted to leave school before finishing my exams. I knew I could get into art school with a good portfolio—I didn't need to stay in school. I hated it. The teachers were so patronizing, talking down to me like I was a child. I thought their rules were stupid. I was ready to be an adult.

Arguing with me wasn't worth the effort. He laughed, with a resigned expression on his face. "Well, I guess it's good you know what you want to do with your life. I didn't have a clue when I was your age."

He was himself for the first time in months. I hadn't realized how much I missed him. He told me how proud he was of me. We talked about death. The topic didn't scare me.

"I'm not afraid," he said, "I'm ready to let go. I'm looking forward to seeing my mum and dad. All the people I love who have died are waiting for me. I know there's something more. I've been close enough times to know that for sure." He held my hand tightly, "I'm gonna miss you, little one," he said, tears welling in his eyes. "That's what's kept me here so many years. You and Sam and the boys and your mum."

"I'm gonna miss you too, Dad, but I'm ready to let you go. I hate seeing you in so much pain."

He looked into my eyes searchingly. "You've been so brave. I'm sorry to have put you through this."

"It made me who I am," I said, emphatically. "Don't be sorry."

When he got tired I helped him into bed. His legs felt like matchsticks. I tucked the blanket around him, and sat on a stool next to him so our faces were level.

"Dad," I said, as I leaned in and put my head on his shoulder, "I don't think I'm going to visit you again."

"That's okay, my love." He gently stroked my pink plastic hair. "I understand; you don't have to."

"I just can't handle this anymore. We've said goodbye too many times."

"It's okay, little one. This is goodbye. This is perfect." I waited by his bedside with my head on his shoulder until I heard his breathing deepen as he fell asleep, and quietly put on my coat and left.

I didn't cry. I even smiled to the nurses as I passed by. It was a relief.

Five weeks after I made the deal with my father, a teacher knocked on the door in religious studies class. "Hi, sorry to disturb you, class. Polly Whittaker? Could you come with me, please?" I packed up my books and followed the teacher to the headmistress's office. When I got there, my best friend Abby was waiting. She stared at me, mute, and wide-eyed as an owl. They asked me to sit down.

I wasn't a stranger to this room, with its dark wood and books. I had many "serious chats" about my behavior and my grades. Only a few weeks before my bright pink hair extensions were the cause of my summons.

"Polly we need to talk about your hair," the headmistress had said.

"Isn't it fabulous?" I replied, scrunching at my new hairdo to make it bigger.

"You're going to have to remove those hair extensions if you want to stay at this school," she said, quite seriously. I laughed.

"What? I don't think so. I only just had them put in," I retorted. "Why on earth would you want me to remove them?"

"They are distracting to other students. It's not fair." She was deadpan. Not an ounce of humor. I couldn't resist the chance to be a smartass.

"Right, because everyone is, like, OH MY GOD Polly's hair is so amazing I can't possibly focus on my schoolwork." She looked back at me stony faced. "Oh, headmistress, please save us from this terrible distraction, how will we ever pass our exams with Polly looking so fabulous?"

"Don't talk back to me like that Polly, or you'll be in

serious trouble. I know you're having a hard time at home right now, and that's the only reason you're not getting a detention." I sneered at her, resentful of her pity.

But this day was different. I wasn't here to talk about my hair. All eyes were on me.

"Hi Polly. I'm so sorry, there's no easy way to say this. Your father died this afternoon.... Your mother has asked that we put you girls in a cab and send you home."

I didn't think I had any tears left to cry, but as Abby put her arm around me I dissolved. Seven years of waiting, over. I was so relieved. I wanted to laugh. But to my surprise all that came out were wracking, uncontrollable sobs.

It snowed the day of my father's funeral. Giant white snowflakes flurried out of the sky. It was unusual weather that seemed to come out of nowhere. Poignant. I dyed my hair black. I didn't think about it. I wasn't being dramatic. I just did it. I stood outside the crematorium and watched the snow fall on the flowers stacked up outside as I read the cards from each person. The outpouring of support from these people I didn't even know moved me. My father had touched many lives.

Hundreds of people showed up to the memorial service. Crowds shuffled in and stood in the back. Every seat in the church filled. Why so many people? What made him so special? It's a question I've asked many of his friends since, and they say the same thing: "Your father was inspiring." He lived his life fully, piloting a hot air balloon like it was a fast car, cracking bad jokes and winning hearts, loving his family, and bringing people together. As I turned back from my spot in the front pew next to my mother, I saw the crowd gathered to mourn my dad, and I realized my goal in life: Inspire enough people to fill a church when I die.

My mother, head held high, wearing a flowing red cape and wide-brimmed hat, stood at the front on the church and read from a Richard Bach book. A story about a creature that clung to the rocks at the bottom of a river, because that's all he knew. But one day he got bored of clinging, and let go. When the creatures downstream saw him float by they thought it was a miracle. He said to them, "I am no more Messiah than you. The river delights to lift us free, if only we dare to let go. Our true work is this voyage, this adventure."

I Love My Life

Polly Superstar

THE MORNING AFTER Kinky Salon I woke up in bed next to Scott. The last thing I remembered about the party was running down the hallway wearing nothing but a pink garter belt and fishnet stockings yelling, "*I love my life!!!*" to straggling guests. My lips curled into a drowsy smile at the memory. I opened one eye and pulled out my earplugs; a city bus rumbled past, and the music from the Mexican shop downstairs added its *umpa thumpa* soundtrack. Scott's head was buried under the pillow. His tattooed shoulder poked out from the blankets. I leaned in and planted a gentle kiss. He stirred, turned over to face me, and slid his warm arms around my naked body. We lay there for a minute, blissful. As the morning took hold, more memories of last night surfaced.

Soon after the doors had opened, the crowd quickly swelled to a lively party, filled with familiar faces. We packed the lobby, mingling beneath the pink fabric that swept in soft curves from the ceiling, exchanging heartfelt hugs and loving squeezes. The glittering mirrored art deco goddess, rescued from piles of junk at the Alameda Flea Market a few weeks earlier, observed us from her sparkly gold frame on the wall. The purple and zebra print velveteen couch hosted a colorful tableau of characters, looking like the lovechildren of Pee Wee's Playhouse and the Marquis de Sade. It had only been a fortnight since we gathered, but it felt like a reunion.

My mind skimmed through memories of the evening. A highlight was snuggling between my two gorgeous lovers, outside on the patio in the warm night air: lips and hands. "I love you, Jimmy," one whispered across my shoulder to his partner.

"I love you too," he replied.

"How lucky are we to have met this beautiful woman?" they kissed deeply, with me tucked between their bodies, their hands exploring me from either side.

"I love you guys!" I blurted, swept up in the love fest.

"We love you too, Polly," they said in unison, smiling lips on my neck, on my face. *I won the jackpot.*

On our way through to the back room, where we would join the naked and horizontal guests at the party, we paused to witness a scene with Nikki at the helm. Wearing a gender-ambiguous ensemble with a penciled-on mustache, she demonstrated her motorboating skills on a topless apprentice. She was quite the expert. She removed her fedora hat, then lifted and separated the breasts in front of her. Placing her face between them, she blew out a loud, "PPHHHFFFFFFTTT," moving her head from side to side. It's not as easy as it sounds. Most people's attempts ended with a quiet "pfhh." Nikki didn't mind showing them again. Uproarious laughter followed each try. She even demonstrated on men, grabbing their pecs and squeezing them together to make a crease, proving that breast size has nothing to do with a good motorboat. Each cleavage, whether male or female, was left with a streak of lipstick, glitter, and a smudge of mustache.

The cabaret was ridiculous—more surreal performance art than burlesque. Scott and I stepped out onto our tiny stage together, pink and blue bulbs surrounding us like a halo, the disco ball sprinkling its light around the glittery room. Our banter felt natural. The crowd sat cross-legged, like kids at story time, and laughed with us. The air was hot and moist with breath. They cheered for the performers like they were in love with them. Backstage, while the acts were on, we kissed.

Norm did a striptease out of a full chicken mascot suit, like the ones you see dancing on the sidewalk outside fast food restaurants clucking and trying to get you to buy chicken wings. Norm was always a crowd pleaser; with his signature smirk and raised eyebrow, he made girls and boys alike squirm in their seats. But nobody expected that he had a *live chicken* in that basket. When he brought it out the crowd went bonkers. Apparently she was his stage chicken and had performed in tons of shows with him. The noise didn't faze her—she actually seemed to enjoy the attention. He held her in front of his junk and backed off stage wearing nothing but the docile Petunia.

I couldn't help but laugh out loud at the memory. "What's so funny?" asked Scott groggily into the pillow.

"I was just thinking about Petunia," I replied.

"Huh?"

"Norm's chicken," I giggled. Scott laughed too as his head pulled out from under the covers. His Salvador Dali mustache, usually so perfect, was squished to one side from being crushed under the pillow. He still sported a little eyeliner from last night's elaborate Harlequin costume. He leaned over and kissed me gently, warm lips and familiar scent. My belly rumbled. "I'm hungry," I complained.

"Me too," he sat up in bed and scratched his head. "Shall we see who's still here and go get some brunch?"

I padded through the bar in my bathrobe. Votive candles still flickered in the corners on colorful altars overflowing with beads and trinkets, plastic red devil bobble heads, sparkly sequin flags, colorful painted bottles, fake flowers, and glittery paraphernalia. The towering tiki statue grinned in approval as I passed. At some point in the evening he'd gained a pink feather boa. The bar was my kitchen when parties weren't happening. I tossed the remaining empties in the trash and retrieved the kettle from its hiding place behind the stacks of plastic cups. I plugged it in for a nice cup of PG Tips. No matter how much I love living in California, I'll never be a coffee drinker. My morning cup of tea is a bit of Britishness I cling to. I waited for the kettle to boil, watching the multicolored Mexican paper decorations fluttering on the ceiling. It had been so hot the night before that we took the door to the patio off its hinges. We hadn't put it back at the end of the party, so the warm morning breeze blew through unhindered.

I heard the sound system click on, speakers linked through all thirteen rooms, a familiar hiss. Then...*Tom Jones.* It was a tradition. If you crashed at Kinky Salon you'd inevitably be woken by the sultry tones of "It's Not Unusual." I ran excitedly down the hall to the dance floor, with its mirrors and glittered walls, and slid into the room sideways, like Fred Astaire, in my pink fluffy slippers, just as Tom started to sing. Scott and I danced around the room, all goofy smiles and arms swinging. Before the song ended, our weary guests had staggered in, looking confused, in various states of undress. Three came from the Pink Room, where they had curled up in the corner like kittens in the soft cocoon. Two came from the lounge, with its swooped "I Dream of Jeannie" multicolor satin ceiling, and piles of comfortable glittery pillowcases. Another four came from the lavish red and gold back-room boudoir, with Moulin Rouge mural and chandelier. We grabbed their hands and danced. It felt like Christmas morning.

Climax

Polly Superstar

WHEN I STARTED being more honest with my friends about my challenges with my orgasm I realized that many women were having a similar experience as I—far more than I ever expected. I would mention it in passing, and their eyes would light up, reaching toward me in gratitude for my honesty. I chatted in a car on a road trip once and discovered four of the five women experienced a similar disconnect from their orgasm.

This realization stunned me: *I was normal.*

I came to a simple conclusion: I needed to practice more, watch more, and learn. So I explored this landscape without holding back. I gigglingly assisted people's intimate interactions with a rubber glove covered in lube. I lay under a couple having sex and watched, close up, the fascinating sight of a cock disappearing into a wet and welcoming pussy. I explored the absolute *delight* I find in being the girl in a bi-boy sandwich, cocks straining toward each other with me in the middle (still my favorite configuration). If it wasn't already absolutely clear, I think sex is awesome, but this frustration and fear of being broken didn't end suddenly with me being fixed.

I still feel broken sometimes.

One night I had a threesome with two girls. It was different because we had all experienced varying degrees of anorgasmia. Immersed in a sea of softness, all I knew was lips, tongues, fingers, and wetness. My hands reached out to caress breasts and slippery crevices as my lips moved from face to face, with smiles, affection, and tender touches. We explored gently at first, then greedily. Moans and whispers surrounded us in a cocoon of pleasure.

When it's just girls playing, I don't have the same concerns as I do when straight men are around. Being with women levels the playing field—nobody's *in it to win it.* When there are cocks in the equation the dynamic shifts. Don't get me wrong—there are plenty of sensitive men who are an exception to this rule. I love men! But so many of them can be needy, wanting desperately to reach their climactic conclusion and leave with bodies and egos satisfied.

As the evening progressed my friends pulled out their strap-ons. One was a perfect replica of male genitalia; the other was a blue, glittery alien cock designed specifically for female pleasure with defined ridges on the sides and a curved end to hit the G-spot. They strapped them into harnesses and pressed them deep into hungry cracks. But it was still different from having an actual cock in the room. These appendages weren't straining to be pleasured in the warm space between our legs. Orgasm wasn't an explicit goal, fulfilling an appropriately satisfying ending to their story.

As *this* story reaches its climax, those same old inadequacies keep coming up. I should give you the money shot. I owe it to you. It's my failure if I don't. I should take you to a moment where I am fixed. Where I am *healthy.* Where I bring down the

178

house with a screaming orgasm and we can all feel better about our interaction. But this isn't simply about my orgasm. Sure, as I get older and more connected to my body I experience orgasms more easily. I can get off in just a few of minutes if I've got my Hitachi Magic Wand. But it's not about my *money shot.* The question that is more important to me is this: why are such a large percentage of women disconnected from their orgasm, and why do they experience such shame about it? Even me—a sex-positive activist with a reassuring sex therapist mother—I still experienced so much shame, it crippled me.

Our culture has taught us that sex is supposed to look a certain way—we watch movies, look at magazines, and read stories, and our sexual expectations become intertwined with these fantasies. When things don't turn out like the movies, where sweaty but perfect bodies rock to that moment of mutual climax in just a few minutes, we blame ourselves.

What I've discovered on my adventure is that my ability to orgasm is vastly broader than I could have imagined. It's not simply a short moment in time, a single, fleeting instant. These days, after years of exploration, reading lots of books, and even participating in a few hands on workshops, I have learned to tune into the subtle, stepping stone sensations that radiate through me. They are waves of pleasure, which pulse and deepen. It's like an opening, surrendering to my capacity for pleasure. They aren't a release—they build, one on the other, until my entire body is flickering with their energy. From this place I have no greedy desire for an "orgasm," but occasionally those blissful stepping stones take me to a rolling, timeless climax that can keep going and going. I have yet to find an end to it. So my understanding of orgasm has expanded from a very specific moment in time, attached to a sensation of neediness and fear, to an arc of pleasure and surrender with no end.

I know now that there is absolutely no problem with how long it takes me to orgasm—the only problem is how ashamed I've been. So no, I didn't orgasm that night surrounded by the soft limbs of pretty girls, not in the way most people understand the meaning of the word. Instead, I released myself from that rapacious yearning. Our rendezvous on that bed was about exploring sensations, pleasure, and love. We nuzzled and rubbed and licked at each other's bodies like over-excited puppies. We giggled and moaned, and we loved every second of it. When we got tired we fell asleep in a pile, each one of us satisfied and loved.

Another Level of Strangeness

Polly Superstar

T HERE ARE MANY allegories in our culture about understanding the truth to be a bad thing: Curiosity killed the cat, Pandora opened the box, Eve ate from the tree of knowledge. We're not ready for the truth. We can't handle the truth. In our strange and beautiful culture, which has so many influences and complexities we will never truly understand, the story that people should stay stupid has held fast for centuries.

The truth about sex is a double whammy. Danger. Stay back. The tradition of interpreting mystic sexual awakening as demonic possession has discouraged any but the most stalwart explorer from adventuring down that disreputable path. The raw power of human sexuality is undeniable, in my experience. The energy pouring off the play spaces at Kinky Salon is enough to charge a battery. One time it actually blew my circuits.

It started in the hallway at a Kinky Salon. A cute triad experimented with a three-way make-out, wordlessly negotiating which lips moved back and forth, keeping all three equally engaged. Adventurous hands went up skirts and down shorts, as the tryst became more risqué. People walked past smiling, whispering words of encouragement and appreciation, and before long, one of the three dropped to his knees to explore what could be found with his mouth at that height. The sexual energy crackled up and down the hallway as the party continued around them with playful conversations coexisting as the scene unfolded. I looked around to see how people were reacting, and apart from a few appreciative glances, everything seemed normal. Well, normal apart from a ménage à trois happening right there in the hallway. I didn't gawk at them—I had no desire to join in—I just paused a few feet away and enjoyed the moment.

As I stood there smiling to myself, appreciating the sense of liberation and openness, something strange happened. An odd sensation overcame me—a flood of energy rose in *my* body. I breathed deeply as a flush of blood turned my face pink. It wasn't embarrassment—I had seen this kind of thing before—I didn't understand why I blushed. I put my hand on my chest to try to calm the sensation. A chaotic swirl descended on me, and I was suddenly incredibly anxious and overwhelmed.

A little flustered, I found solace in the bathroom, closing the door behind me to gather myself. I lowered the seat of the toilet and sat down, and held my cool hands against the hotness of my cheeks. The volume of the music outside made the bottles on the shelf rattle with every beat. A sensation pulled at my chest, part longing, part bliss, part confusion. Outside I could hear the triad giggling. I experimented, closed my eyes, and surrendered to the sensation in my chest, and as I did the longing and confusion slipped away. Bliss filled my body, pouring into me—warm honey filling a jar. When it reached capacity I found my head spontaneously nodding in affirmation, as if puppeteered.

As I opened my eyes I realized a glow had settled on the edges of everything. A fairytale sparkle. I stood up and looked at myself in the mirror, blinking back. *Did someone spike my drink?* I had experienced just about every kind of high in my rebellious youth, but this didn't feel like a drug. My senses heightened, but there was no jangly toxicity in my bloodstream. I was just very aware, and very...awake.

What the fuck is happening?

I gathered myself, took a deep breath, and stepped back out into the party. Information flooded my senses. I scanned the rooms and realized that I had become intensely empathic. I always had a good sense of people, but this seemed different. Some people were relaxed and happy, but I can also sense that some were scared, overwhelmed, or frustrated. I had gone from being hooked into a low battery in need of a charge, to being plugged into a high-voltage power supply. I didn't even realize that this kind of resolution was possible.

I saw Scott and whisked him into the office. "What's up?" he asked, looking concerned.

"I'm just really...*feeling* this crowd." I tried to gather my thoughts. How could I possibly describe this sensation? It was imperceptibly different. The windscreen had been cleaned, and now I could see, but in an instant the memory of my previous state melted away. I had no reference points to compare it to.

"I get it," he said, reassuringly. "There's a lot of energy here tonight. I'm feeling it too." He took my hand. "We're conduits for all the kundalini being generated; those play spaces are really firing up the grid."

I wrinkled my nose at him—I've always been a little resistant to his New Age language, but he just laughed at me and cocked his eyebrow comically. "It's *science, missy,* whether you like it or not." He took me in his arms and held me very closely, and we stood in silence, heartbeats synchronized.

I heard of kundalini for the first time at a rave in London. A friend of mine guided me through a kundalini-raising meditation while we were high on E in a chill space. I sensed the energy, but just put it down to the drugs.

My second encounter was with a dakini—a teacher of sacred sexuality—who helped me tune into my sexual energy when I first started exploring my orgasm more consciously. She taught me breathing exercises and showed me how to tune into the energy of sex.

"Kundalini is the creative energy of the cosmos," she had told me. "It's personified as a sleeping serpent at the base of the spine, which can be awakened and tapped into using techniques humans have known about for centuries. Ancient cultures weren't afraid of sex. They perceived divinity, creativity, and sexuality as inextricably intertwined."

I had never experienced anything like this before—a spontaneous blast of energy that rocked open my senses. I didn't know why it happened, that life force blasting through my consciousness. That uncontrollable nodding of my head. Was I saying yes to something I didn't even understand?

Suddenly it seemed I had lived my whole life in a haze of numbness. A self-protecting bubble I created to shield myself from a pain of life. I guess I needed those defenses when my father was dying, to stay functional—to be able to face school and my teenage life. But that was more than fifteen years ago.

I shed it like a snake.

Numb

Polly Whittaker

"NO WAY, MUM. You have to drop us off here. I'm not getting out of the car in front of the club with you driving. Please, don't embarrass me." In the backseat behind us my best friend Abby and her new girlfriend Kat giggled nervously. Kat had transferred into our school just before my father died. She was strong and confident, and a little intimidating. Young love bloomed. I was happy for them. I preferred to have lesbian friends than deal with boys.

"Polly, I want to see where you go on these Saturday night adventures." My mother tried to make light of the situation, but her voice sounded worried.

"You can see it from here. *Look.*" I pointed toward the boarded up snooker club at the end of the street. "There's the door at the end of this road. But *please* drop us off here," I pleaded.

"*That* place? It doesn't look open. Shall I wait here for you just in case?"

"Mum, just go. It's a squat—*an abandoned building.* They aren't going to light a sign and open the door. We have to knock."

"Okay, fine," she sounded defeated. "I don't have the energy to argue with you. Just be careful, okay?"

"Of course, Mum. I'm not an idiot!" I said defensively.

She pulled up on the corner and I kissed her on the cheek as I left the car, leaving a black lip print. I linked arms with my friends and clacked down the street in my stiletto boots, little metal padlocks banging against my heels as I scurried inside out of the cold. My fishnet stockings didn't give me much protection against the chilly wind, and my PVC coat barely covered my ass. Underneath I wore a metal chainmail bikini, which froze against my larger-than-average teenage breasts. I turned around to see my mum leaning over the steering wheel with her head in her hands. I regretted being so stubborn and resolved to apologize tomorrow.

We knocked on the door of the empty snooker club, and it opened to reveal a pale-faced man with crimped black hair covering one eye. We proudly presented our membership cards, and he ushered us inside. "Hello, girls. Nice to see you again."

We giggled.

Downstairs opened into a cavernous room, but the smoke was so thick we could barely see. We dropped our coats off in our usual corner and stopped to tighten each other's corsets and fluff our enormous hairdos. All three of us had huge hair extensions backcombed to twice the size of our heads and reaching down to the backs of our knees. Kat's were purple, Abby's were blond, and mine were black.

The early atmospheric set droned loudly: foghorns, the tolling of church bells, obscure organ music, and eerie sound effects. Not unlike a haunted house. The opportunity to dance would come later; for now we would buy some sodas, drink down a little, and then pour the vodka we had stashed in my bag into the can. We sat in the corner, watching people arrive. I knew their names, but none of them knew me. I was just a kid playing dress-up. The club was called WRAITH, and the people who attended had been hanging out together for years, as it moved around from squat to squat. They talked about seeing Siouxsie play the Bat Cave back in '85. I had already missed all the best times.

I hated the '90s.

I sat on the edge of a hard, black wooden bench looking out into the smoke-filled room. My feet hurt, pinched in my stilettos. I wondered how I would last the night. Abby and Kat sat next to me chatting. I couldn't hear them over the loud music. I sat and quietly contemplated the blackness of my heart. This *was* a goth club, after all.

Last week a guy had fallen onto his knees crying in the middle of the dance floor. Genuinely sobbing. He had a necklace made of real barbed wire, and blood ran down his neck onto his shirt as he moved. We thought he was the *coolest*. Being unbearably sad was something we all related to. We found a place where we had permission to express our darkness. They welcomed the shadow side of life here. It was honest.

At home the atmosphere was pure tragedy. Any sadness from me only made things worse, so I spent my life being the peacemaker, consoler, and distracting entertainer. At school, irritating teachers told me to "Smile, Polly. What's wrong with you?" At WRAITH we could escape from the need to pretend we were okay.

A girl sat next to me and introduced herself as Sadie. Her hair looked like Tina Turner in *Beyond Thunderdome*, spiky on the top and long in the back. We made small talk for a while. I felt awkward. Sadie was as young as us, but she'd been hanging out at WRAITH for a few years and knew everyone. I stifled a yawn. I hadn't been sleeping much— insomnia wracked my nights.

"Do you want some speed?" Sadie offered.

"What's that?" I asked. She pulled out a little bag of white powder from her purse.

"It perks you up, stops you being tired."

"Okay. I'll try a bit," I replied.

"Here, just put it in your drink," she instructed. I held out my coke can cocktail, and she tapped in the powder from the tiny plastic bag. The coke fizzed up and almost overflowed. I sucked at the foam as it gushed over my hand.

Twenty minutes later I became lightheaded. A buzzing sensation hummed all over my body. My heart beat faster than usual. I held my hand on my chest and took a really deep breath. Sadie looked at me sideways. *"You starting to feel it?"* she asked. I nodded and smiled. My feet didn't hurt anymore.

My favorite song came on, and I stood up to dance. So did Sadie. My legs trembled at first, but the sensation didn't last long. Sparkles of energy flew up my legs, up my spine, and burst out of my head in a fountain.

I danced, and my arms felt like feathers as they swung around my body. Like wings. My feet tingled. My fingers tingled. My face tingled. I didn't stagger anymore, even though I'd had a lot to drink. Perfectly balanced. Graceful. Confident. Numbness washed over me, and I realized the aching pain in my chest had gone.

I don't know how many hours passed, but Abby and Kat fell asleep cuddled up in our pile of coats in the corner. I sat and laughed with Sadie. The DJ pressed the button on the smoke machine for so long our hands became invisible in the thick mist. People coughed, and on the dance floor they stumbled into each other blindly. We laughed so hard, tears threatened to ruin my perfect spider web makeup. Once the smoke cleared I noticed a puddle of liquid coming from the bathroom. The toilets had overflowed again, and raw sewage crept its way across the floor toward us. It happened every week. The building had old pipes, and the influx of people every weekend was too much. We scurried to the other side of the dance floor to avoid it.

We'd been talking all night. I didn't remember much, but it was so easy to talk. I smoked a whole pack of cigarettes. My jaw was stiff, and I had chewed the inside of my cheeks raw. I drank nearly half a bottle of cheap vodka, but I wasn't drunk. I had never been able to talk like this before. To really communicate. Writing poetry would be amazing.

I was creative, connected, *inspired.*

"So, do you live with your parents?" Sadie asked, making small talk as we settled into our new spot.

"With my mum, yeah," I said. It was weird to say it out loud like that. I realized what might be coming next.

"Where's your dad?"

I paused.

"He's dead."

"I'm sorry; that's awful." Her voice genuinely filled with concern. "When did that happen?"

"Last week, actually." I laughed out loud. I couldn't help it.

"Are you joking?" She looked at me, confused.

"No...no, I'm not."

"Fu-uck. Are you okay?"

"Not really." I said, honestly, shaking my head and looking down. The speed in my bloodstream made me strangely

189

detached. A blissful numbness. She put her arm around me and gave me a squeeze.

"*That's mad.* Well. I guess this is as good a place as any to come when someone dies."

The Cosmic Scouring Brush

Polly Superstar

I'VE ALWAYS BEEN a very pragmatic, grounded person. I don't believe in anything I haven't experienced firsthand, although I never rule things out just because they're unlikely. I like being open to possibility, and a sense of curiosity, rather than shutting down ideas until they're proven true by science. In my opinion, magic is just science we haven't figured out yet. Aliens, fairies, crop circles, astral bodies, telepathy, I say *maybe. Why not?*

How about things *I've* experienced—the energy of an altar, kundalini, the power of equinoxes and solstices, the subtle changes in cycles of the moon, acupuncture, nature spirits. Is it all in my head? MAYBE. I say YES to it all. Give me wonder over scientific proof because only time will tell. In every era there are Galileos who say things that seem crazy, but later are proved to be objective truth. Nobody tries to argue that the earth is flat anymore. With that in mind, let me tell you about the time I met a guru.

Every long-term relationship is bound to hit a rocky patch that pulls its existence into question. This is true whether it's an open relationship or a monogamous one—either way, people hit the wall, and trust is brought into question. If you can make it through these challenges, your relationship can get stronger, and your sense of companionship can deepen. You learn about each other's fears and failings, and you can reach a whole new level of intimacy.

For us, the wall was a woman called Sarah. She was dark haired, wide eyed, slender, and quiet. The complete opposite of me. She was also monogamous. While that might seem like an obvious problem, it's not as simple as it sounds. While she preferred monogamy, she was willing to *tolerate* my relationship with Scott.

Scott wanted so badly for things to work—to have both of us. Looking back I understand—sometimes you do anything to hang on to love, even if it doesn't make any sense.

The series of events that left me heartbroken, crying on the floor of Mission Control as Scott walked away, aren't important. We had neglected our relationship, focusing too much on work. We took each other for granted, living, working, and playing in the same place. We produced sex parties *every* weekend while simultaneously trying to push forward our plans for Superstar Avatar. Things got claustrophobic. Our intensely intimate relationship was a helix spiral of connection on every level, but some days it seemed more like a noose. Then, along came Sarah, and it was easy for her to push the crowbar into the cracks. I could see what she was trying to do, but Scott didn't believe me.

"If you leave, this is it," I said, and I meant it. "We can't come back from this. It's over. This is *not* the relationship I want." Tears streamed down my face.

"That's not true, Polly," he said, in a conciliatory tone. "It'll be okay. I'll be back on Monday. It's just a weekend at a hot spring. I still love you. That hasn't changed. This doesn't have to be such a big deal." He tried to reason with me.

"It *is* a big deal," I yelled, frustrated. "Don't you understand what I'm saying?"

"*You're* making it a big deal," he replied, calmly. "Look, I'll be back. Everything will be okay."

"Don't do this, Scott. Pease. Don't go. If you walk out now I lose all my faith in us."

But he did. He left. And I sobbed on the floor. I cried for as long as a person can cry, and then I was alone. I stood up, and looked around. I had no idea what to do. I walked, in a daze, to the back room and lay on the huge expanse of beds. I broke into sobs, and stopped. My relationship was over. All the dreams, all the shared experience, that unimaginable depth of love. Over. I thought we were unbreakable. These were thoughts I didn't want to consider. But he left, and I was alone, and I didn't want him back.

My cellphone rang. It was Tara. She's a quirky magical punk-rock shaman who really gets me. I answered, glad to have someone to talk to.

"Hey, Polly. Wanna go see a guru?" She sounded perky.

"I don't know, T. I think I just broke up with Scott." I explained to her the incidents of the morning, and her tone changed.

"Come on, Polly," she said emphatically. "Let's go see a guru. It's exactly what you need." She had seen the situation play out over the last few months, watching me as I sank into the quicksand of my own life, trapped and scared and not knowing what to do. She'd seen the arrival of this woman in Scott's life. She heard me talk about how hard things were, how scared I was.

I had never met a guru before. The idea of it seemed strange, but getting out of the house with Tara and driving somewhere out of the city sounded like good medicine. Fifteen minutes later she was on my doorstep wrapping me in a warm hug. Tara is tall and strong—a dancer—with long dark hair, almond eyes, and slender, gentle hands. We met through Zari when I first arrived in San Francisco and became close as sisters. They were both part of that Burning Man fire-art group The Flaming Lotus Girls. We had all bonded in the desert. I sobbed onto her shoulder for a few moments as she stroked my head and whispered in my ear. "It's okay. It's gonna be okay."

"Let's get out of here," I said, wanting to leave Mission Control and the bitter memories of the last two hours.

We drove for about an hour, with Tara's compilation of songs by *strong women who don't take any shit* blasting loudly on the stereo. We ended up at a retreat center in Marin; it had bamboo floors, tall ceilings, and exposed architecture, all nestled in impeccably manicured grounds. We arrived late, so we snuck into the back and settled onto some cushions, sitting cross-legged and trying to blend in. Everyone wore white except us. The guru sat on the floor too—red dot on her forehead, white powder streaked above her eyebrows, dark skin, and a gold nose ring. They called her Amma, but she wasn't that famous Amma who hugs people. Amma just means *mother.* She stopped her introduction to say hello and welcome us, which made me even more self-conscious. People turned and smiled as we sat down.

I don't belong here.

I sat for a while dealing with the discomfort. It would be rude to leave now, but how could someone like her possibly

have something to say that was relevant to me? My hips stiff-
ened uncomfortably sitting on the floor, but I had no choice. I
had to listen.

Behind her on a presentation board she displayed an Indi-
an-looking mythological figure. A blue-faced creature draped
in gold. An alarmingly foreign looking deity with teeth bared,
tonsils exposed, and tongue protruding. Its multiple arms displayed a range of indescribable looking objects. "Pratyangira
has manifested as a lion. You see her here? She looks pretty
scary, huh?" The crowd laughed. "But she isn't scary. She just
looks that way sometimes. She represents an aspect of the
mother that is very old. So old it's before everything. Before
mother, before father. This place is deep within; in a place we
call the void. In this place there is no fear, no wanting, no pain.
There is not even time or space. Just mother's love. That is all."
Amma had an easy way of explaining things. "This is a time
when the masters are coming down from the mountains," she
continued. "The time for secrets is over. No more gurus. *Everyone is a guru.* When a god manifests in our world it is called
an avatar. Vishnu walked the earth many times as Rama, as
Krishna, and many more. But now is the time of avatars. We are
all avatars of the divine. We are discovering our superpowers
on this planet like Superman. All of us. We are remembering."

Superpowers? Avatars? Suddenly, I could relate. I sat up
taller on my pillow, smiling broadly, connected and inspired.
"We are at the end of the fourth Yuga—the Kali Yuga," she
continued, "and now is the time we all discover our true nature
as divine."

A woman in the front row raised her hand, and Amma gestured for her to speak. "What happens in the fifth Yuga?" she

asked. Amma laughed a big belly laugh as she responded.

"There is no fifth Yuga."

The crowd didn't laugh this time. There was an awkward pause as what she said sank in. She smiled broadly, unfazed. I liked this woman a lot. She seemed so real, so honest. She kept joking with her husband, who clicked away on a laptop for the duration of her talk. Hours passed, and I didn't even have discomfort at sitting cross-legged anymore. The incident with Scott had been pushed to the back of my mind. This was the perfect distraction.

"Now, enough talking, this is what you really came here for." She said as she stood up and rolled out a mat on the ground. It spanned about six feet square, and on it a yantra had been drawn—a geometric mandala—painted in red and orange. In a very matter-of-fact tone, she went on to describe how this mat was an anchor to the void, and that by stepping onto it we would clear deep karma and release fears. Be with the Mother.

I looked at Tara quizzically. She shrugged her shoulders, stood, grabbed my hand and pulled me up to join her, to wait our turn for the "magic mat to the void." Why not? I love this weird kind of shit.

"If you get lightheaded, that's okay. Don't worry; it's quite normal," she explained to the crowd. "There will be people here to catch you if you fall. So just fall back. It's okay."

I watched as the first few people had their experience. They stepped onto the mat and had their moment. They fell back and were caught. They smiled, bowed respectfully to the guru, and then sat off to the side in lotus pose. They looked peaceful with their hands resting palms upward and blissful smiles on their faces. Soon I reached the front of the line.

The assistants ushered me onto the mat and stood me in front of Amma. I smiled at her. For a moment we were simply two people. Then something shifted. I felt it in my solar plexus first. A knot of energy, tightly wound and ready to burst. She put her hand on my forehead, and her eyeballs rolled to the back of her head. Suddenly I spiraled dizzily. The knot unraveled, and the world turned upside down. I forgot which way was up. I heard someone say, "she's going to fall," as my legs buckled underneath me. I collapsed forward, into the arms of Amma. She caught me and held me close to her chest; with my chin resting on her shoulder she spoke an indecipherable language in my ear. Everything went black. I lost all sense of time and space. They had to help me to the side because I couldn't walk. I couldn't even sit. I curled up in a ball. My hands started painfully cramping, bent over in little lobster claws, and my arms bent tight at the elbows. All I could do was breathe while this incredible discomfort passed. My face tightened, and the sides of my mouth drew down in an exaggerated frown. My entire body tingled, similar to that sensation you get when you fall asleep on your arm.

I lay with my face on my knees, alarmed by this sudden, unexpected, and rather bizarre physical reaction. The people around me sat with satisfied smiles, while some sort of cosmic scouring brush violated my inner being, and ground its way through the deepest, darkest parts of my soul. I breathed through the tingles and the cramps, wishing I had somewhere to hide. When it passed, I went outside and sat under a tree on the lawn. Tara followed me out.

"What the fuck just happened?" I asked her.

"I think we met the void," she said, smiling and putting her

197

arm around my shoulder as she sat beside me. "You okay?" She looked concerned.

"Yeah. I think so. That was…fucking weird."

Later that evening I got a call from Scott. I still felt distant, but my experience with Amma had done something to me. I hadn't processed what happened yet, but I had shifted. Although I was still hurt about having my feelings disregarded, when I heard his voice I didn't take it personally anymore.

"We took some magic mushrooms in the forest today," he said.

"Why are you telling me this? I don't understand, Scott. I just want to go to sleep. I'm exhausted."

"No. I have to talk to you now. It's important. All day all I could think about was you. I'm so sorry I left you. This is all wrong. I shouldn't be here. I should be with you. You are my queen. This whole thing has been stupid. I've been in denial. I don't know what I'm doing. I'm scared. I'm scared of us. I'm scared of how much I love you. Scared of how intertwined our lives are. But I've been sitting next to her in the hot springs and I…I don't even know who she is. I feel so distant. But you're my queen. *You're my Queen.* You make sense. I love you. I can't imagine not loving you. It's over with her. I'll be back tomorrow and I don't want to see her anymore. You're right. It doesn't make any sense. She doesn't get it. I love you. *You're my Queen.*"

When Scott returned to San Francisco we reunited with tears and kisses. A new lightness had entered my being. I wouldn't describe the situation as happy—we still had a lot of work to do—but we survived.

It took a few more weeks, but eventually, he did end his relationship with Sarah. She wanted to be monogamous. He didn't. That's always a recipe for heartache. If I hadn't seen the guru, I don't know if I would have had the strength to make it through. When it finally happened, he cried like a grieving child. I couldn't be happy with him so sad, but I was relieved. I comforted him, and had more compassion for his pain than I would have ever imagined. The whole experience brought us closer together. We came out the other side stronger and clearer, meeting each other again on new ground. We honeymooned for a while, both thankful to have our future back.

I joined Amma's mailing list—her husband signed me up at the end of the day and gave me a knowing hug. The look in his eye told me that my bizarre reaction wasn't unusual.

I read the newsletters as they came in, and I followed their stories as they traveled around. Then one day, about a year later, I noticed they were touring California again. Excitedly, I scrolled down the list of cities they planned to visit, hoping they would come somewhere close. Their San Francisco visit had a date, but not a venue. I knew exactly what to do.

Maybe it was a little crazy. Mission Control would hardly be considered an appropriate place for a guru. Surely they would choose a peaceful location with a well-manicured lawn up in Marin somewhere. Not a sex party venue on a dirty stretch of Mission Street. But something compelled me. I sent them an email telling them we would be honored to have Amma visit us, and almost immediately I got a response saying *yes*.

How do you prepare for the arrival of a guru? We cleaned the floors and put out fresh flowers on the altars. We prepared a chair and draped it with pink velvet. We rolled out a rug and pulled cushions from around the space and piled them on the floor. The smell of flowers hung in the air as we waited for her arrival.

Amma came up the stairs with a scarf over her head. She focused on a small idol that she held close to her face. Her entourage helped to guide her. Clearly, she was overwhelmed by the intensity of Mission Street with its cast of crack heads and Mexican gangsters. She whispered quietly to her statue as the hustle and bustle of arrival subsided, her scarf shielding everything around her as we exchanged hellos with her husband. She didn't see us—her eyes rolled in her head.

Her hand gently touched my shoulder. "Where are the pictures of the Masters?" she asked, referring to those photographs of gurus that they have at ashrams. She wanted to see familiar faces, to ground her self in this strange place.

"We don't have any," I said, apologetically. She looked confused and overwhelmed. I started to think this might have been a mistake. I felt guilty for bringing her to this swirling palace of kundalini. For a moment I spiraled in my own self-doubt, but then I remembered. At her talk she had spoken about everyone recognizing their divine power, about everyone being avatars. My confidence rekindled. I leaned in and whispered in her ear. "We are all Masters." Suddenly her energy shifted, and her eyes settled on mine as she smiled, knowingly.

We ushered her into the front room and seated ourselves on pillows. She sat tall and smiling. Scott made some tea, and we chatted and made ourselves comfortable. "I know this isn't the kind of place you usually visit," I said, sipping my tea. "What made you decide to accept my invitation?"

"When I check my email I don't read them; I scan their energy. Yours was shining gold. I could see the sun. I knew this was right. This is where I need to be." She laughed for a second before she asked. "What kind of events do you do here?"

"Creative, artistic...er...*sexy* parties." I said, unsure of how she would respond. She surprised me by giggling.

Once the guests started arriving she seemed comfortable and confident. She answered people's questions and did her speech about avatars and superpowers. We smiled, honored and humbled by her presence. She pulled rose petals out of a bag. "You think you are here to see me," she said, smiling, "but it is *me* who is here to see *you*." She pointed to us and we laughed together. She paused, suddenly serious, and her eyes filled with tears. "Look at all these beautiful faces. I am here to honor you, divine beings." She wept, and threw handfuls of rose petals into the air above our heads, letting them land gently on us. Showering us with Mother's love.

Then we went up to meet her one at a time, face to face. I sat by the side and observed closely, transfixed as she cycled through the frequencies of different goddesses. One moment she was Kali embodied, fiercely loving, then wise like Sarasvati. She blessed each person, giving them a dose of the energy they needed. These were not the people she usually saw. I knew that. This crowd was smattered with strippers and professional dominatrixes, prostitutes, queers, and perverts. My beautiful freaky family. But she had no prejudice. She held them in her embrace, equally. Tears streamed down my face as I witnessed each encounter. These people deserved this. They deserved to be seen as sacred, as divine. We weren't outcasts anymore. We were not the unloved. Mother recognized us. All our shame was absolved.

Nuclear Family

Polly Whittaker

W E ALL HAVE deep, dark secrets we cling to. Things we're ashamed of. They become so intertwined with our identity that we forget where we end and they begin. Acknowledging they exist gives us the opportunity to let go of those mysteries we believe define us.

When my father died, my relationship with my big brother Simon changed dramatically. Maybe he had a newfound sense of responsibility toward me, now our father was gone. He was twenty-nine—thirteen years older than me—and had played a big role in raising me. My big brother always made time to play with me and be my friend. He stuck up for me and teased me. I experienced the infinite joy of a child when I was with him.

When I turned sixteen our dynamic shifted. I stopped being the silly kid sister, and he started to listen to what I had to say, to take me seriously. I don't know if I actually changed, or if it was just his perspective. He invited me to go out to a bar with him. We drank cocktails and created a new relationship as grown-ups. I was delighted to have his attention in this new territory.

My brother's approval became the most important thing in the world. He didn't know it at the time, but he became a father figure to me.

It's tough being a teenager—the no man's land between childhood and becoming an adult is a tricky place to navigate, no matter what your circumstances are. It's when you find your power, and learn to wield it. My desire for my big brother to love me became so powerful it was disorienting. In the post-death tornado that comes from bereavement, confusing emotions danced me into a shadowy corner. We had both lost so much; perhaps he was as confused as me.

There was only one place where I saw my power. With a flick of my hair and a flutter of my eyelashes I could convince men of my innocence in any situation. The inspector on the train would believe the story about losing my ticket. The nightclub security guard would trust that I should be on the guest list. At fetish clubs, I sat tall on bar stools, patent leather thigh boots encasing demurely crossed legs, while men bowed at my feet to worship me as a goddess. For a teenager who slowly watched her father die, that overwhelming sense of powerlessness was all consuming. Discovering the potent effect of my young female sexuality gave me one domain where I could be in control.

One night, a few weeks after the funeral, my mum had gone away for the weekend, leaving Simon and me in the house alone. She was absent a lot once my father died, incapable of facing the life he left behind. I invited a friend over, and we drank the drinks cabinet dry of green ginger wine, Campari, and Southern Comfort. In the haze intoxication, my grieving teenage brain concocted a plan.

I rested my hand on the doorframe of the kitchen, where my brother sat drinking a beer. When I was a kid I had dropped a can of coke down the stairs and then opened it without understanding the explosive outcome. I wasn't usually allowed

203

soda. If you looked carefully, you could still see the brown stains on the painting that hung on the wall behind him. The chair Simon sat in was the same one he had comforted the small me in. It had been a moment both hilarious and touching. He had laughed as he wiped the tears from my eyes. But that was ten years ago, in happier times.

"Hey," I said, snake hips and hungry eyes trained on him. As my brother looked up, I configured my body to its most alluring stance. I was a counterfeit seductress. I knew all the moves. My friend giggled beside me. I saw a flicker of desire in his eyes, and as I switched off the light by the door and plunged us into darkness, I knew I had the upper hand.

I remember the feeling of the cold linoleum against my back as we kissed sloppy drunk on the kitchen floor, all three of us, in the shadows. The excitement of being desired echoed through the blur of alcohol. He was older than me, but I was in control. I didn't care if it was wrong. In a single audacious act I proved how rebellious and subversive I could be, and I expressed my love for my brother in the only way I knew how.

I remember that feeling of power draining from me as his hand reached into my panties. But by that point I had something to prove. *"There's that Whittaker pussy,"* he whispered into my ear as his fingers slipped inside. In the confusion of love, lust, and power, I remember wishing it was over. He remembers thinking I was beautiful.

I woke up the next morning with a dull ache pounding through me. It wasn't just the hangover from the sticky-sweet cocktails. It was shame. It caught in my throat and strangled me, an invisible rope to hang myself by. I didn't tell a soul. My dirty secret would only prove my weakness, and I preferred the bravado of my perceived power to the truth of my humiliation.

Is it common for half siblings to experiment in this way? I don't judge now whether this was right or wrong. The real truth is often an expanse of circumstances and emotions that aren't so black and white.

Sexual shame is such a common reaction for teenagers, but it wasn't something I had experienced before. The distressing humiliation, followed by a burning-hot desire to turn back the clock and do things differently. I thought I was immune to it.

In the years following my father's death, my family broke apart. Simon vacillated back and forth between deep love and intense anger, pulling me close and then pushing me away violently. People don't think straight when they're mourning. They lash out. Or they hide. Like a galaxy that floated too near a black hole, the fabric of our reality ripped, and we were flung to different parts of the universe. My family is, to this day, estranged. I'm the only one who manages to maintain relationships with everyone. The rifts made during that time stay in place more than twenty years later. My loving family, each one of them a genius with a huge heart, had suffered so much for so long—we just went nuclear.

My mother became a hollowed shell of the woman she had been when I was a child. Overtaken with grief, she developed severe agoraphobia. She stopped eating. Pale and stick thin, she would faint, landing on the ground with a scary-sounding crunch, and we would have to carry her to the couch. Worried about her deepening alcoholism, my sister had confronted her, but her promises not to drink proved empty when I found her suckling on the teat of a wine box in the closet of the spare room. My brothers were angry with her for coping so badly. There was the obligatory conflict over the will.

My mother's stoic face, which had remained so brave and strong for so many years, disintegrated before our eyes, and we were left with a woman we didn't know. Then, *she left us.* She couldn't cope. She didn't mean to abandon us, but she did. She sold our family home and moved 300 miles north, to the other end of the country. She escaped the toxic conflict with my brothers, and the memories of my father, which haunted every corner of London for her.

A year later my brothers' mother, Marjorie, died too, and they went mad with anger and grief. They became an impenetrable wall of pain, and for a while they stopped talking to me.

Desperate and depressed, by the time I reached my twenties I had disappeared into substance abuse. I easily scored drugs from my local bar, and I made myself into a human test subject for mind-altering substances. Cocaine, speed, ecstasy, 2CB, ketamine, GHB, MDA, acid, and mushrooms were consumed in various configurations on a regular schedule. The rave generation ruled, and I lost myself dancing on podiums in the squat clubs of London.

Dark Night

Polly Whittaker

ONE NIGHT a small group of us partied at The Fort—our little house in Camden Town near the projects. We were high on 2CB. I stood in the hallway listening to the wind. It whipped around the building and spiraled upward. A hot, summer wind. The windows rattled. The door shook. I closed my eyes and a skeletal figure manifested in the spiral hallucinations, with dark eyes and a body of fluttering, gray, torn fabric. It circled me, spinning around the house. It laughed through the cracks under the doors, swirling round and round in the dark outside. I breathed and listened. Death didn't frighten me. I had seen too much of it when my dad was dying in those terminal wards. It surrounded me for years. The wind slowly grew louder and bigger until the whole house moved at once—the windows, every floorboard, the door handles, the pipes, all in unison. One big roar, as if the whole house might fly away and land me at the foot of the yellow brick road. Then, it was quiet and death was gone. I blinked my eyes open. They rolled in their sockets for a moment as I tried to focus.

I heard voices through the door as Abby and Ben chatted and listened to music. Ben was my new boyfriend. I met him at art school. A year younger than me, he was fun and outgoing, the singer in a band. I started seeing him shortly after I broke up with Phoenix, and I tried to negotiate a more open relationship. I thought we were magical and perfect and unstoppable. I wasn't jealous when Ben made out with my friends. I found it exciting.

Upstairs Damon and Scarlet argued. They always argued. Scarlet worked as a dominatrix at our local dungeon, beating and humiliating men for money. I admired her. We all tried our hand at being professional dominants, but it's not as easy as you'd think. Most of us made a bit of extra cash answering the phones and ordering around the submissives. We gave them absurd tasks to do like polishing the table legs and washing the doorframes. That dungeon was always sparkling clean. It had tons of kinky equipment, mirrored walls, and multiple themed rooms, all in modern black and shiny silver. My group of friends had pretty much taken over. We had wild afterparties, dressing in outfits and tying each other up. Abby worked full time in the office, scheduling the girls and answering the phones.

Damon was Scarlet's boyfriend—a kooky guy I knew since my days as a goth. By this point we'd graduated from Goth to fetish. We were *kinky.* Sadness was sooo '80s. Shiny and modern, we were the Y2K generation.

Last on the list of people in the house that night was Bella. A very pretty thing, a couple of years younger than us, she brought out my maternal urge. She had a perfect oval face and big pouty lips. She'd just done her first photo shoot for Penthouse.

As I stood there in the hallway my cat rubbed against my leg. I picked him up and he purred for a moment, then wriggled from my grasp. Cat fur stuck to me. I shook my hands. *Was it still there?* I couldn't tell. I was *really* high. I realized I'd been standing in the hallway for a while. I couldn't remember what I was doing there.

Scarlet and Damon had gone quiet, so I went upstairs to investigate. I found Damon sitting with his back against the wall in my bedroom. He had a weird, evil expression on his face.

"What are you doing up here, Damon?" I asked nonchalantly. *It's probably just me. I'm high. He's not really evil, that's silly.* He didn't answer. He just stared at me. "Are you okay?" I asked, starting to feel a little uncomfortable. Next to him sat a plate of leftover meat from the dinner we had earlier. He picked at it with his fingers.

I found Scarlet under the bed.

"*I'm okay.*" her shaky voice reassured me, "I'm okay, I'm okay. I've got me fags, I've got me cocktail, I've got everything I need under here." She held onto her cigarettes and her cocktail reassuringly.

"Scarlet. Seriously. You're scaring me."

"I'm fine, I'm fine, I've got me fags, I've got me cocktail. I'll be fine. Everything is okay." Clearly, everything was not okay.

"*Slut,*" came a voice from behind me. I turned around in time to see Damon throwing a piece of meat under the bed.

"*Damon!* What are you doing?" I asked, aghast at what I had witnessed. He laughed. It was the first time he had broken his weird evil character since I'd been upstairs. I saw Damon again, just for a moment, my funny friend.

Just as I said, "*Stop it, Damon,*" his eyes glassed over and his energy shifted, back to evil.

It took me half an hour to talk them into a truce. Scarlet eventually came out from under the bed, and Damon stopped being evil. Well, for the most part. Satisfied that no more meat would be thrown, I ventured back downstairs.

Perhaps taking that third pill was a mistake. 2CB can be a

strange drug. It's empathic, like ecstasy, but if things are fucked up it gets amplified. If there's tension, or underlying drama, you will *all* feel it.

I opened the door to Abby's room and found Abby and Ben sitting on the edge of the bed. They seemed guilty somehow, like they were hiding something. *It's probably just my imagination.* I sat down on the couch. The music was really loud, and I couldn't hear what they were saying. Abby giggled as Ben leaned in to whisper in her ear.

"WHERE'S BELLA GONE?" I had to shout. They shrugged. I looked out across the hallway and saw the light on in the bathroom. *She must be in there.*

I sat back on the couch and listened to the music. It seemed overwhelmingly loud. The patterns on the couch swirled around me. I lost the motor function needed for smooth eyeball control, and my eyes flickered as they moved. It nauseated me. I closed them for a moment, but that felt worse: I descended down the vortex spiral of hallucinations and thought I might vomit. I snapped my eyes open again and tried to pull myself together. Swirly patterns overtook my field of vision. On the other side of the room Abby and Ben seemed to be flirting. We had explored making out with each other when we were high, and Abby and Ben often ended up together, but this seemed different. She gazed at him with such...*affection.*

What is that look? Am I imagining it?

The bathroom across the hallway drew my attention again. The door stood open, and I kept seeing Bella move back and forth. *What is she doing in there?* I wanted to go and find out, but I couldn't move. I breathed deep as a wave hit me again. I wanted to tell them to turn the music down, but I couldn't find the words. For a moment, I disappeared into the pattern of the couch. Just a pair of eyes in a swirl. Falling back. Falling into the void. My eyes rolled in the back of my head as I surfed the edge of my consciousness.

When I returned I realized that Bella had come out of the bathroom. I turned my head to see her standing in the hallway. She held her hands out in front of her, as if in supplication. The light coming out of the bathroom rimmed her silhouette, like a statue of the Virgin Mary, with arms outstretched and rays of saintly energy pouring out from behind her. It took me a moment to realize she was covered in blood.

"BEN, TURN THE MUSIC DOWN," I yelled. They ignored me. "Abby, *please*, TURN THE MUSIC DOWN!" They glanced over, but they couldn't see Bella, gliding across the hallway toward me. "TURN THE FUCKING MUSIC DOWN!!!" I sat up, trying to shake myself back into the world and dampen the hallucinations.

Bella slowly floated forward, looking directly at me, her head cocked to one side, with a sorrowful expression, her arms reached toward me, palms upward. Her make up streaked down her face in long gray trails. Blood splattered her white dress. Suddenly she was through the door and sitting down beside me.

"*I'm sorry, Polly,*" she said, bleeding onto the couch.

"GUYS! TURN THE FUCKING MUSIC DOWN." They saw Bella, and the music clicked off suddenly.

"*I'm sorry, Polly.*" She sat next to me, rocking back and forth, holding her wrists out in front of her, bleeding onto her knees.

"Jesus, Bella, what have you done?" There's nothing like the sight of blood and an accompanying burst of adrenaline to

211

sober you up.

"I'm sorry, Polly," she said, looking down.

I grabbed hold of her arms to inspect them; squinting to make sure I had a real picture of what was happening. Slashes oozed blood from wrists to elbows.

"I'm sorry, Polly."

Abby and Ben sat by her feet, examining her wrists with concern.

"What do you think?" I asked them pragmatically. "Do you think we need to call an ambulance?"

"I'm sorry, Polly."

"It's okay, honey," I said, smoothing her hair. "It's okay. Don't worry. We'll take care of you." But truthfully, I didn't know how to take care of her. I examined her wrists again. There were lots of cuts, as if she spent time on it like a work of art, each tragic red brushstroke an expression of her sadness.

"I'm sorry, Polly."

I went to the bathroom to find a towel. There were streaks of blood everywhere. On the sink and the mirror. Straight razorblades scattered around. *She brought her own razorblades. She prepared for this.* I retrieved a towel from the shelf and returned to the scene, pressing it firmly onto her wounds. Abby sobbed as Bella stared ahead vacantly.

"What did you do that for?" Abby cried. "Why would you do that?"

Bella didn't answer.

Suddenly Scarlet stood in the doorway surveying the scene. "What's going on in here?"

"Bella cut herself," I said. "We're trying to figure out if we need to call an ambulance."

"Bella! For Christ's sake! Are you trying to top yourself? Let's have a look."

I peeled back the towel, and Scarlet peered at Bella's wrists.

"Nah, she'll be all right. That's not gonna kill her. I've seen worse. Have you got any bandages?"

Taken aback by her blasé attitude, I agreed that Bella's injuries, while dramatic, weren't serious enough to take her to the hospital. Not in the state we were in. She'd have an armful of lovely scars to commemorate the evening, though.

"Let's go to the shop and get bandages, Polly," Scarlet held out her hand to me. "Come on."

"Are you sure?" I studied Bella's wrists again. She started to look embarrassed.

"I'm sorry, Polly," she said again.

She's wearing white. She brought her own razorblades. She's not going to die. She planned this. A cry for help. Why did she do this tonight? Why did she do this to me? I started to get angry.

"Yeah, let's go," I said, grabbing Scarlet's hand.

I was halfway to the 7-Eleven before I realized that I was only wearing my underwear. Panties, bra, a tiny slip, and flip-flops. Blood streaked across my slip. Being outside felt good though, the air on my skin. Camden hummed with people, even though it was past 4 AM. They stared as we walked past. I didn't care.

The shop was bright. Too bright. I squinted around the aisles.

"*Can I help you?*" asked the shop assistant.

"Do you have any bandages?" I asked politely. He stared at the blood on my slip.

"Have you...*hurt yourself?*" he asked.

"Not me, it's my friend. She's cut herself. I need bandages."

I couldn't believe how well I was holding it together. Scarlet checked out the big display of baked goods.

"Polly, can we get some donuts?" she asked. "Wait. Did you bring money?"

"Scarlet, let's focus. I'm asking for bandages."

"Right, sorry." She stood next to me and tried to look serious.

"We don't have bandages, sorry. Will a Band-Aid do?" said the man.

"No, that's not going to be enough," I replied.

Scarlet checked the shelf of medical supplies. "How about a nappy? We could tape it to her arms," she suggested.

"Are you kidding?" Clearly she wasn't.

"*Sterile and absorbent!*" she said, triumphantly waving the package in the air with a smile and a flourish.

"Do you have any tape?" she asked. The man watched us, incredulous.

"Sure, we have tape, aisle three." I located the tape and stopped at the donut display.

"Can I get six donuts too, please?" I asked, politely. Scarlet and I started to giggle uncontrollably. "And a pack of cigarettes." The man observed us stony faced.

"What kind?"

"Um...Lucky Strikes. It's that kind of a night. I'm feeling lucky." I replied, smiling.

We left the shop laden with supplies. Duct tape, diapers, donuts, and cigarettes. As the sky started to turn pink, we sat on the roof of The Fort. We washed Bella's face and disinfected her cuts. She wore my pajamas and had diapers taped securely to both arms. She was pale and sad, but the bleeding had stopped. We smoked cigarettes and ate donuts as the sun rose.

This experience, disturbing as it was, didn't stop my spiraling drug abuse. Somewhere along the way I lost my ability to see that I'd had enough. Or maybe I just didn't care. If drugs were available I couldn't say no. I wasn't the kind of addict who got high every day, but I binged every weekend, and hid behind the excuse that I was "having fun."

Before the prohibition of drugs, every village had a shaman or a witch. A wise healer who helped guide young people through the confusing and vulnerable world of drug use. In the past, intoxicants were sacred, and partaking was a powerful, spiritual experience. The only guide I had was a worn-out CD of the Ozric Tentacles—a psychedelic prog rock band whose songs were like mini shamanic journeys.

In modern Western culture we don't have the support we need, and we're left on our own to explore the potentially hazardous world of mind-altering substances. Rather than being walked through our first drug experiences with a mature adult, teenagers are force-fed government information videos, instilling them with fear. We're told that drugs are bad. We risk spending time in jail if we are caught; yet *we still do it.* Trashy magazines paint a glamorous world of celebrity drug use, thinly veiled in casual judgment. Humans are curious by nature, especially teenagers, and making something illegal only makes it more alluring.

Let's not forget, we've been brewing, fermenting, smoking and snorting medicines, seeking out magical fungus, and combining unlikely ingredients since the dawn of time. These shamanic concoctions have helped us travel to alternate states of consciousness, giving us a broader perspective on human existence. If taken with awareness, mind-altering substances can be incredibly life affirming, and personally transformative.

Sparklepony and Peepshow Mini Golf

Polly Superstar

MY USE OF substances has changed since I was a teenager. I no longer use drugs to numb my pain, or for pure hedonism. At my parties I am always sober. Well, maybe a cocktail or two. Recreational drug use is something I rarely partake in. Cocaine and speed make me numb, and I don't need that anymore. Psychedelics, on the other hand, can provide a deeply connected experience, if explored consciously.

On this particular occasion we were camping in the Black Rock Desert. That's the location of Burning Man, but some people go there at other times of year. (It's a badly kept secret, but it is supposed to be a secret, so I won't tell you when we go.)

The desert is a good place to gain perspective. Flat, gray, cracked earth as far as the eye can see, and huge skies flanked by purple mountains. At night, stars light the sky bright as day. Big Nature at its most majestic.

This camping trip was an excuse to play mini golf. Not just any mini golf—*Peepshow Mini Golf*. It's interactive anti-theater—one of our more ridiculous creative manifestations. We've set it up in many unlikely situations. We played in the iPhone line outside the Apple Store in downtown San Francisco for a total of 36 hours, dressed as clowns. But we weren't really buying iPhones—we just did it for the *media circus.* A trip to Los Angeles climaxed in a parking lot in Hollywood, where we challenged a DIY bike gang to a mini golf showdown. For that trip we dressed as food mascots. I was an ice cream sundae. Scott was a taco. We called it the Food Drive.

Here's how the game works: It's a portable mini golf hole with dancers who distract the putter. Getting from one end of the course to another is a chaotic blur of dry humping, honking, and screaming. The putter reaches the finish line by *any means possible.* Once they reach their destination, and putt the ball in the hole, the spinner wheel comes out and directs what happens next. Sometimes it's a "high five" for everyone on the course and all the bystanders, spreading out in all directions. Or it might be a conga line, with the putter leading the way. "Group hug" is a good one too, although being at the center of a giant clown hug can be terrifying.

Out in the desert, Peepshow Mini Golf got crazy. There were no rules. The clowns danced on the course, coming up with new ways to distract the putters. The game became simple—*to play as long as you can.*

We set up the course outside our tent, crudely painted in red and yellow stripes, and lit with rope light. A few other tents scattered around nearby, and as the last orange light of dusk left the sky, we cranked the music. We hooked up a generator to a powered speaker, and blasted gangster rap, then cartoon theme tunes. *"M-i-c-k-e-y-M-o-u-s-e! Mickey Mouse!"*

I found a stack of firecrackers, and started throwing them at people's feet, trying to distract them from putting. It was a ridiculous sight: Clowns with their pants around their ankles, shaking their bits and shuffling around the course. Firecrackers going off all around. A madness took over. I could see the faces of my friends encircling the course, beaming in the glow of the flashing circus signs. In the distance cars gathered. The desert dwellers. Dusty people in dusty cars, hoodies pulled up; locals, curious about what we were doing. They parked just outside the glow of our lights in the darkness, and sat on the hoods of their cars watching. I went over, offered them swigs from my bottle of tequila and made friends. I dressed as a clown, and they dressed all in black, but we found common ground in tequila and firecrackers.

This happy scene came to an abrupt end when I burned my hand. Perhaps, in hindsight, the combination of tequila and firecrackers was a bad idea. I clutched my hand to my chest, fighting back tears. *I'm so stupid. What am I doing here? This behavior is dangerous and idiotic.* I crawled into my tent, found my medical supplies, and licked my wounds.

The next morning I woke up grouchy. My hand hurt, and I wanted to go home. Scott was already up, making breakfast, whistling a perky tune as the hot morning sun seared through the thin fabric of the tent. Soon I would have no choice but to get up, as the tent became an oven in the desert heat. I contemplated how I might change this sorry situation.

Scott had bought me an inflatable rainbow unicorn while he had been in New York on a recent trip. It sat on the top of my bag. I pulled it out and blew it up, and had an idea. *When this unicorn is with me I will always be safe.* I tucked it under my arm and stepped out of the tent, my confidence in the day revived.

As the sun reached its peak in the sky we were swimming in the nearby springs. The unicorn made a great floatation device, and by this time someone had named her *Sparklepony.* I floated in the cool water watching the dragonflies zip around the sky above me. I've always loved dragonflies. They are so beautiful and so alien.

Scott called me over to the bank, and I swam toward him. *"Wanna go on a journey?"* he asked. A group of excited friends looked at me in unison. They had been plotting.

Given my recent mysterious kundalini overload at Kinky Salon, and my experience with the guru, I was curious to explore the potential of those esoteric erotic secrets in an altered state. Delving into the mystery sounded appealing.

The proposal being made that day, by the side of the pond, was a hit of a little-known hallucinogenic called *Bromo-Dragonfly.* Extremely potent and long lasting, taking this particular chemical concoction would be a commitment. I thought about my burned hand, and the reservations I had been having. Then I contemplated my new friend Sparklepony. *When this unicorn is with me, I will always be safe.*

We divvied up the little white tabs of paper and looked each other in the eyes knowingly as we placed them on our tongues. I took a moment to sit by the side of the pond on my own, Sparklepony tucked under my arm, watching the dragonflies as I said a little prayer for my adventure. When the flying dragonflies left iridescent rainbow trails in their wake, I knew it was starting to take effect.

Ten hours later, after a slow and steady climb, the high *finally* reached its peak. We could then expect to ride it for about six hours, full tilt, and then slowly come down for another ten hours. Since my prayer at the side of the pond, it's been a bit of a blur. Back at camp, the heat had been overwhelming. Stuck

219

under our shade structure I got claustrophobic, so at every opportunity I ducked out from under the tarp, with Sparklepony wedged firmly under my arm, and ran around like a child in a playground. But my pale skin and freckles are not suited to the desert sun, and people kept pulling me back into the shade.

"Sparklepony! You're going to burn."

"Sparklepony! Are you wearing sunscreen?"

"Sparklepony! Are you drinking water?"

This went on all afternoon. I ran in and out from that shade like a yo-yo. We did a sunset photo shoot with Peepshow Mini Golf, but I had to wear shades because I couldn't figure out how to put on clown face. I could barely stand still for the photos.

By the time night fell, I was having full-body orgasms. Energy rolling through my body in waves, sending fountains of sparkling rainbow light out from every extremity. I had never experienced this before. My body flooded with pulsing, cosmic, erotic power.

Scott set up Peepshow Mini Golf. I couldn't do anything but watch from the sidelines. The clowns were obscene, pulling panties to one side and bending over to expose themselves, tea-bagging each other with dusty balls. A crowd gathered.

While we took a break some friends rolled up with their young children. They wanted to play mini golf. The sight of children on the course so soon after the recent display of smut made me feel strange, but the parent of one child was a dominatrix clown, and the other was an absinthe bootlegger. They seemed to be entertained by the scene.

One of the children took a liking to Sparklepony. I gave it to her to hold for a minute, but she wouldn't give it back. A panic attack rose within me. *I need Sparklepony or I won't be safe.* I grabbed the inflatable back from the little girl, tucked it safely under my arm, and skulked into the shadows. The children danced, sent into a frenzy by the music and the energy. They grabbed hold of pieces of the course, rocking them back and forth until they snapped. Their parents were wide eyed.

"Is this okay?" they mouthed to Scott, over the music.

"It's perfect," he laughed.

A dust storm started to rise. It blew though in gusts, swirling around us as the children destroyed Peepshow Mini Golf. They jumped up and down on its remains laughing.

As my body convulsed gently in waves of energy, our little bubble of reality detached from the rest of the world. We were riding a novelty spike so high it created multiverses. The edges of reality gave way, and the rules of matter became malleable. I watched as a friend doused a toilet paper roll in gasoline and set it on fire. They kicked it around like a football, cackling. The dust blew through full force, and everything became dark apart from the flame. I pulled my goggles down over my eyes, covered my face with a scarf, and clutched onto Sparklepony. *With this unicorn I will always be safe.*

Eventually the chaos, the laughter, the swirling psychedelic madness all became too much for me. I sought refuge in my tent. I lay back onto the mattress and was overcome with bliss. My body responded with another undulating wave of ecstasy. My back arched in response, and another cosmic orgasm blew me open. I shook and moaned and gasped as my spine rested back down on the mattress in post-coital rapture. The floodgates had opened. Erotic energy pushed through my body in waves, opening doors to my most intimate places. Wave after wave, I fucked the universe.

When my body began to tire, the energy didn't abate. I lay there and allowed the exhaustion to take over. It was 2 AM. I'd been high for fourteen hours. I had two more hours of peaking before it even *started* to wear off. I wouldn't be done until lunchtime tomorrow. My body shuddered again, but this time it was too much. I wanted it to be over. I wanted to go home. I clutched onto my unicorn and took a deep breath. *"Don't worry,"* a voice said, *"with Sparklepony you will always be safe."*

When I opened my eyes the tent crawled with insects. A writhing mass of centipedes, beetles, and ants of all sizes. They swarmed over the roof of the tent, swirling and crawling. Then I realized they were on me. They crawled up my arms and my legs. They swarmed onto my face, in my ears, and up my nose. They wriggled up inside me between my legs. I didn't panic or move—it didn't occur to me. They engulfed me, and I dissolved. The tent dissolved. The insects disappeared, and I became the desert. I was dust, flat and expansive, looking up at the bright star lit sky. The tent had gone. I had gone. All was quiet.

We are the desert.
We are the sky.
We are one.

I descended inward, pulled in by a chittering sound, and came face to face with slithering bat beings, dangling upside down from a blackened tree, guarding the gateway to the underworld. *I must be dead.*

"What are you doing here?" they asked me.

"I think I'm dead," I replied.

"No, you're not dead. We would know if you were dead.

We would be expecting you. But this is a surprise."

"Well, if I'm not dead, why am I here?" I asked.

"We don't know," they replied.

"Death doesn't frighten me," I told them.

"So you say. But this is not your time." They started to chitter again, and the sound lifted me up and through the ground, back to my bed in the tent. For a moment the surroundings were unfamiliar. It was still dark outside, but *centuries* had passed.

"This tent?" I thought to myself. *"This was so long ago. Lifetimes."* Sparklepony rested on top of me. My stomach gurgled with the intensity of being human. My body felt like a sack of meat, squishy and squelchy. I reached behind to make sure I hadn't had an accident in the bed, figuring that if I had shit myself it would probably be time to call for help. But I was good.

With this unicorn you will always be safe.

A rolling, celestial orgasm took me back into the other worlds. I stood in a room floating in space. Huge, arched windows revealed starry skyscapes. There was a table in the center of the room, on a raised dais, with strange beings seated around it. They invited me to sit with them. Some were physical beings, three dimensional—almost human—others were different. They shimmered. I sat next to a wide-faced, humanoid creature with blond hair and strong arms. He welcomed me and introduced himself. *"Am I dead?"* I asked.

"No," he laughed, "you're here to learn."

He taught me how to use sound to manipulate time and space. I traveled to a blue bubble, which was the beginning and the end of time; quiet and cool and glowing. I forgot that I was human.

I am pure experience.

When I returned to the tent I felt cold. It was still dark.

Another century had passed. I was amazed to be alive, and even more amazed that I hadn't shit myself. Exhausted, my body still convulsed with rolling energy. I heard a rustling at the tent door, and Scott's face appeared. He wore a bunny suit, and carried a violet glow stick. He climbed into the tent and held me close, the violet light shimmered pulsing pastel rainbows onto his face. He told me the story of how he rescued a couple who had lost their car in the dark of the desert by clicking the button on their car keys. *"Whup whup."* The car lit up in the distance. I couldn't even begin to explain what I had experienced. As the sky started to change color and the Bromo-Dragonfly finally began to ebb from my system, he wrapped me in his arms and slept.

I didn't sleep. My satori had scattered, but the shuddering remained. It became toxic. When the morning sun started to burn into the tent, I sobbed. My consciousness fragmented into a million pieces, and I didn't know how to reassemble. I couldn't process what happened. Fear of death completely took over. I had to get off the desert or *I would die.*

As the day began and the temperature rose, Scott put me in a car with the air conditioning on. I sat in the front seat with my head in my hands, crying. My friends packed up the camp. They looked over at me, concerned. I felt silly, but also genuinely terrified. *If we don't leave this desert I'm going to die!* The Bromo-Dragonfly was still in my system. I had a few more hours until the effect wore off completely. I wasn't traveling interdimensionally anymore. I was just sitting in the car, *waiting to die.*

They slowly loaded up and checked the ground for any tiny bits of trash. We left the desert as we found it, and drove toward the road. It seemed to take forever. *I'm going to die here.*

We finally made it to the road, but that was worse. We sped headlong at seventy miles an hour, winding through heart stopping passes and past sheer drops. *We are going to die!* We finally made it to Reno, and checked into the hotel. *I'm going to die.* I peeled off my sweaty, dusty clothes. I'm going to die. I took a shower. *I'm going to die.* I looked at myself in the mirror. *You've done it this time, Polly. You went too far. No coming back from this one.* I considered biting a chunk of flesh out of my arm. It would be so satisfying. So real. But then, I had a moment of clarity and went back into the bedroom, sinking onto the soft bed.

"Please don't leave me alone," I said to Scott. "I think I might do something...weird."

"What do you mean?" he asked, exhausted.

"Just don't leave me alone. I might...chew my own arm off." We both laughed. *I'm going to die.*

I laid on the bed, and Scott brought out his medicine bag. Essential oils. He anointed my forehead and the bottom of my feet with lotus oil. Shimmering violet. He spritzed me with fir. The forest. Green and gold. He brought me back into my body as I sobbed. But I wasn't going to die.

"I don't think I ever need to do that again," I said to Scott as I struggled to eat the scrambled eggs room service delivered. "I went out so far this time. I thought I wouldn't come back."

"Well, I'm glad you did," he said, holding my hand. "I need you here. You scared me, Polly."

The clean sheets felt like heaven as I slipped into the bed. Cool and soft. My exhausted body sank into the bed and almost thirty hours after my prayer to the dragonfly, I finally fell asleep.

I went in seeking answers, to connect, and to gain a deeper

understanding. I wanted to know what it meant when energy flooded my body at the parties, with life force tingling in my fingers and toes, but the answer was unexpected…and *complicated.*

For years I had told myself the story that I wasn't afraid of death. I had been around it for so long as I watched my father die, I thought I was immune. But my fearlessness was a sham—a smokescreen I created to avoid the truth. That universal, creative, erotic energy blasting into my body shone a bright light straight through me, revealing where I had been lying to myself. A helicopter chased me across an empty landscape at night, with a spotlight pointed at me. Beneath me there was a shadow so dark and so crisp, I couldn't deny its existence.

The truth was, not only was I afraid of death, it terrified me. Fear had gripped a hidden part of me, holding on tight for years, but in that moment I pried its boney fingers loose.

The phrase *la petite mort* is an idiom for orgasm. It means "the little death," and refers to that moment of transcendence, when we are taken out on a wave into a more expansive reality. Was *this* the fear that had held me back from my own orgasm? Had that deep, unspeakable terror stopped me from allowing my consciousness to experience that little death? My façade of bravery and strength slipped away. I didn't have to beat myself up for being broken anymore. I gave myself permission to be afraid, and to face the distressing truth—that death is fucking terrifying.

A year later, I went back to the Black Rock Desert, but this time for Burning Man. It was Sunday night. With Sparklepony tucked under my arm all week, I was safe. As we prepared to leave camp for the night I was in a panic. I couldn't find her anywhere!

"I can't leave without Sparklepony!" I wailed, tearing my tent apart in a desperate search. My friends were all waiting, but I refused to leave camp without my unicorn. I was afraid that something would happen. Without her I wasn't safe. I knew it was silly, but I couldn't help it.

My campmate had a plan. She'd been waiting for this moment. She came into my tent and presented me with a unicorn horn and a pair of shorts with a tail.

"Check it out, Polly. You *are* Sparklepony!"

It's a revelation. I don't need no plastic unicorn to keep me safe.

I am Sparklepony.

The glacier of dread melted into a puddle in seconds. I put on the outfit and contemplated my reflection in the dusty mirror. In that moment I realized that I'm not safe, that life is dangerous, and that one day I will join my father in death. But there was a new resolve in my eye. A twinkle only I really understood. I had taken responsibility for my fears, and donned the garb of my own magical protector. I was ready to enjoy life, complete with its joys *and* terrors.

XXX Haunted Funhouse

Polly Superstar

ALTHOUGH OUR infinitely complex culture has been spiraling and shifting for centuries, there are some widespread customs that don't seem to go away. Halloween, Samhain, Day of the Dead, All Saint's Day. A time to honor the dead and acknowledge the coming of winter as the calendar moves into the dark half of the year.

A time to stare fear in the face.

It was an unusually warm night for October. Mission Street crowded with people dressed in the cheap costumes you buy at Halloween Superstores—the ones that come in the plastic bag with the photo in the front, showing you how great you are going to look. Those photos are a lie. The costumes never fit properly.

I stood inside the gate of Mission Control and watched the parade of bad costumes—sexy nurse, sexy witch. Unlike the guests of Kinky Salon, Halloween is the one time of year normal people have permission to dress outrageously. I enjoyed the cool air and chatted with the door guy, gratefully taking a break from the demanding party upstairs. We played a game: trying to spot the Kinky Salon people through the crowd on Mission Street.

"Zombie showgirls," he said as he pointed toward a group of women getting out of a taxi.

"Oh, you're good," I said, as they zipped across the road, tottering in our direction on their high-heeled shoes, feathers flying. Soon their green faces smiled at us through the gate, and I ushered them up the stairs. They left us in a wake of glitter and the scent of peach body lotion. The door guy put up his hand for a high five and I reciprocated. I noticed a couple across the road watch as the showgirls were ushered inside, and predictable as clockwork, within a minute they stood at the gate full of curiosity.

"Hi," they said, with a tone that said, "*We're cool.*"

"What are you here for?" asked the door guy.

"Errr, the party?" they replied sounding a little confused.

"Wrong answer, I'm afraid," he responded, his voice full of authority.

"Oh, come on," they tried to persuade him, but I knew it wouldn't work.

"Private party, I can't let you in," he said, bluntly.

"How do you know we're not invited?" asked the woman, in a flirty tone.

"I can tell because you aren't dressed right, and you don't know what you're here for," he replied courteously, but with a slightly sarcastic tone. The guy started to get defensive.

"Dude, you're turning us away for not being dressed right? These are $500 jeans!" The door guy looked at me, his eyebrow cocked in amusement, and I tried not to laugh.

"How much your jeans cost is not relevant, sir. It's a private party."

In a vain attempt to maintain his credibility in front of his date, he yelled, "You're a fucking asshole!" and then stumbled away from the gate and disappeared back into the bar across the street.

"I better head back up," I said with a sigh. "Wish me luck. It's mayhem up there!"

"Good luck! If anyone can handle it you can, Miss Pandemonium," he said, and reached for a high five.

I went back up and found the party in full swing. We'd spent the previous week transforming Mission Control with spooky decor, covering the lobby in spider webs and pink glittery skeletons. I pushed my way through the extravagantly dressed crowd. Bride of Frankenstein, complete with a tall, black wig and fringed burlesque outfit trimmed with skulls. Ronald McDonald. Bert and Ernie from Sesame Street with bondage harnesses strapped across their chests. A white unicorn with a short, chubby horn pulled a rainbow scarf out of his butt as people cheered. The faces of the crowd shone.

For a moment I wished I could just enjoy the party, have a cocktail, and forget about being responsible. Hosting parties every weekend was getting to me. I was already exhausted from putting up all the decor, and the night had barely begun. But a crowd of this size wouldn't take care of itself—it needed to be managed. "PEOPLE JAM!" I yelled. "Can we please clear the lobby? *Move along.* The rest of the space is much more fun. Why are you all hanging out here? Clear this area please." People shuffled in different directions, trying to find a spot where they weren't in the way.

As I stood at the top of the stairs wondering which direction to go in, the music transitioned from Disney's Haunted Mansion theme to loud surf guitar music. The energy ramped.

The party was a Halloween spectacle—a total of thirty performers created an ongoing show with scenes unfolding all over Mission Control. Zombie strippers, vampires, and scary clowns, plus tour guides to show people around. I hadn't experienced it myself yet, so I joined a group that was gathering at the start of the tour.

"Welcome to Kinky Salon's Triple X Haunted Funhouse," the tour guide's voice boomed over the crowd. "If you please follow me, I can reveal to you the horrors that lie within." Tall and handsome, he wore an impeccably presented top hat and tailcoat. "The site where this building now stands was once a cemetery, and some say the bodies were never removed. The lost souls walk these halls for eternity." He led us down a hallway covered in colorful but spooky circus banners, with a zigzag of pennant streamers. The partygoers followed him obediently, with their plastic cups held up high in the air to avoid being spilled. He gestured for us to enter a room. The *zombie quarantine*. Biohazard posters were pasted unevenly around the room with diagonal stripes of yellow caution tape. A plastic wall separated us from scantily clad figures swaying back and forth. They pawed at the plastic leaving bloody handprints. A man in white protective overalls stood guard with a huge plastic squirt gun spray-painted silver.

"This room was once a strip club," the tour guide announced in his commanding voice, "but it became infected by the radioactive waste from a meteorite that landed nearby. All the dancers became infected; their lust for human flesh was so great. Luckily, the authorities moved in and created this quarantine, so you are all completely safe." One of the zombies reached out from behind the plastic wall and made a loud "uuuuuuhhhhhhh" sound. The girl closest squeaked in alarm, then laughed.

"Are you sure this quarantine will hold?" I asked, feigning a dramatic tone.

"Yes, ma'am," he replied. "This is the latest technology. It's totally safe here." He shook the plastic to demonstrate.

"Uhhhhhhhhhhhhhhhh," the zombies responded in unison.

"Please don't touch that, sir," the guard said in a stern voice. "Stay back for your own safety."

We all giggled as we left the room, but clowns blocked our path. One was seven feet tall, built like a football player. He leered at us as we tried to pass. Running around him at a lower level was a tiny clown, no more that five feet tall, giggling and shaking a rattle in people's faces.

"EEEEEAAAAAIIII!" squealed one of the group. "I hate clowns!"

The tall clown stood over her staring coldly into her eyes, daring her to cross him. The rest of us squeezed by screaming and left her there to face him alone.

We shuffled into the next room, and the guide closed the door behind us. "Ladies and gentlemen, here the greatest horror of all is also the greatest beauty. I give you Dracula's brides." He switched on a light, and the shapes of three women became visible. They crawled on top of each other, making moaning sounds. They were naked from the waist up, their faces and breasts covered in blood. They lifted their heads, bearing fangs, and bit at each other. "Trapped for eternity, these ladies of the night are destined to live without satisfaction, if you can call it a life, for they claw and bite at each others breasts, but their veins run dry. Forever wanting, forever yearning, for the taste of..."

"Coooooock," moaned one of the vampires. The room descended into laughter; even the vampires couldn't keep straight faces.

The next room was the dungeon. Tied up in a brutal-looking

contraption was a man in a latex gimp suit, complete with a zippered mouth and full-face mask. A dominatrix towered over him in eight-inch heels, using a vicious looking crop to administer stinging blows to his nipples—the only part of his body exposed. He flinched with each impact.

"The pain slut," announced the tour guide. "Who knows why he must endure such tortures? Encased in his latex tomb, the only way he knows he is alive is through the brutal administrations of his loving mistress."

"Thank you, Mistress," the gimp said in a muffled voice.

Suddenly, red lights started to flash, and zombies poured out of the quarantine zone, terrorizing their way through the crowd. The guard tried in vain to beat them back, but the zombies overtook him, pulled him to the ground and tore off his protective suit. Blood flew in the air splattering some guests, causing screams of laughter. Within a few moments the guard stood up, taking on the appropriate zombie stance and muttered "uuuuuhhhhhhhhh," as he joined the zombies on their quest for human flesh. We hurried through, laughing and screaming in our escape.

The tour guide led us to a laboratory, with bubbling lights, anatomical posters, and a terrified patient lying on a gurney. A crazed-looking doctor greeted us. "Velcome," he said in a creepy accent. A beautiful nurse in a very tight, very short uniform stepped by his side and smiled menacingly through her ruby red lips. In front of them the woman on the gurney shook her head back and forth in protest. The doctor spoke in a hysterical tone about his pioneering work in the field of genital re-engineering, while the nurse rubbed his chest and spoke words of encouragement into his ear.

"Yes, doctor, you're so clever, so brave, so brilliant." They both had unconvincing Eastern European accents. The patient looked at us in terror and silently mouthed the words "*Help me*" as the doctor continued his monologue. The nurse brought out various sex toys to demonstrate the groundbreaking operation he was about to perform. The scene degenerated into chaos as the doctor held the dildos aloft, and dry humped the nurse against the table, laughing maniacally.

We scurried out to find a sacrifice in full swing. A demon stood on stage holding the victim by her throat, while the validity of her status as "virgin" was debated by the crowd. "She's not a virgin; I saw her in the back room earlier this evening!" someone yelled. The audience laughed and jeered in approval. The "virgin" struggled in the grip of the demon, wide eyed with distress, pleading with the audience to help her, scantily clad in an innocent looking white slip.

"KILL HER ANYWAY!" yelled a voice from the back of the room.

"Feast on her blood!" screamed another.

The demon didn't need any more encouragement. His helpers tore her scant white dress from her body and suddenly she was naked and screaming. He lifted his ceremonial knife and slowly plunged it into her heart, fake blood squirted in all directions. She screamed one last, bloodcurdling cry as blood dripped in rivers out of the side of her mouth. The demon held up her limp body and his helper stepped forward with a goblet and filled it with her blood. The demon's assistants passed the goblet of blood into the crowd, and invited them to drink. I knew the dark, thick, ruby-red liquid was a mixture of chocolate syrup and strawberry syrup—I made the concoction earlier that day and placed it behind the curtain so that it could be reached at just the right moment. Some people sniffed at the glass suspiciously before taking a tiny sip. Others poured the contents into their mouths without hesitation, letting it drip down their chins and smiling with bloodstained teeth.

For a minute, a low reverent chanting filled the air while the goblet made its rounds. I could see Scott; his tired smile as huge as my own. I stepped toward him, and he put his hand around my waist and gave me a loving squeeze. He took the microphone and spoke with a reverent tone. "Happy Samhain, everyone. I know you're a bunch of tree-hugging pagans." The crowd cheered, and passed the goblet up to Scott. He held it out high above his head, and paused for a moment. "To the dead." He whispered, and took a long draw from the glass, letting the sticky liquid pour down his neck. I signaled to the DJ to start playing, and licked the blood off his chin as the music started.

I smiled, looking around the room at the faces of all the people having fun. Another great night. Everything was going smoothly. Nobody had any idea about the nagging doubt that occupied me. It pulled from deep inside. Was it really my destiny to entertain and clean up after these people for the rest of my life? Was I wasting my time? Did they care about the bigger picture? Sure, this was fun, but was it important? Should I be paying closer attention? Those transcendent experiences, where I felt connected to the mysteries of the universe, made me feel strangely isolated.

Most ironically of all, with all these sexy parties, *my sex life was suffering.* I looked over at Scott and watched him flirting, feeling a pang of jealousy. It had been months since he had looked at me that way. We talked about it, and he reassured me I was being paranoid, that he still thought I was sexy. But we didn't make out like we used to, with hungry mouths and ravaging hands. Our relentless party schedule had started to shift the way we related. Sex, for us, was becoming work.

Global Emissaries of Cultural Change

Polly Superstar

NOW HERE'S A TWIST. Just when I had started to fear that our work with Superstar Avatar would never go anywhere, we got an email out of nowhere from Scott's friend Miya. He had mentioned her name before—an eccentric Japanese educator and respected writer, she had been a longtime fan of his work, but an air of mystery surrounded her. Cryptic language and puzzling clues riddled her email. It told us to prepare for a trip to Japan. I didn't believe that it was real—we had been working for so long and with so little return—but when I found myself sitting on the plane to Japan a few weeks later, I felt reinvigorated with a sense of giddy optimism.

Miya invited us to present Superstar Avatar to her colleagues in a grueling, three-week schedule of workshops and talks. Following her advice, we changed the name to Beauty Engine, which she thought would be a more relatable name for her community. She arranged meetings with teachers in a variety of different fields, and the tour ended in Kyoto for the celebration of the ten-year anniversary of her organization. We would be keynote speakers. She saw us as ambassadors of the West, and saw Beauty Engine as a rainbow bridge joining together cultures and creating a universal language of creativity.

The teachers she worked with wanted to learn these methods, to help them connect with Japanese teenagers who had fallen out of the incredibly strict, traditional schooling system. In a whirlwind, we went from the edge of failure to the edge of success overnight.

There was just one complication. We couldn't let them know about our sex parties. This community of Japanese educators would not understand. A fearful voice in my head told me that if people knew I threw sex parties, they wouldn't take me seriously. So we kept it quiet—our dirty little secret—and pretended we were something we were not.

On our first day in Japan I needed to check emails for Club Kiss, which would be taking place in San Francisco shortly after our return. A teacher offered us a computer in her office. Scott stood behind me, in a casual attempt to block the view of the screen as our two worlds collided.

"You have everything you need?" asked a curious teenager who peered over my shoulder, smiling enthusiastically.

"Yes, thank you," I said, as I speedily clicked off the page that only moments earlier had displayed a large, erect penis. Luckily she didn't see it. Those swingers are always sending me pictures of their cocks—even though I specifically ask them not to. We both bowed our heads politely to each other. Scott chatted with the teacher on the other side of the room and started to wander.

"*Stand behind me,*" I hissed. He looked at me confused. "*Stand behind me!*" I said again, wide eyed and panicking, gesturing to the computer. He stepped back into the spot that blocked the screen from the teacher, and I clicked back onto the cock shot and replied to the email.

The tension between the duality of our lives was glaringly evident. How could we be global emissaries of cultural change in an unfamiliar country, and open our home for strangers to fuck every weekend? These two undertakings seemed irreconcilable.

"Hi everyone. We are honored to be here today," Scott said, and paused while Miya translated. About twenty teachers, mostly women in their forties, sat in a circle. We planned to introduce them to the concept of Beauty Engine—the life game previously known as Superstar Avatar—by leading a little interactive experience. We hoped to reveal the mythic personas underlying their everyday lives—to show them tools for a creative approach, to make day-to-day life more playful.

"Okay! So let's find out who is here today. Let's just introduce ourselves one at a time. Say who you are and what makes you *unique*." He smiled and paused as Miya translated, and then looked back at a circle of blank faces. No reaction. Not a twitch. *Did she translate right?*

"Someone jump in. *Don't be shy,*" I said, looking over at Miya. She translated. Still nobody spoke.

"Okay then, how about you?" I pointed to the one person who wasn't looking down. Her eyes snapped downward to stare at her lap. "What's your name?" I asked. "What makes you unique?"

She mumbled something in Japanese and we waited for Miya's translation. "*I am nothing. I am nobody. I am not unique.*"

The next three hours were excruciatingly painful. Nobody warned us about the old Japanese proverb: "The nail that sticks out gets hammered in."

We threw out our carefully laid out plan, and pulled out a

whiteboard. We wrote: *Nature. Music. City. Creativity. Struggle. Family. Art. History.* We got them to close their eyes, and then we read out the words one at a time, asking them to raise their hand if this word represented something important in their lives—something they identified with. We tallied the results on the board next to the words, and then they opened their eyes and looked at the results.

I was an untrained art therapist. I had no idea what I was doing. Did this have anything to do with Superstar Avatar anymore? I was out of my depth, in a strange country, with a three-week tour ahead of me. *I was freaking out.* But I had to exude confidence and professionalism. I was an emissary of co-creation. A leader in the field of social design. I was full of shit, actually. A liar. I threw dirty, filthy sex parties. I had seen more people fuck than a porn director. But nonetheless I sat in a room full of faces looking to me to learn about our *framework for social evolution.*

"Is there anyone who wants to tell us more about how they answered?" said Scott, gesturing to the whiteboard. As he waited for Miya's translation I could see he was struggling too. Again, nobody wanted to speak.

"It looks like a lot of people identify with nature. Who raised their hand when we said *nature*?" I asked, looking around the room. "Do any of you want to talk more about that?"

An old lady who hadn't spoken yet started to speak. Her eyes were tiny black beads in wrinkled sockets—like a character from the Hayo Miyazaki movie *Totoro*—a caricature of a wise old Japanese lady. We had to wait for the translation. "She says she talks to the trees and the plants. She feels the branches that connect her to the sky and the roots that connect her to the earth." Scott looked at me with a raised eyebrow. Miya turned to her and said something in Japanese, which she didn't translate. The woman stood up and walked toward us, holding Scott's gaze directly. She raised her hands to waist level and started to wave them gently, as her face settled into a gentle smile. She spoke, but the tone sounded different than any Japanese I had ever heard. I realized that she was demonstrating how she talked to nature. I could almost sense the plants on the windowsill of the classroom bend in her direction. This went on for a couple of minutes, and then her energy shifted. She looked down, bowed her head, and sat back in her chair. We were dumbstruck. How could we follow that? Miya explained to us that she had spoken in an ancient style of Japanese and that translation would not be possible. There was no denying that was a "mythic" persona of some kind.

Three hours later, when the class was nearly over, we had run out of ideas. Miya leaned over and whispered in my ear. "Is it okay if I do something to end the class?"

"Yes, please, thank you, that would be great," I smiled, relieved.

She moved the chairs to the side of the room and got everyone to sit on the floor. She didn't speak, and the group followed her lead wordlessly. We sat on the ground as she started to walk around the circle on tiptoes nodding her head and looking intently from one person to the next. She raised her, hands and the walk turned into a dance—a rhythmic pacing with a beat mimicked by her hands. The group lifted their hands and copied her movements.

"Beauty Engine, Beauty Engine," she said in a whispery sing-song voice, as she continued to pace around the circle.

"*Beauty Engine, Beauty Engine.*" After a few rounds, she held out her hand to a woman, who understood the invitation, and without being told what to do, she lifted herself up from her seat on the floor and started to pace around the circle. Miya sat down as the woman's movements turned into a gentle dance.

She chanted "*Beau-ty En-gine,*" putting the accent on a slightly different part of the word in her own sing-song tone. "*Beau-ty En-gine, Beau-ty En-gine.*" Her hands lifted up around her face, and she wiggled her fingers. The people in the circle copied her movements. After a few moments she invited another person to join. One at a time they partook in this strange ritual. At one point, they invited me to the center. I felt ridiculous and awkward as I snuck around the circle on tip toes whispering "*Beau-ty En-gine, Beau-ty En-gine.*" This was the most absurd thing I had ever participated in. What was going on? We had spent all day trying to get these people to come out of their shells, and then Miya worked her magic without saying a word and all of a sudden they were dancing around the room. By the end the whole group danced together. We ended with a collective "*Whoop,*" and applause.

Being in Japan made me feel clumsy and clueless. It's a mystery how a country that looks so similar, with high-rise buildings, televisions, malls, and fashion magazines, could be so different. There's a "hive mind" activated that Westerners have a tough time tuning into. When something needs to be done, people often spring into action simultaneously, seeming to understand their task in the bigger job without needing to be told. On busy streets people don't bump into each other—they flow like water.

Our trip ended with a big presentation to a packed audi-
torium. We waited backstage, watching the stage on the little
black-and-white TV in our fancy dressing room. By this time
we were comfortable talking about Beauty Engine. We rolled
out our rainbow labyrinth mat in front of the stage, and invited
people to walk it with us. We told them the story of the Beauty Engine as a global language to bring together art projects
from all over the world. After the presentation, sitting out in the
lobby, I noticed a few people crying. I asked Miya what was
happening; she told me it was the anniversary of the Hiroshima
bombing. They hadn't mentioned it before, but that was why
they had asked us to speak, as emissaries with a message of
peace from America. I gulped back a glass of water to quench
my suddenly parched throat; glad I didn't know that before we
went out on stage.

Afterward they brought us upstairs to a suite, where the
people who had attended our first workshop created flower arrangements to represent the aspects of the *Beauty Engine.* We
sat, amazed and humbled, as they explained why they had se-
lected each flower, placed it in a particular way, and how it
reflected a part of the Beauty Engine. A giant lotus flower
blooming out of tiny, fragile white blossoms represented *community,* with the large flower signifying the collective power of
the group. A dynamic centerpiece with flowers twisted around
a curved metal frame represented *activation,* with the many
different flowers showing all the diverse resources coming together for creative collaboration.

It was a strange tangent, but clearly they got it. They got *us,*
even if I wasn't sure if I did anymore.

243

Trapped in a Utopia I Don't Want

Polly Superstar

THE MOMENT we arrived back in San Francisco, the memories of Japan slipped like a dream after a morning cup of tea. We returned to Mission Control and the relentless schedule of sex parties, opening our home to horny guests every weekend.

Which life did I want? In Japan I felt indescribably awkward and inauthentic, but I must admit—I enjoyed the challenge. I wanted to do *important* work for the future of culture. Back in San Francisco I was a slave to Eros. I was his janitor: keeping the safer-sex supplies stocked, tucking the sheets neatly on the beds, steam cleaning the couches, and folding the towels. I was his secretary: promoting the parties on social networks and organizing the volunteers. None of it was fun for me, but at least I was comfortable in my own skin. I was never ashamed of my slutty history, but in Japan I had to hide who I was. These two lives were at odds with each other. I couldn't do both. I had to decide what was important to me.

I loved the original idea of Superstar Avatar—giving people the tools to live more playful, creative lives—but it had slowly developed over the years into something I didn't recognize anymore. Instead of superheroes and counterculture, it was second-rate self-help. It had become a self-referential, esoteric, intellectual dead end. It didn't make sense to me anymore. Even if the trip to Japan opened up opportunities, would I want to follow them? If I admitted this wasn't fun for me, then what might that mean for my relationship with Scott? Our work together? Our life together?

When I started this journey I thought that sex was the most important thing in my world. I was a rebel. I wanted to explore my own orgasm as much as I wanted to witness a revolution. It was all such a *struggle*. Then somewhere along the way sex became *normal*. Even crazy, kinky, group sex was simply a natural backdrop to my life.

But something shifted again.

I found it difficult to reconcile the parties with my transcendent experiences of sex. I didn't feel any judgment toward my promiscuous past, but I didn't feel it served me anymore. As I became more energetically sensitive I realized that sexual interactions could both invigorate and drain me, depending on how I approached them. At the parties, I rarely had time to tune in to a sexual interaction in a way that was rejuvenating.

In addition to this energetic shift, my waning sexual connection with Scott was becoming more obvious. Even if I felt good about playing, I didn't want to be insensitive and have sex right in front of him. It didn't seem fair. As a result, the play space at our events was no longer a place where I could feel comfortable.

I started to get resentful.

I was simultaneously experiencing sexual energy that was like some sort of universal, cosmic transmission, while *my* sex life diminished. I threw events every single weekend, a rotating door of liberation, but for me it was so different I couldn't relate anymore. *I experienced sex the same way some people experience religion.* What did that mean for day-to-day life? For my relationships? For my sexuality? *Wasn't I allowed to just have fun anymore?* It didn't feel fair.

During the next few months the situation slowly deteriorated. Soon, it sounded like this inside my head:

I am dying a slow death. From the outside it's all glitter and lipstick, sex and flirtation, but inside I'm suffocating, choking on all the sickly giggles and batting eyelashes.

Hot and sexy.

Come on.

Switch it on.

Your audience is waiting.

Everyone owns a piece of me. I am the walls of Mission Control, touched by a thousand hands. Don't look at me in the daytime or you'll see how I've weathered.

I have watched so many people have sex I don't even register sexy anymore. I'm not even having sex because it feels like work.

Or it feels like church.

Either way, my body is public property in this place. If one more person tries to touch my boobs without asking I'm going to scream in their face, hit them, cry, walk out the door, catch a cab, go to the beach, sit in the sand to watch the black ocean nuzzling the shore, the stars glitzing up in the sky. I'm trapped in a utopia I don't want.

I want to be artistic, do something new, tap into that raw creative life force and reach another level. Get away from the sticky hands pulling me back. It's ironic. Sex is a tool of liberation for so many people, but it's become a prison for me. I cast the line out into the shadows and caught the most unexpected gift of all: I'm immune to the magic. What does that mean? The script that binds me frees all these people.

We've reached that shimmering mirage on the horizon and found a muddy puddle. We traveled so far to get here. What now? I want to break it open, smash it to pieces, but I'm too scared to imagine what that might mean.

I had so much hope in the early days. I was a pioneer in the Wild West, blazing the trail, rewriting the script. I am filled with a million happy memories. If I think logically I can't imagine why I would feel the way I do.

Just get on with it.

Do the work and stop complaining.

The idea flutters in my mind for a moment: *move out of Mission Control. Start over.*

But where would we live? How would we survive?

I'm afraid.

I'm afraid I will lose everything.

Like last time.

Heartbreak

Polly Whittaker

I WAS INFATUATED with Ben. He was a charming goofball who always knew how to make me smile. When our relationship began it was breezy and fun. We would do ecstasy and go out dancing, as high on young love as we were on the drug.

I tried to negotiate a little openness. We didn't have sex with other people, but I enjoyed flirting and making out with people at parties, and didn't want to stop because I had a boyfriend. My first baby steps into opening up felt liberating and natural.

I didn't see it coming.

I went home to Ben one day gushing with enthusiasm about something banal, oblivious to what was happening. "I'm really glad things are going so well for you," he said as he reached out for my hands. "Listen, there's something I have to tell you." His brow furrowed.

"What's going on?" I asked, anxiety rising.

"Listen, I think I have to move out. I'm…I'm moving out." I looked over his shoulder. Packed bags filled the hallway. I had been so excited to tell him the news about my new job I hadn't even noticed them.

"W-what? What are you talking about? Where are you going?"

"I'm gonna go stay on the couch at the dungeon for a bit until I get myself sorted. This…just isn't working anymore."

My jaw sat open for a moment. How did I miss this coming?

"You're breaking up with me?" I asked, needing to make sure that what I heard was right.

"I don't know. Polly, I'm confused. Things are very confusing living here. I need to leave." Then his tone shifted, and he suddenly sounded annoyed. "Besides, I'm tired of watching everyone making out with my girlfriend."

"Please, don't go," I wailed. "We need to talk. We can figure this out."

"I'm sorry, I *really* need to get out of here. Nothing you can say can change this." He picked up his bags and went to the front door, "I'll be in touch."

A few weeks later I got a call from Scarlet. "You realize that Ben and Abby are fucking, right?" Scarlet always had a way with words.

"No they're not," I said, as the blood drained from my face.

"Polly, don't be an idiot." My mind raced. Surely this was just Scarlet drama mongering.

"Abby would never do that to me," I told her emphatically. "I am absolutely sure of it."

"Well, they're spending a lot of time together. I'm here at the dungeon every day. I see them."

I hadn't visited the dungeon recently—the idea of bumping into Ben was too much to bear. Abby went there every day, to work on the phones. "Yes, they're friends," I said. "I know they hang out. I know he's staying there. But that doesn't mean they're fucking."

"Well, if they're not fucking then I'm the Queen of Sheba." There was an awkward silence.

"I really appreciate that you're trying to help, Scarlet, but please don't gossip about this kind of stuff. It's very hurtful."

Her voice softened. "Listen, Polly, I just care about you, that's all. I don't want to see you having the wool pulled over your eyes by these cunts. Everyone knows about it but you." The last sentence planted the seed of doubt in my mind. *Everyone knows about it but me? How long has this been going on?* I remembered the look of affection on their faces that night when Bella had cut her wrists. How they seemed so wrapped up in each other.

A few hours later Abby came home from work. She seemed distant, and I suddenly realized that she'd been like this for weeks. My obsession with my heartbreak had clouded my perception.

I sat in the kitchen as she made a cup of tea. "So...what's going on with you and Ben?" I asked, straight to the point.

"What do you mean?" She looked shocked at the question.

"I dunno. It's stupid." Fear gripped me. What if Scarlet was right? Did I even want to know? "Look, I heard there's something going on between you and Ben. The people at the dungeon are talking about it. Is it true?"

"No, of course not," she looked me in the eye. "Nothing's going on between me and Ben; you're being paranoid." That was all I needed to hear. I collapsed in tears.

"I'm sorry, Abby. I just don't know what's real. I know you wouldn't do that to me." She held me in her arms as I cried.

Over the next couple of months Abby got more and more distant. The stories about her budding relationship with Ben persisted, but I continued to defend her. When she moved out of The Fort I finally accepted that I'd lost her.

Nearly six months passed, and we hardly saw each other. Then she invited me out to a meal at a restaurant, to tell me the truth over dinner. I can't remember how the conversation went—it's all a bit of a blur. I was drunk. I guessed what was coming by the tone of her voice on the phone. She said she loved me, and how hard this was. Then she told me they were in love.

I walked away from the restaurant and left her standing in the rain waiting for a cab. I crossed the road and turned around for one final glimpse: Arm outstretched, she stepped toward the curb to get the attention of a passing taxi. A car passing by drove through an enormous puddle and greasy water projected into the air. It drenched her from head to toe. She looked defeated, hair wet with dirty water, makeup streaked down her face, trying to be dignified as she stepped into the cab. I stood on the corner in the pouring rain and laughed out loud, satisfied at the universe's impeccable timing. She deserved that. As I laughed my heart grew calluses.

My decade-long friendship came to a brutally sad conclusion alongside the end of the romance. I lost the person I loved and trusted most in the world, who had been with me through everything. I guess everyone goes through some sort of heartbreak; it's part of growing up. I've never fully recovered from this one. Sixteen years later I still miss her. I don't blame her for what she did—I understand that I was a difficult person to be close to. My father's death left me adrift, self-absorbed, depressed. I was demanding and blind. I was so obsessed with my own experience I didn't stop to listen. I neglected her needs and took her for granted. I thought she would always be there.

It's a story so predictable it could almost be funny if it wasn't so tragic. What happens if you let your boyfriend make out with your best friend, and they end up falling in love? It's the classic argument for monogamy. *Keep your man close, with his cock under lock and key, or you'll lose him.* Truthfully, my desire for openness might have accelerated the process, but I think Abby and Ben would have ended up together either way.

A broken heart can be a beautiful place. It's full of opportunities. All those shards scattered about, reflecting images you never saw before. Fleeting glimpses of possibility. When your ego is pulverized into an unrecognizable mush, it becomes compost for your future. You have the chance to reimagine yourself.

I decided love needed to play by my rules. Our culture lays out the story of how we are supposed to fall in love: Princesses are rescued, hearts are won, and love is offered as the reward of every satisfying storyline. "You complete me" is seen as romantic, rather than dysfunctional codependence. The kind of fairytale love story we are force-fed every day by movies, books, and dreary songs about "*dying without your love*" seemed absurd to me. They made me angry. Conforming to the social rules laid out for me meant giving up my freedom for an illusion. Determined not to fall into that trap, I wanted to explore, to adventure.

I put my heart in a freezer, and stayed single for a long time. It was nearly five years until I met Scott and fell in love again. I thought I had it all figured out by then. I didn't even realize how much baggage I was carrying until I started to unload it.

Fuck Your Boner

Polly Superstar

"**F**OR FFFFFUCKS SSSSSSSSAAAAAAKE!"

"Polly, please. Don't yell. You're stressing me out," Scott said as he reached for new light bulb. The party would be starting soon, and our ancient computer had crashed *again* when I tried to print out the volunteer list.

"Sorry. This computer is being a *bitch*. I didn't realize you were there. I'm not yelling at you."

"Seriously, Polly, this attitude of yours will ruin the party."

"*My* attitude? *Really? You're* the one who's been cursing at blown light bulbs for the last half an hour." My phone rang as Scott grouchily left the room, muttering under his breath.

"Hi, I'm sorry, I'm not going to be able to make it tonight. I have a cold. I was supposed to be on coat check," said the voice on the other end of the phone.

"Okay, no worries, you take care of yourself!" That was the third call I had received from volunteers flaking. I hadn't told Scott how short staffed we were because I didn't want to stress him out any more than he already was.

Tired and irritable, we went to grab a sandwich before the doors opened and Scott made an announcement. "So...Kati's gonna be here tonight," my jaw tightened. Kati had been on

253

the scene for a few months—a pretty thing with dark hair and dark eyes. She was friendly and gracious toward me, which was nice, and I relished the alone time I got when Scott was out with her. But tonight we were short staffed, and I knew what was coming next.

"Mmmhmm," I tried to be nonchalant, my mind racing to figure out how to respond without reacting.

"Well, I'd like to hang out with her tonight." His tone was defensive. I looked at my sandwich, cycling through painful emotions. "I think I deserve a night of fun," he said, plaintively. "When do *I* ever get to enjoy the parties?" He looked at me with a sad puppy-dog face. Then it shifted into a glare. "*Aren't you going to say anything?*" I paused, trying to quiet the anger rising in me. But it was no good.

"Let's just recap to make sure I understood," I said with a sarcastic tone. "Instead of helping me with an understaffed party you want to go off and *fuck your girlfriend* instead?"

"I didn't know we were understaffed tonight," he replied apologetically.

"No, well, you wouldn't, because I'm the one who works all month organizing these parties. And instead of asking me what's going on and seeing where you can help, you're just making demands. What about *my* night off? When do I get to enjoy the party?"

"Don't be mad at me just because I have someone nice in my life."

His comment cut a little close to home. I had been having a hard time since we got back from Japan; I found it difficult to reach out and meet new people. I hadn't had anyone else in my life for months, and I retreated into work. I was disconnected from the community, and confused about my relationship with Scott.

"That's such a fucked-up thing to say to me, Scott."

"Well, it's true. I'm tired of your jealousy," he said quietly.

My frustration bubbled over into anger, and I exploded with rage—shouting and crying—I don't remember what I said. I found his accusation insulting, and I was mad because I knew deep down, he was right. I always wanted an open relationship, but recently I had awoken to a sobering realization: I saw the way Scott looked at his lovers, and *I wasn't getting that passion* from him anymore. After almost a decade of being together our sex life had stultified, and I have to admit that I *was* jealous. I wanted him to look at me with that intensity again, but all I got these days was tired Scott, stressed Scott, depressed Scott. He saw me as a symbol of all our failures, and resented me for it. I felt undesirable. Unlovable.

Scott doesn't respond well to conflict. He shuts down. I shouldn't have yelled, but I couldn't stop myself. "I can't have this conversation with you right now," I said as I stood up. "I have to get ready for the party." I twirled around and left him to finish his sandwich alone. Scott hates it when I walk out on an argument, but I needed to get my head together. Back in my room I cried into my pillow, abandoned and resentful. When Scott returned he stomped around outside my door, turning on lights and prepping the space for opening. I knew my time to cry had run out.

I stared at my reflection in the mirror and took a deep breath. My eyeliner smudged down my face in a big smear. I sniffed, not even trying to stop the cascade as tears filled my eyes again. My shoulders shook involuntarily as I wept. I heard a gentle knock at the door. "Polly? Are you okay?" It was an unfamiliar voice. The volunteers were already arriving.

"*I'm fine,*" I snapped. "Just give me a minute."

"We need the guest list, people are arriving." The voice sounded apologetic.

"Oh *shit,*" I said to myself as I grabbed the guest list from the desk, wiped my eyes, and opened the door a crack, thrusting the paper out to the waiting hand in the hallway. "I'll be out in a sec; *I'm fine,*" I said, repeating the rather unconvincing statement.

My room was a mess. The aftermath of a frustrated costume frenzy. Frilly panties exploded from my dresser in a cascade. Outfits ripped off hangers and cast aside in piles. My box of tights spilled over and vomited its colorful load off the side of the bed. Of the 3,500 square feet of Mission Control outside this door, these 200 square feet of space were the only part that was actually mine. It was my office, my closet, my living room, and where Scott and I slept.

I picked up a tissue and wiped my eyes, rolling my shoulders and gently moving my head from side to side, shaking my hands like a surgeon about to operate. I picked up the eyeliner and started again, trying to reassemble my face. My eyes were puffy and the salty tears made my skin sting. I was going to have to pull out all the stops on my glamour superpowers to cover this mess up. I dabbed the charcoal-gray eye shadow over my eyelids, figuring an intense smoky look would do the job. I covered my eyes with glitter, camouflaging any telltale signs of tears, and dabbed pink gloss on my lips. I practiced smiling at myself in the mirror, tuning my acting skills. The music in the front of the building began. Someone pressed play on our standard play list with a song so familiar it made me want to punch the wall.

I pulled on my stockings and attached them to my garter belt, momentarily losing my cool, fiddling with a difficult fastening on the back. I opened my eyes wide to try and prevent tears from welling up. I pulled on my boots and stood in front of the mirror again. I tugged my wig on my head. The bangs came down low, almost covering my eyes, making it easy for me to hide.

With a sigh I finally stepped out of my room, putting on a smiling face and making my way down the hallway. *"Hot and sexy, Polly, hot and sexy,"* I reminded myself, bitterly.

In the lobby the vibe was bright and friendly, with volunteers chatting and guests arriving. The doors had opened minutes ago, and guests were already mingling. A volunteer waved me down as I walked by. "I need a Sharpie. Where would I find one?" Happy for a mission, I headed to the office.

I swept through quickly so as to avoid having to talk to anyone yet, and made my way to the cupboard of office supplies. Hurrying back through the lobby wasn't so easy the second time, and a few people insisted on slowing me down to say hi and exchange cheek kisses. I smiled and dealt with the pleasantries, excusing myself by waving the Sharpie and gesturing to the bar. None of them realized there was a problem.

Halfway down the hallway a volunteer stopped me, her eyes filled with concern. *This must be the woman who heard me crying through the door.*

"Are you okay?" she asked.

"Not really." The pressure in my chest returned and tears pricked my eyes.

"Need a hug?" She offered sweetly.

"Not right now. Thank you," I smiled weakly.

"Well, if you need anything, I am here. *Anything,* you just say the word."

"I really appreciate that," I said, with just enough sincerity to get her off my back. I was genuinely grateful for her concern, but a hug was the last thing I needed.

I found a million and one things to keep me busy and save me from having to exchange anything other than basic pleasantries with anyone. I eventually found Scott out on the patio standing on a chair changing the bulbs in the fixtures and angling them for the perfect lighting. He put on a green filter and the whole garden took on a rich, verdant glow. The door shut behind me, and I took a moment to appreciate the cool air on my skin. I closed my eyes and listened to the sound of the fountain gurgling. You couldn't hear the party from out here—not yet. It was almost peaceful, even with the sounds of Mission Street echoing in over the wall.

"Did the bulb go out here too?" I asked quietly.

"Yep, it's crazy," he said as he finished the job and stepped down off the chair, smoothing his hands on his jeans. He hadn't even dressed yet.

"I'm sorry," he said as he stepped toward me and took me in his arms. "I don't know why we thought it was a good idea to try and negotiate that just before the doors opened. I am in such a weird mood I couldn't drop it. I didn't mean to get angry with you; I'm sorry. You shouldn't listen to me when I'm like that." He paused to look in my eyes. "I love you," he said, smoothing my hair out of my face and leaning in to kiss my tear stained lips.

"I love you too," I said, not needing to cry anymore.

He stepped back and looked at me intently for a moment.

"Well, you're a hot mess," he said, laughing a little in spite of it all.

I shrugged and wrinkled my brow. "I feel like crap," I sniffed.

"Let's just take care of each other tonight, okay?" he said. "Let's be gentle and loving. I don't want to leave you to do all the work. We need to support each other. I know that."

It was a stalemate with one solution—we both had to let go. As people swarmed in the doors and the party lurched forward we had no choice, and we both knew it. The details of our disconnect could be analyzed and articulated later. In that moment we had to release all our small, scared thoughts, and focus on the bigger picture. If we held on to these lingering toxic emotions, people would feel it and the party would suffer. We could wait, the party would not. My heart melted a little as he pulled me toward him, allowing the familiarity of his touch to ease my scared and bruised ego, quieting its bitter voice to a whisper. His hand touched my face as I sang an internal lullaby, softly sending that part of myself to sleep.

Suddenly the door to the patio flew open, and a couple peered out at us, unsure whether or not to come outside. They mumbled to each other and closed the door again, deciding not to interrupt our intimate moment. We laughed at this impromptu disturbance, accustomed to our most personal interactions being public, and released at least some of our tension in a gentle kiss.

The party was uneventful. I wandered around the space from room to room, checking in on the different scenes. I used to love these parties. I loved the atmosphere of openness. But these days I was always working. In the first half of the night

I had to organize the volunteers and host the cabaret; then in the second half there was always something annoying to deal with—a drunk to kick out or a blocked toilet. The events had been slow of late. I tried not to think about it too much.

The party still had a couple of hours left before it wound down, but I couldn't relax. I was separate from the crowd, and melancholy.

"Hi there," smiled a handsome man as I poured myself a glass of champagne at the bar. The tiki statue stared down at me from the bar, accusingly. The guy trying to flirt was cute enough, but exuded a desperate vibe as he tried to be nonchalant about sitting next to me.

"Hi," I said, with a big smile. It's my job as the party host to make sure everyone feels happy and welcome, but I wasn't going to take one for the team. Not tonight. "Excuse me, I gotta run and check on the DJ," I lied as I stood up and swept out of the room.

I used to be promiscuous. I used to get a kick out of sex without consequence. It was fun. I would have played with that desperate man like a cat batting around a mouse. But these days I was looking for more than a drunken late-night encounter. It seemed inane. I wanted to practice that universal, ecstatic experience, to explore the energy of sexuality in a conscious way. I'm not talking about the physical reactions—the increased blood flow to the genitals or the dilation of the pupils. I mean the *magic*. That unexplainable and mysterious energy that can flow between people. It's that kind of sparkling connection I craved. But I wasn't finding it.

Oh, the irony: I threw sex parties every weekend but *I wasn't getting laid.* I was having a hard time meeting new people, and

Scott and I *weren't fucking,* but we had to host these parties to-gether. It was a weird kind of torture. Looking at the situation from an outside perspective, we were crazy to think that our sex life *wouldn't* be affected by living at Mission Control. We had talked about therapy. We looked at workshop brochures togeth-er, and read about techniques for rekindling our connection. My confidence in our ability to push through it remained strong. Our love for each other remained unquestionable. But it wasn't easy.

I found Scott in the office, sitting on the couch looking tired. "Hello, sweetheart," I greeted him as I sat next to him and snuggled into his chest.

"Hey. You okay?" he asked as he put his arm around me.

"Mmhhmm. Just tired."

"Me too." He leaned in to kiss me on the lips, soft and gentle. We paused for a moment, allowing the closeness of our bodies to send ripples of comfort through each other.

"Is everyone out there fucking?" he asked.

"Yeah, looks like it." I rested my head on his shoulder.

"Well, how uninspiring. Can't they think of anything else to do?"

"I guess it's what they came here for," I replied.

"What about community? Love? Art? Humor? None of that seems to matter to them anymore," he said bitterly. We paused for a moment, contemplating our fate.

"I think I'm just bored," I complained. "I just want to shake it up."

"We could always just put on the babyheads," Scott sug-gested with a wry smile.

By the time we arrived in the back room we were giggling uncontrollably wearing giant papier-mâché babyhead masks on our heads. We peeked into the entrance to the playroom, and found it packed with sweaty, fucking bodies. Stepping in, we stood at the end of the beds pretending to make out with our giant heads clonking against each other. From inside the babyhead mask I couldn't see much. It was hot in there, and the inside of the mask smelled musty. I got down on my knees and mimed giving Scott a blowjob. His hand guided my head up and down. Then we found a spot on the corner of the bed, and I turned my babyhead mask around, continuing the show, but now with my head backward. I reached out my hands in front of me to find bodies to caress. They squealed and wriggled away. After a few minutes we pulled off our masks to find that all but the most dedicated had stopped what they were doing to watch our little display. We laughed, sweaty faced, after our exertion. Scott grabbed the side of his cheek with his fingers to make a squelching sound in time to the music.

"Wow. That'll make you lose your boner," said a couple on the bed, looking at us accusingly.

We laughed. We don't care. Fuck your boring boner.

Rats in a Cage

Polly Superstar

EIGHT YEARS after the first party at Mission Control, the hopes of Superstar Avatar seemed lost, and the parties were overwhelming. Pure willpower wasn't enough anymore. I became distant and troubled, and my ability to be the perky host, always *hot and sexy,* had officially run dry. My enthusiasm waned, and it affected my promotion of and participation in the parties.

I sat in my office on a rainy spring day. Shelves of papers caved in on me, as I went through the monotonous motions of copying and pasting an invitation to the various social networks. In that moment I had a realization. It might seem obvious, but at the time it was a revelation: I needed to figure out an exit strategy.

My brain whirred, seeking solutions: I could see the problem. *Mission Control.* The never-ending pressure of the events put a huge strain on my relationship with Scott. We had settled into this unhappy routine—without romance. We loved each other deeply, but how could we possibly enjoy our connection when we were like rats in a cage? We had to separate out work and play, find that place where we felt sexy again. We hosted these supercharged erotic parties every weekend and didn't explore them ourselves. It didn't make any sense. It was crazy.

What if we trained people to run the parties for us? Or found a manager to take over my job? We must find a way to pull out of this sorry situation without losing everything.

"It's time to make changes, Polly," came a voice in my head. "Don't be afraid of losing it all. It's the only way. Be ready to let it all go."

"Let it all go?" I thought to myself. "I don't think so. I can make a plan."

"If you let it all go then only what's real will survive. You won't lose it all. Just your illusions."

I wasn't ready to hear this. I shut out the voice and pushed back my chair, looking around the cluttered office, helpless. I got down on my knees and started to pick up the orange tickets that littered the floor. Every weekend this room converted into the coat check, and it never seemed to recover completely. Having a simple task to do improved my mood. For the next five minutes I could forget about this alarming proposition from the voice in my head. I could forget about the $500 rent-increase letter I received from the landlord, and the credit card bill, and the horrible review I found online for Club Kiss that called me "bitchy" and commented on how I had put on weight. I could forget about my dreams of being a pioneer for cultural change, forget about the vision of life as art, life as an infinite game. Forget about the troubles in my relationship. Forget about my failure. Just pick up these tickets, and stack them neatly in a pile in my hand.

The phone rang.

"Hello?"

"Hi, is that Polly?" said a friendly, unfamiliar female voice.

"Yes, hi. Who's this?"

"Hi, this is Heather. I emailed you yesterday. I just wanted to follow up and talk to you about the possibility of throwing a Kinky Salon in Austin."

The phone call surprised me. Over the years I had received countless emails from people looking for an event similar to Kinky Salon in their town. I kept my ear to the ground and asked around, but the answer was always the same: There's nothing quite like Kinky Salon anywhere else in the world, as far as I knew. But this email was different. Heather had been a regular at the parties for years, and she wasn't just asking me to connect her to a party in Austin; she wanted to throw one. I didn't expect her to be so enthusiastic. I listened to her talk, allowing her excitement to infiltrate into my exhausted soul.

"The thing is—Kinky Salon really did change my life. I can't imagine life without it. I would love to bring that vibe to Austin. The people here would eat it up. It's that combination of sexy and artistic. I think it would really work here, and I'd love to try and make it happen, I really would. I'm quite serious."

I started to consider the idea, and something inside me fluttered back to life: a half-forgotten dream. As I listened to Heather chatter in my ear about sexual liberation and conscious community, I remembered. The global network of parties, the sexual revolution, breaking down centuries of sexual repression, pleasure, transformation, community, cultural change. I had forgotten how passionately I felt about it. In my ironic status as sex party hostess who's not having sex, I pushed all my dreams to one side with bitterness and regret. But Heather reminded me why it's important, regardless of my personal difficulties.

Maybe somehow this might even help me.

I sat and pondered. What are the elements that create a Kinky Salon? I broke down the simple structure: The rules at the door, the friendly greeters, the funny cabaret, the ridiculous costumes. *It's like a game.* My years of working on Superstar Avatar made it seem obvious. Why not share the structure, and watch Kinky Salons crop up all over the world? Maybe even find a team to run the events at Mission Control too. Pull ourselves out of this sticky mess. Move out of Mission Control and get an apartment. Somewhere with a real kitchen, and a bathtub, and some personal space to call mine.

I realized *I was homesick.* It overtook me in waves, bubbling up from a place I had forgotten. Homesick for the family home I lost when I was sixteen. Homesick for a home that wasn't constantly being invaded by hundreds of horny partygoers. Homesick for a life I never managed to achieve. It clawed at me, dragging me under. *I have to get out of here.* The sensation took over in a rolling wave of need, which made me nauseous it was so intense. *I need to go home.* Not to England—that place isn't home to me anymore. But a place I don't know yet. A home that's waiting for me.

To my surprise, over the next few months I started getting more inquiries. *London came next.* I never imagined they would want Kinky Salon in my hometown. I assumed the people were too self-conscious to combine their sexiness with ridiculousness the way we do in San Francisco. And the culture over there depended too much on recreational drugs to understand the need for our "don't get too intoxicated" rule. But I was wrong—the proposition excited them. They were Burning Man people, who traveled across the world each year for the festival. They learned the value of play and freedom in that dry and chaotic Petri dish, and they wanted Kinky Salon.

A flurry of activity followed. Scott and I threw a series of workshops, teaching some die-hard fans the basics of how to throw a Kinky Salon. We worked harder than ever, seeing the possibility of an exit from Mission Control, if our events reached a global audience. I started to write a guidebook, based on the workshops we had created, and I built a website to share the information. We spoke to event promoters across the world, listened to their needs, and advised them on their strategy for launching their very own Kinky Salon.

In my quiet moments, self-doubt still racked my being. Did any of this have value? Was I just kidding myself with all the talk of transformation and community and healing through sexuality? Was the whole thing just an intellectual justification for hedonism? Was it a mistake to expand outside the walls of Mission Control? If I let the whole world know about the sex parties, would my dreams of cultural change be dead forever?

It wasn't long before I faced a grim reality. *These Kinky Salon chapters would never earn us any money.* If we tried to charge people to use the Kinky Salon script, they would just copy the idea and change some things around, give it a new name, and do it anyway. We had a choice—we would either hold on tight to the brand and get more involved in running the parties in other cities, or we would *give it away for free.* The first option wasn't really possible. Running the events at Mission Control already took up all of our time, and we didn't have the resources to fly around the world throwing parties.

"It has to be free. Give it away. Trust that you'll be taken care of." It was that voice again. I wasn't sure I wanted to listen. It didn't make any sense. I was working harder than ever

267

at an unsustainable pace. If I couldn't make money from this, how would I survive? I resented the suggestion. It was crazy.

One day I sat working on the Kinky Salon guidebook, and I hit a wall. I had written about the charter, and how to greet people when they arrived. I had covered the chapter on the PAL system, our structure for accountability at the parties where everyone's responsible for the person they came with. I didn't know what came next. I became overwhelmed and crippled with uncertainty. I heard from somewhere that a good way to break through writer's block was simply to write. Forget the project you're focused on and just write. So I wrote about my father's death. "*It won't go in the book,*" I thought to myself. "*It's just a way of kick-starting the writing, that's all.*"

I sat down and it came out of me like a flood, memories I had half forgotten, stitches of history interconnected in a huge tapestry. I realized that it had *everything* to do with Kinky Salon. My childhood, my family, my escape from London, my relationship with Scott, and our mad plan to change the world. My quest for family and for healing. This was *all* part of the journey.

The idea was ludicrous.

That's all you need, Polly. A memoir? That's just another time-consuming project that doesn't earn you any money. Just stick to the plan. *Why can't you ever stick to a plan?*

The Shadow of Scarcity

Polly Superstar

SENSE OF LONGING deafened me. A need so profound it made me want to go shopping. I craved to be lulled by fluorescent lights and bad indie rock at Hot Topic. The ache in my solar plexus quashed momentarily as I filled the empty void in my life with stuff. Purple glitter nail polish for a dollar. That would do the trick.

An urgent, desperate cry for wholeness permeated my entire being. A desire to follow my muse rather than my wallet. But I was afraid. If didn't cling on tight, would I end up with nothing? No love, no money, no life: a failure.

Close your eyes tight, and hang on for dear life. Pretend it isn't happening. Drink that bottle of wine and watch some TV.

Although my circumstances might be different, I know I'm not alone in experiencing this feeling—our culture supports us in being sociopathically grabby. We are told that there is not enough to go around and someone, somewhere will be left out in the cold. The only way to stop that from being you is to hold on tight to what you've got, and grab whatever comes your way. Whether you're touching someone's ass without asking or skimming profits from old ladies' pensions, it boils down to the same mass cultural misconception: scarcity. It makes everyone so needy.

Bernard Lietaer, the distinguished economist, suggested that this fear is the result of an archetypal suppression of the goddess. After 5,000 years of violent oppression of the feminine, it just seems *normal*. *"...Starting with the Indo-European invasions - reinforced by the anti-Goddess view of Judeo-Christianity, culminating with three centuries of witch hunts - all the way to the Victorian era."*[xii] He suggests that the characteristics we've been told are natural, like greed and fear of scarcity, are a powerful manifestation of worldwide archetypal shadow. That sounds to me like woo-woo California theory, but this guy was responsible for the convergence mechanism for the euro. He knows his shit.

I'm an economics nerd. It's weird, I know. But there are lots of parallels between economics and sexuality. The basic ideas of ownership versus sharing, and scarcity versus abundance, are core dichotomies in both. That cultural shadow doesn't just influence our wallets; it fucks with our hearts too.

Our economy is based on the idea that banks distribute wealth, but really we are the ones with all the value. Banks just give us the tools to trade, and claim ownership of things. If we had a money system that encouraged sharing instead of hoarding, the world would be a very different place. It's not people that are greedy; it's the money systems that make them that way.

It's the same thing with relationships. Our culture tells us that monogamy is the moral high ground. We find our mate and clamp our seal of ownership on that person. Jealousy and neediness are seen as culturally acceptable, even natural. Being attracted to another person is grounds for divorce. The cultural framework that dictates our relationships has bred a world of fearful, distrustful, possessive nutcases.

We cling like blind kittens reaching for our mother. Reason and rationality dull our intuition. We ignore the signs. Even when it feels wrong, we listen to logic. *It's naïve to follow your heart.*

I didn't want my life to fall apart. I had imagined a perfect, magical destiny opening up. I thought mystical forces guided me. I wanted to float in on a hot air balloon and have everyone believe in me. Instead, the cracks in my fantasy became too obvious to hide, and the cruel shadow of scarcity spread over me.

Fuck

Polly Superstar

"FUCK FUCK FUCK fuck fuck." I looked at the computer again, hoping I had missed something. However hard we tried, we always seemed to be struggling. The downward trend in attendance continued as our energy waned. The parties just weren't as fun when we were unhappy. We were snapping at volunteers, and the bad vibe was spreading. People started to gossip.

"Ffffffffffuck," I said again. My shoulders hurt from stooping over the computer. This isn't how I wanted to spend my Friday night, but *I had no choice.* If we didn't straighten out these books we would be losing even more money to bank fines and credit card fees. I tried to readjust my seat to get comfortable— I had a vicious yeast infection that no amount of yogurt eating or inserting of garlic in intimate places seemed to help. My pussy itched like a motherfucker.

I stood up, snapping the lid of my laptop closed. I needed a break. I jiggled the handle of the door, but it stuck.

"Fuck."

Not again. Mission Control seemed to fall apart faster than we put it back together. Having events every weekend wore on the space as badly as it wore on us, and the pressure to keep up with repairs was constant. I found the pliers sitting on the side table, under a pile of dirty laundry, and expertly maneuvered them on the broken handle.

"Brrrr." The sound came from my mouth before I thought it. Mission Control was freezing outside the cozy pink cocoon of my room. I flicked the light switch. It came on for a second and then popped and went out.

"Fuuuuuuck."

I fumbled around in the dark and found the kettle, knocking over a tiki mug and a small dusty fake plant on the shelf, but I didn't care. Tea would help. I waited for the kettle to boil. The bar served as a kitchen when events weren't happening— limited as it certainly was, with a microwave and toaster oven tucked under the counter. I blew warm breath on my hands, and it mingled with the steam from the kettle. My eyes adjusted to the dimness until I saw the silhouettes of the furniture around me—the velveteen chair in the shape of a giant shoe, the rocking tiger toy that people love to ride when they're drunk. With the pretty, twinkly lights of the bar turned off the place looked dreary. A little bit spooky, even. I scratched my pussy knowing it would make it worse, and winced at the discomfort.

The kettle reached its boil and clicked off. I poured the steaming liquid into the biggest mug I could find and dunked in a tea bag. I heard the front door open and clank closed. Footsteps came up the stairs. A chirpy whistle told me it was Scott. I whistled back. We used this call-and-response code to find each other in the expanse of Mission Control.

Things were difficult between us. Although there was never a lack of love, the resentment we had toward each other was increasing. Just taking the afternoon off relieved it. We kissed in the dappled sunlight in the park and ate ice cream and fell in love all over again. We slept together every night in a tight ball, fetal and spooning, clinging on with hope. If we could escape from this place we might be able to find balance again, rediscover our relationship.

Scott found me in the bar standing with my cup of tea. His eyes squinted. "What are you doing here in the dark?"

"Bulb went." I answered, sounding distinctly grumpy.

"What's wrong with you?" he asked.

"I'm having a bad night," I replied and sipped my tea.

"Jesus, Polly, I have to have a life," he sounded frustrated. "I just went out for one drink."

"I don't care about that; I'm just having a hard night. It's got nothing to do with you."

"Well it certainly sounds like it does. You're mad at me for going out," he fumed. "Why won't you admit it? I can't keep up with you. You're working yourself into the ground."

"This doesn't have anything to do with you," I spat. "Why does it always have to be about *you?* I'm just stressed out. I've been trying to do the books. We're fucked. You don't even know how fucked we are living in your fucking fantasyland. We have taxes to pay and credit cards to pay off and you're... you're just *fucking useless*...I just...I can't take this anymore." I started to cry. Scott stared at me stony eyed in the darkness.

"Well, I don't have to stay here and listen to this. You're the one who's fucked, Polly, because you're the one who doesn't know how to take care of yourself. You're so fucking pigheaded. I don't need to be bossed around by you." He twirled around and stomped off down the hallway. The door slammed closed behind him.

The sound of the Mission bus went by as I sobbed violently. The tiki statue on the bar stared down at me, teeth bared in a mocking grimace. I fell to my knees and howled. Something inside me cracked open, and I didn't stop it. I let it rip me apart. I bathed in that gorgeous and terrifying place where the future dissolves and you're left swimming in the unknown. All previously understood expectations became meaningless. I was at my purest, my most powerful in this place, because anything was possible. Even the scariest, most unfathomable ideas become attainable when you have nothing to lose.

After a while I was hoarse and numb and quiet. No thoughts could pierce this silent place. My exhausted body was home to a soul cleansed by fire. I basked in that moment before liberation.

Then, suddenly, my phone vibrated in my pocket. It made me jump. I sniffed and wiped my nose on the back of my hand and pressed the little green button. "Hello?" It was Scott. "Angel?" His voice sounded full of concern.

"Yeah, I'm here."

"Silly thing," he said.

"Hmm." I was frosty and distant.

"I love you, my angel," he said.

"Where are you?" I asked in a small voice.

"I'm coming home. I'm sorry. I had to walk it off." He sounded tired. "I'm coming home now."

My tea had gone cold. I went to the bathroom and washed my face, patting it dry with a musty towel. I heard the front door and stood in the hallway sheepishly waiting. He arrived with a bunch of flowers. He cocked his head to one side as he handed them to me, and then reached out lovingly with his other arm to pull me toward him. Pink roses. They smelled powdery.

"Thanks," I said, all of a sudden feeling ridiculous.

"You deserve them; you work so hard." He whispered in my ear, "Come on, let's go into the warm. It's fucking freezing out here."

He led me to the bedroom, and as I sat down on the edge of the bed he closed the door behind him.

"Don't do that!" I said, suddenly animated, but it was too late. The door clicked closed and he looked at me, startled by my sudden reaction. "The handle broke—we're locked in now," I explained. I couldn't help smiling.

"Well I'm not going anywhere," he said, "but I do have to pee."

"Pee out the window," I suggested. We both giggled. Just a little.

We sat on the bed in each other's arms. He broke the silence by cooing affectionately and stroking my head—after a few minutes I fell fast asleep. He shuffled me under the covers, and I slept curled up like a kitten, holding myself tightly. He wrapped his arms around me in a protective bubble.

That night I had a dream a lion had escaped from the zoo and chased me. In my dream I screamed, panicked, not knowing where to run. The lion followed me, slowly and steadily, across courtyards and through buildings. Its jaws dripped, and its eyes trained on me. I saw him attack people with his giant claws. They were flung sideways, bloody and broken. But he stayed on his task. He wanted me. I screamed and ran. Eventually my fear propelled me into a building and up some stairs. Trapped in a room at the top of a turret in an old Victorian house, the lion padded back and forth outside the door. His enormous claws scratched the wood. I sat in the turret, and panic engulfed me;

I had nowhere else to run. But then, in the way it sometimes happens in dreams, I became lucid. I heard a voice. It said, "Let the lion eat you." Suddenly I understood, and became fearless.

I opened the door. The huge, golden lion came toward me with teeth flashing. He pushed me to the ground and his paws rested on my shoulders, pinning me down, his teeth just inches away from my face. His hot breath smelled of meat. I watched his mouth open wide and for a moment all I saw was his fearsome teeth. I was ready. With a roar, I was consumed.

I woke up with a start, confused for a moment as my consciousness transferred from dream state to waking. Scott sat in my pink bathrobe quietly tapping away at his laptop, peering intently at its little glowing screen. Remembering last night, I pulled the blanket over my head and moaned.

From under the covers I heard Scott say, "Tea?"

"Uuuuh," I replied.

He fumbled with the pliers on the broken door handle, cursing a little under his breath, and came back a few minutes later with a steaming mug of PG Tips.

"Come on, funnyface," he said encouragingly, and pulled back the covers.

I sat in bed and drank tea in silence while Scott puttered around the room getting dressed, my mind blank and strangely calm. The Mexican radio from the store downstairs came on with its enthusiastic voices muffled through the floorboards. The ice cream cart went by outside, with little bells going *ching ching*. Trucks shuddered past, making the building shake.

I always say that my environment is a direct reflection of my state of mind—you can easily tell what mood I'm in by how chaotic my living space is. This morning I was a mess—clothes were strewn about in colorful mounds of stripes and spots, piles of magazines and books covered every surface. Powder and glitter from a makeup accident the week before covered my dresser. Little pots of color with no lids and pencils that needed sharpening piled up in the dust. Usually the sight of such disarray would stress me out, but not this morning. It didn't even register. Something was rising in me. By the time we sat down to talk I was resolute. "I quit," I said. "I don't know how it's going to work, but I quit."

Scott hid a half smile. This was something Scott had suggested a dozen times already but I didn't think it possible.

"I give up," I continued. "The more events we do the more burned out we get. Even if we could afford to pay someone to help, who would it be? The problem with this equation is Mission Control. It's too big and too expensive. I can't do it all myself. I'm going crazy."

The smile left Scott's face. "Hey, that's not fair," he said. "I work my ass off around here. Just because I'm not good at all the admin stuff doesn't mean you're doing it all yourself."

"Admin stuff? Is that what I am? Some sort of secretary? While you're off working on all the fun creative stuff I'm here making sure there's a roof over our heads."

We flared up for a moment, staring at each other defiantly.

Holy shit, this is tearing us apart.

"Sorry," I said. "Really, I'm sorry. You're right. I'm being a bitch." We sat and took some deep breaths together, and he reached over to hold my hand. "This place is destroying us. There's no escaping it. We have to leave." The words left my mouth and hovered in the space between us. "We have to pack our stuff up, and get the hell out of here. I don't want to do this anymore."

"I know," he said. Then after a pause. "How?"

"Fuck, I don't know." I looked around the room, piled floor to ceiling with nine years of my life and pictured how hard it would be to get organized enough to leave. "Let's burn it down." I laughed.

"Burn it; *yeah,* that's a great idea," Scott grinned. We sat for a moment gleefully imagining burning Mission Control to the ground. It would be so easy, so clean.

"Okay, I'm going to make another cup of tea," I said as I stood up. "Do you want one?"

"Sure."

I went out into the bar and set the kettle to boil. Even though the sun shone brightly outside, Mission Control felt like a tomb. I imagined my escape.

"We will need a storage space," I thought to myself, "somewhere to keep everything on hold until we figure out our next move. We can pack all this stuff in boxes. It wouldn't be that hard. Take the tiki statue down and put him in bubble wrap, take down all the African masks and the velvet paintings, disassemble the altars and carefully pack them away. We'll need to be organized. I'll write labels on the boxes with the name of the room and the contents to make them easy to find." I imagined the boxes and the labels, and packing them away, putting them in a truck and storing them in a warehouse; little coffins containing the body of Mission Control.

Scott found me quietly crying over my tea. "I was imagining packing Mission Control in boxes," I said. "It's the saddest thing ever." He looked at me forlornly. We held each other, like bewildered children standing by the roadside after a car wreck.

Over the next few hours we formulated a plan. Once I get

an idea in my head I don't wait around. Swift action would be necessary—if we left it too long we might change our minds, make some excuses, and find ourselves trapped again, as we had done so many times before. The first step was to announce the move to the community. I sat in front of the computer and started to type:

"It's with a heavy heart that we announce the impending closure of Mission Control and the end of Kinky Salon as we know it. After an incredible nine years of community, creativity, and LOVE, we have decided that it's time to close this chapter to make way for The New."

I Wept for All My Failures

Polly Superstar

FOR THE FIRST TIME since my teen years, I had no idea what I was going to do with my life. I looked back and saw a decade filled with hope and lost dreams. I wept for all my failures, for all the people I had let down.

"Don't be afraid of losing it all. It's the only way. Be ready to let it all go."

"Okay, *fine,* irritatingly wise voice in my head. I'm ready."

We announced that we would throw parties for another six months, with the hope that our impending closure would encourage people to come out, pack the events, and then give us a nest egg to move forward with. A couple of weeks after the announcement, when the messages expressing sadness had trickled to a stop, I received a surprising email from a guy called Jason James. He said:

"Why not give Mission Control to the community and let us run it?"

Who is this guy? I'd seen him around at parties but just as a face in the crowd. I appreciated the sentiment, but I had every reason to be skeptical. Clearly, he didn't understand what he was proposing. It's one thing to volunteer for a couple of hours at a party, but did he understand the amount of manpower necessary to run Mission Control? These party people would hate to lose their playground, but who would want to take responsibility for it?

At that point, skeptical or not, I had nothing to lose. So I humored him and let him organize a meeting. Scott refused to come. He said he was done. I went out of curiosity, but mainly to confirm my low expectations.

At the meeting, people piled on top of each other in a friendly puddle of pillows in the middle of the room, giggling as they arranged themselves. We had pulled out the pillows when we ran out of chairs. Kind faces smiled at me, row upon row. I glanced around, a little bashful at the support. Whatever came of this, it felt good to be with these people. It was comforting to be surrounded by friends, although I had to admit I didn't know the names of half the people present.

I shrank down, embarrassed by how bad the room looked with the lights on. A hole had mysteriously appeared by the door a few weeks earlier, and the walls badly needed a paint job. The archway of soft pink and blue lights by the stage hid a multitude of patches and scrapes. Once the disco ball was swirling its lights around the room the place looked perfect, as long as you didn't inspect too closely. But with the overhead lights on, the room looked distinctly shabby.

Jason James stood at the front: tall, softly spoken, with a certain boyish charm, and a flop of light brown hair. "Maybe we can start by saying a few words about why we want to help save Mission Control." A murmur of approval rippled through the crowd.

A girl I'd seen a million times at the parties raised her hand. She looked a little shy as the attention of the crowd focused on her and she started to speak. "I've never experienced anything like Mission Control before. I can't put my finger on what it is that's different here, but it feels like home to me. The parties, the community, it changed my life. I can be myself here. I'm not going to let go of it that easily." She shrugged her shoulders. "That's it, I guess. Why let it go if we don't have to?" There was a pause as eyes flicked around the room, seeing who would speak next. One at a time I heard their stories. They told inspiring, life-affirming accounts of personal growth. They gave rousing speeches about sexuality and cultural change. Visions of the raw power of sexual energy and the creative life force of the universe. They spoke bravely and honestly. A few of them cried.

"How *didn't* Mission Control change my life? Very nearly every significant friendship started under this roof. It's where I learned community, service, and accountability."

"I've actually had quite spiritual experiences here. The level of connection and love in the community is incredible. People are there for each other in a way I've never experienced before."

"I was a shy introvert when I started coming. I learned how to talk to people, a sense of style, self-confidence, how to negotiate. I would really miss the community and the freedom. Where else can you wake up naked with a group of people, start singing, and have breakfast?"

"I met most of the people I call my friends through Mission Control. I consider these people to be a big part of my extended family. I have never felt more accepted and loved in my life."

Who were all these people?

I began to understand.

"Kinky Salon was a life changer for me. I never knew such magical people existed. If I ever find words to describe the feeling, I'll let you know."

While I busied myself being obsessed with the things going wrong, I lost track of what went right. My frustrations were so compelling that they took all my attention. Meanwhile, *they* had created something beyond my dreams. *This happened while I was looking the other way.* I stopped, dropped everything, and expected it to end. Instead I found myself being held. This wasn't just about Mission Control anymore. It wasn't just about parties.

I wasn't expecting this.

"The Kinky Salon community are the most loving, genuine, happiest people that I know. I honestly have no idea what my life would be like without Mission Control."

Chosen family. Meaning. Freedom. Creativity. Culture. Love. Self-expression. Dreams. Hope. Healing. Life as art. The sexual revolution. *Did that really just happen?* I listened to story after story, and it sounded like these dreams really did come true. I just needed to stop and pay attention.

Sometimes you just have to try to break something to find out it's unbreakable.

We could leave, and Mission Control would survive.

We wouldn't have to pack away everything into sad little boxes to gather dust in a storage space. The tiki could stay smiling on the bar. The Judgmental Tiger could keep watch in the lobby. There were so many people who wanted to help. People with motivation and skills. At the end of the meeting they scrambled for the clipboard to sign up.

I wanted to streak through San Francisco yelling "Merry Christmas, Mister Potter!" at the top of my lungs, like that guy in the movie *It's a Wonderful Life*. But all I could do was smile and say "thank you," over and over again, as tears welled in my eyes.

"What are you going to do with your life now you have all this time on your hands, Polly?" Jason asked, smiling a satisfied smile as we wrapped up the meeting.

"I want to tell my story. Write a book. It's going to end right here, at this moment."

"A happy ending?" he asked cheekily.

"I wasn't expecting it, but yeah. I guess it is." He leaned down to hug me.

"Well, I can't wait to read it."

Mission Control
Changed My Life

Polly Superstar

I TOOK MISSION CONTROL for granted. I undervalued, and even resented it. I became so attached to Scott's vision of Superstar Avatar that anything less seemed insignificant. I didn't appreciate what Mission Control had become. Even when the parties started to spread around the world, when people spoke to me with such enthusiasm, I still saw it as second rate. Disappointingly gauche. A vulgar, substandard thing, to be ashamed of. A failure. But looking back now I realize—Mission Control reflected like a mirror, and the failure I saw was *me*.

The voice in my head had told me, "If you let it all go then only what's real will survive. You won't lose it all. Just your illusions." The reality that revealed itself was simple: I had worth.

San Francisco is a pioneering town, and I've learned to be proud of the contributions I've made to its culture. I understand now that Mission Control is part of a lineage of events and communities that are changing culture's relationship to sexuality. But it doesn't end here. Generations after us will continue to heal the scars from centuries of denial and the prohibition of sexual expression and freedom. As we try to make sense of our place in the universe, and how we can have a healthy, balanced culture, I believe that our relationship to sexuality will be a sure indicator of our progress.

Mission Control has become an important stepping-stone in this cycle of the sexual revolution; I can see its value now. I can see my value.

Sex Is Art, and Art Is Everything

Polly Superstar

I DON'T PRETEND to know anything, but here's what I believe: Sex is art, and art is *everything*. I apologize for going all California on you, but that mysterious cosmic force that gives life to everything? It's sex. The pulse of your heartbeat? Sex. The spark of inspiration? Sex. Electrons spinning in atoms? You guessed it. Sex. The urge to create art? Sex. Don't worry about the semantics—you know I'm not talking about the simple act of coitus. Sex is a means of self-expression that operates on many different levels. It can be physical, energetic, spiritual, and intellectual. To me, this makes it art. And making art is like having sex with the universe.

I am an antenna. Every cell in my body, every fiber of my muscles, is a tool for communication. It's not just how I express who I am, it's how I *discover* who I am. I stand on the hilltop, like Sutro Tower—San Francisco's iconic retro landmark of the golden age of television—beaming my transmission to the world. Sometimes I feel a bit silly standing up here on this hill. But I can't get down. When I try, hands push me back up.

It's scary. Sex is where we hide our fucked-up-ness. Or I have. Sex is where *I hide my fucked-up-ness,* and digging into that compost is where I find my truest art.

288

Sex is my crowbar—it opens me like an oyster, exposing my soft inner membranes to the world in words and images, attempting to tell my story through crude expression.

I've given up on grand visions, on projections; all I want is what's real. Give me *this moment.* Tender parts revealed. Truths exposed. No questions, no doubt. Finding my place on that fragile thread of history. The weight of ages giving me a platform to stand on. A history of blood and battles fought so I don't have to. The glory of living in a time and place where I can be myself is such a luxury.

I notice the stepping stones I took to reach where I am today. My father's death. The disintegration of my family. The loss of my best friend. My move to America. Scott. Mission Control. The moments where I broke apart, and then put myself back together.

Experiencing a sense of sexual inadequacy is a story I share with many women. Perhaps I wouldn't have been so explorative as a teenager if orgasm had been easy for me. Perhaps the fetish scene wouldn't have been so appealing to me. Perhaps I would never have deepened my understanding of pleasure to experience the sensations I can now, if I hadn't been so steadfast in my quest.

All the doubts and fears I experienced—that downhill spiral of years of wondering if anything I did had value. Without it, I would have never had the amazingly life-changing realization that *it was all worth it.*

A side effect of trying to do impossible things means a lot of the time I will fail. Failure is inevitable. If you never fail, that means you never tried to do something impossible.

Is it worth it? Hell yes, it is! I live for this. But is it really a *happy ending?* Kind of. I'm not going to pretend to you that I suddenly have the sun shining out of my ass. But it's four years later, Mission Control still exists, and I live in a cute little apartment around the corner with a bathroom and a kitchen, soft carpets, and central heating, and that makes me very happy.

The volunteers keep Mission Control running smoothly so I can follow my next dream, which is to tell this story. I have to admit I didn't think they could do it. But they've done more than just maintain the space; it's actually improved since we left. The whole thing has been so inspiring I decided to stick around. I still throw parties there, and they organize all the logistics—I get to show up once a month and be the hostess. It's heavenly. I actually get to enjoy the parties now.

And can you believe it? Kinky Salons have sprung up all over the world, and they're still expanding! At the time this book goes to print they're happening in Austin, London, Copenhagen, New York, New Orleans, Portland, and Berlin—beacons of sex culture. Each one is a little different, because we gave over control to the volunteers rather than clinging tightly to the end product. They're not incorporated or licensed. It's not a franchise. It's a family of events, all offering the experience of a Kinky Salon. I went to the one in London, and it felt like home. So, Mission Control really did become a central hub for a global network of parties, just like I dreamed. But it's nothing like I imagined it would be. I thought I would be in charge of it, but instead I'm in service to it.

When the Mission Control team took over and Scott and I moved out, our lives changed dramatically. With the barriers to our happiness removed, we invested time and energy in being together. We even took a vacation—our first ever—a romantic trip to Thailand to see our friends get married. We kissed under palm trees and made love in the heat of the day with the fan on full, mosquito net billowing in our rustic beach hut. It was all so perfect—the struggle, the triumph, love winning in the end. What a great story. That's how movies end. Love should have been my reward, my payoff. It would have been textbook.

But that's not what happened.

I didn't want this story to finish with my relationship with Scott ending. I've been having a tough time admitting that it does. I considered writing a different ending—it's my story after all—but I realized that being real was more important.

In April 2012 I wanted to have a party to celebrate the tenth anniversary of our first kiss. Remember that event down in Los Angeles, with the incident in the giant inflatable ball and the penis puppeteer? It seems like a lifetime ago. I wanted to commemorate the decade of deep love we had shared, and acknowledge the incredible things we had achieved together. But when I suggested it, something unexpected happened. Rather than reminding him of all the good times, it seemed to dredge up the traumas. We had been in survival mode for so long it etched into our behavior and our habits. Angst had become so intrinsic to our relationship that we couldn't exist without it. The resentments that had built up over so many years finally brought us down. It cracked. It crumbled. We never did celebrate that kiss.

Scott has been my biggest teacher. Words aren't adequate as a means to express all the things I learned from our life together. To open up, to inspire each other, to love unquestionably, to experience that love deepening, and then to *let him go* when the time came.

I've rewritten this ending many times over the past year as

I've moved through different phases. At first sadness and anger filled the pages, then grief, then surrender. In the last couple of months, I think I've reached a new place, and rereading these stories has helped. I'm ready to close this book and start a new one. I'm ready for new stories to write.

Hold Me

Polly Superstar

I WAS SITTING in the bathroom at Mission Control. The clock said 2 AM, and I was crying. Uncontrollable sobs, as if someone I love had died. I knew tonight would be hard, but I had no idea it would be this bad. Scott and I only broke up two months ago, and we were trying to be grown-ups. Our holiday party had always been a favorite of ours—we'd had so many special times over the years—so we decided to host it together. But seeing Scott leave with his new girlfriend had been too much. I couldn't pull myself together. It had been half an hour already, and people kept jiggling the door handle and knocking. I ignored them. Sooner or later I would have to face the music, so I stood up and got a piece of tissue and looked in the mirror, wiping the black streaks from under my eyes. I went over the list of things I needed to do in my head. Pay the DJ, thank the security guy, leave money for the cleaner, put the cash in the safe.

I straightened my outfit, unlocked the door, and stepped out into the empty hallway. It was late, and the party was nearly over. I walked toward the lobby, and as I turned the corner I ran headlong into a couple I had been chatting to earlier in the night. I didn't know them well. They looked at me with concern.

"Are you okay?" She reached out to hold my hand. A tsunami of emotions swelled uncontrollably in my chest. He stepped beside me and put his arm around my shoulders as I broke down.

"Oh shit, Polly," she said, her voice full of concern. "Come in here," she pulled me through a doorway into a room encircled with beds. She found an empty space on the bed by the door, and they laid me down and climbed either side of me, cocooning me between their bodies. Naked, fucking people surrounded us, lit with the orange glow of the lanterns, which cast flickering geometric shadows over their skin. I sobbed gently into their chests as they held me tenderly, allowing me the space to be broken. Nobody else in the room could see what was happening—they continued their trysts unaware.

"I'm sorry. Tonight was just so hard," I blubbed. "I didn't expect this to happen. I'm...such a mess."

"It's okay," he said. "Be a mess. *We've got you.*" She stroked my head comfortingly.

The swirling sexual energy of our neighbors surrounded us. A warm sensation started to build in my chest. Sweet honey dripping into my consciousness. The moans of pleasure increased as the energy in the room ramped up. A woman in the corner cried out as my tears stopped. I opened my heart, let the sensation flood into me, and regenerated. I buried my face for a few more minutes, breathing long and slow as we listened to the noises of the people around us.

"Thank you," I said to the couple holding me, sheepish and grateful for their support. "Thank you so much."

"Thank *you,* Polly."

We lay there quietly for a while, but then I realized I

couldn't stay there forever.

"Oh shit, I have to finish up this party...*uuuuh*.... I don't know how I'm going to do it," I admitted. "I'm such a wreck. How am I going to go out there?"

"You don't look that bad," said the woman, licking her finger to wipe the streaks from under my eyes. "Besides, that could just be your post-orgasm face. We fucked you so hard we made you cry." We all giggled.

"Yeah," I agreed, "you just fucked me so hard."

"Look at you," he said, ruffling my hair. "You're all disheveled. Your hair's a mess, and your makeup's all over your face. You look freshly fucked to me."

I didn't even know these people, but in that moment they *were* Mission Control. They were the anonymous face, and comforting arms, of the community reaching out to hold me, protect me, and love me.

Goodbye

Polly Superstar

BEFORE WE GO, I have one more tale to tell. Another Burning Man story. I've been every year since my first adventure, and I can't imagine life without my annual pilgrimage. I think of the Burn as something akin to the Telesterion, in the great hall of Eleusis, where thousands of ancient Greeks were initiated into The Mystery with secret rites: Our souls are baked. Sometimes it's hell, complete with screams, flickering flames, and demons. Sometimes it's ecstatic, sublime, whimsical and nuanced.

I walked across the desert at night with a group of friends. We were high on ecstasy, our hearts cracked open. The raw and fertile soil of our souls ready to receive the seeds of our own evolution. The city spanned across our horizon in an arc of light. Blinking neon and crackling flames opened up to a moonless sky. We were laughing and dancing our way slowly from nowhere to nowhere, when suddenly I saw the unmistakable shape of a hot air balloon on the horizon. It was lit from the inside for a moment, its majestic curves revealed fleetingly in the night sky. A few moments later, through the din of music and chaos, I heard the noise. Kshhhhhh.

"GUYS. STOP." I pointed at the horizon. "*It's a hot air*

balloon." They stopped and squinted into the distance through the mélange of lights and motion.

"Polly, you're high. There's no hot air balloon out there." I gestured in the direction I saw the apparition, jumping excitedly up and down.

"COME ON. I *swear.* I saw it." I started to march them across the desert. As we walked I told them the story: "My father was a hot air balloonist. I spent my entire childhood watching hot air balloons fly. We would go on these balloon meets where we would join up with all my dad's friends in a field somewhere. Always super early in the morning. Something about the weather being better for flying at that time of day." I had my eye on the patch of sky, and squealed as I saw the balloon light up again. "THERE! Did you see it that time?"

"Yes, yes we saw it!"

"Oh my god we have to find it. My father...my father.... He was a famous balloonist. He was the chairman of the BBAC, the British Balloon and Airship Club. He won a special award, which he handed off to Richard Branson after he had it for a year. On stage as he passed it over, he said "nice pickle," talking about Branston Pickle. It was a joke. My father's sense of humor. I don't know if Richard Branson laughed or not." I was talking at a million miles a second, stories of my childhood pouring from me. Memories of Serendipity, my father's balloon.

We strode across the desert, watching as every few minutes the balloon revealed itself, getting larger each time. My friends listened to my stories and kept up with my pace. "The thing is, *I never got to fly.* My mother wouldn't let me. There was an accident before I was born, and she got hurt really badly. She said it was too dangerous. My brothers and my sister—they all got to go up, but I was too young. I was supposed to go up when I was sixteen. That's when she thought I would be old enough. But he died. He died, you guys. He died when I was sixteen. *I never got to go up.*" I started to cry.

"Come on, Polly. You're going up in that balloon."

"Fuck yeah, I'm going up in that balloon!" I wiped the tears from my eyes and picked up the pace. Stories continued to pour out of me. The time my dad tried to skim the balloon across a lake and ended up with a basket full of mud and weeds. The time a farmer sued him for scaring his pigs. His failed ploy to get my mother to fly by amassing a crew of hot women. The time a baby bull chased my mum across a field. The way I would take my shoes off and run around inside the balloon when it lay on its side, a giant multicolor dome all to myself. The time he flew so late in the evening we missed the barn dance at the farm. The way I would roll around on the balloon at the end of the flight to help deflate it, as it billowed up around me. The way the balloon had descended into the cloud of his ashes, solemnly poured from the urn moments earlier, making his friends choke, breathing him in, becoming one with him. The last laugh. Always a joker.

By the time we arrived we were breathless and excited as the balloon gently lowered out of the sky and landed on the desert floor next to us. I repeated the stories to the man standing where my father used to stand, in the center of the basket, hand on the propane lever. KSHHHHHH. The hands of my friends pushed me into the basket, excited faces lit by the propane flame. I rose into the air and watched the city getting smaller beneath me. Twinkling lights, sounds getting softer. I held onto

298

the edge of the basket. So familiar. Hard leather stitched onto wicker. I stood in these baskets a million times. I played pretend. I wore goggles and imagined being a pilot as the basket stood in the back of the trailer. I hid, hoping I could fool them into letting me rise into the sky with my father, but they always discovered me and pulled me out.

But not this time. I was free. Skyward. The city became a blur as tears fell from my eyes down to the dusty desert floor hundreds of feet below. For a moment all my memories of my father converged into one and he was there, smiling, knowingly, looking out at the city with me, the wind rustling through our hair, that sense of freedom just to be in the sky, in the quiet. *This is why he loved it up here.*

When I landed, my friends ran to greet me. I was crying so hard I couldn't breathe. A thousand tears I never shed. They pulled me out of the basket and thanked the pilot. I couldn't stand. They huddled around me, a ball on the ground, and smothered me with love. They petted me and cooed lovingly.

"WOOOO!" I yelled. I couldn't keep it in. "WOOOOO!" They danced around me, picking me up and dancing with me. We watched as the balloon rose back into the air. We waved. He waved back. Goodbye! *Goodbye Dad!*

Never Not Broken

What are you so afraid of?

I'm afraid of being alone. Isn't everyone?

You are never alone.

What if I'm not good enough?

You're the one who always talks about being fearless.

I don't know which direction to go in.

Don't worry, you can't get it wrong.

I miss him.

I know you do. That's a normal part of letting go.

It doesn't seem fair.

It isn't.

My heart hurts.

It will heal; it'll just take a little time.

I feel so alone.

But you're surrounded by love!

What if I never find love like that again?

You won't. Love is always one of a kind. Next time it will be different.

What if I'm just broken?

We're never not broken; that's what makes us invincible.

I'm afraid.

Listen to the voice of love, not the voice of fear.

Oh, fuck. How do I tell the difference?

Be brave, little one. You can do it.

Wait a second.... Who am I talking to? Is this Dad? Is it Sparklepony? Is it GOD?

No, silly. It's me...Polly. The person you're becoming. Don't worry, the future is amazing.

The Dream

ISTILL DREAM about my dad. Usually I see him from behind and recognize the slant of his shoulders and the shape of his head. As I approach he turns around.

"Dad. What are you doing here? *I thought you were dead.*" I am so happy it's him.

"No. I'm still around." He smiles at me, the familiar creases of his eyes wrinkling as he reaches out to hold my hands. "I miss you." His hands are warm. All of a sudden the scene seems familiar. I remember.

"I'm dreaming, aren't I?"

"Yes, but that's okay. We still get to see each other. It's nice to see you."

"It's nice to see you too, Dad. But I don't understand. Why did you have to leave?"

"Don't worry, little one. *I'm always here.*"

He hugs me and I surrender into his chest, comforted and safe. It doesn't matter if I'm dreaming.

Epilogue

A S THIS BOOK goes to print there's one final surprising subplot to share. In October 2013 we received an eviction notice for Mission Control. There was no explanation. A 30-day notice was thrust into our hands, and we were told to leave. Our lease had ended, so we had no recourse available to us. We had no choice but to accept the inevitable.

As I write this, we have just finished packing Mission Control into boxes, and shipped them to a storage space. We don't know what the future holds. The crew of volunteers who run Mission Control are committed to finding a new space, and the meantime, we are hosting events in temporary spaces to keep the community alive. Who knows, by the time you read this we might have a new home.

It turns out that Mission Control isn't simply the walls and pretty decor; it's people.

Historical Timeline

Robert Lawrence, Ed.D.

1963: In the swinging '60s, it was the San Francisco Sexual Freedom League—run by Margo St. James of COYOTE (Call Off Your Old Tired Ethics) fame—that handed the hot torch of sex to Margo Rila.

1973: Sex, gender, orientation, and national artists mixed it up at Betty Dodson's Castro Street apartment.

1975: George Moscone and Willie Brown made sex between consenting adults legal in California (CA Assembly Bill 489).

1980: Professional sex educators exemplified by Drs. Maggie Rubenstein and David Lourea knew something bad was happening to our community health. An artist sweated himself to death in two weeks, and no one would touch him.

1982: The first American AIDS clinic was established in San Francisco.

1984: Dianne Feinstein halted sex in commercial public venues.

1989: Buzz Bense opened his commercial venue at 890 Folsom to a group of clubs.

1990s: After a well-publicized police bust, some of the groups at 890 Folsom became the core of the Coalition for Healthy Sex (CHS). They were influenced by the Sexual Health and Attitude Reassessment Project (SHARP), from the Institute for the Advanced Study of Human Sexuality, the K'Thar Sissies, and an AIDS prevention dramaturgic model written by Dr. Clark Taylor and Dr. David Lourea. CHS made handshake agreements to operate safer-sex-oriented public assembly events with SF officials with the help of the Mayor's Office, the Health Department, the Fire Department, and the Police Department, plus Chuck Frutchey and Dan Wohlfeiler (who represented the SF AIDS Foundation and Stop AIDS Project, now stakeholders in any public sex environments, especially those where men had sex with men).

1991: Mark I. Chester held Sex/Art Salons where everyone performed or made sex/art on stage. Queen of Heaven parties moved to the Mission, where upwards of 350 people would attend safer-sex performances, art making, and a new alternate safer-sex community love. Mother Goose, EROS, The Blow Buddies, 848 Community Space, and later Power Exchange, Black Sheets, and Apple Betty shared that moment in history. Sex in commercial venues was again allowed in SF but needed to have open doors, enough lighting, public assembly compliance, safer-sex supplies, and monitors for condom use.

1993: Queen of Heaven moved to 848 Community Space as the only open-gender, pansexual, safer-sex art orgy in town. Queen of Heaven was involved deeply in the beginning of San Francisco's current sex-as-art movement.

1996: The performance aspect at 890 Folsom was lost to commerce with sex as the only interest. Most of the groups like EROS or The Blow Buddies had gone commercial to support the larger community.

1999: When Polly arrived in San Francisco, 848 Community Space was the only venue left for gender-mixed, performative sex, art, and creativity.

2000: Polly found Mission Control and moved in on December 31.

2003: Polly and Scott threw the first Kinky Salon.

Notes

[i]   You can find out all about Folsom Street Fair here: www.folsomstreetfair.com

[ii]   Do yourself a favor and go to the Burning Man Festival: www.burningman.com

[iii]   To find out more about the work of the Sisters of Perpetual Indulgence: www.thesisters.org

[iv]   Check out the incredible talent at House of Harlot—the best latex fashion design in the world: www.houseofharlot.com

[v]   A great book to find out about the history of San Francisco is *Erotic City: Sexual Revolutions and the Making of Modern San Francisco* by Josh Sides.

[vi]   The biography of Wilhelm Reich, father of the Sex Positive movement, is a fascinating read: *Fury on Earth: A Biography of Wilhelm Reich* by Myron Sharaf.

vii Ida Craddock was an activist and a sexual spiritualist. You can get a glimpse into her reality by reading her writings in *Sexual Outlaw, Erotic Mystic* by Vere Chapell.

.

viii Learn all about the crazy history of sexual revolution that happened during the Enlightenment with *The Origins of Sex: A History of the First Sexual Revolution* by Faramerz Dabhoiwala.

ix The Showtime TV show *Polyamory: Married and Dating* is a bit sensationalist, but it depicts polyamory quite positively. Here are a couple of the many newspaper articles that have discussed polyamory in a positive light:
New York Times 10/3/08: "Hopelessly devoted to you and you and you"
New York Post 10/2/13: "3 no longer a crowd as open relationships see a boom"

x Don't miss the incredible book *Sex at Dawn* by Christopher Ryan and Cacilda Jetha on the prehistoric origins of modern sexuality. It's one of my all-time favorites.

xi This is the primer on polyamory. If you want to open up your relationships read *The Ethical Slut* by Dossie Easton first.

xii This quote came from an interview with Sarah Van Gelder. You can find it online if you're interested.

Gratitude

An extra-special heartfelt thanks goes to Scott. His willingness to let me write these stories and share them with the world has been inspiring. He never even hesitated. He understood that the tough stories can be the most important ones, and always supported me in being authentic in my writing. That's real love. My gratitude is endless.

Thank you to the people who helped me with my writing. I couldn't have done this without my über-talented support crew: Russell Gonzaga, Jason Squamata, Fer Dumpert, Erik Davis, Michele Novick, Nina Stavinga, Stephanie Pascal, and Dominic Tinio. And the folks who cheered me on and kept me going, reaching me in my writer's hole and keeping me sane: Pouneh Mortazavi, Melanie Venus Rose, PK, Eddie Kestermont, Jessica Berlin, Andie Grace, Annie Sprinkle, Carol Queen, Violet Blue, and Nifer Kilakila. Plus my family: Mum, Sam, Simon, Adam, Aunty Penny and all the rest of the clan.

Finally, this book would have never been written without the support, love, and unending generosity of Jason James, and the Bridge and Crew at Mission Control—Elle Beigh, Ken C, Charley Chaz, Pepper, Joe K, Jocko, Bix, Arwen, and Zev.

Acknowledgments

A. Lady, Aaron, Aaron Cutchin, Abigail, Absinthia, Adrian Roberts, agoodbadhabit, Alayna Rae, Alejandra Francisco, Alena, Aleph, Alex Lewis, Alex Pope, Alice Kaerast, Allison Jung, Amber Lee Baker, Amy Rasmussen, Amy Sheridan, Angie, Ann¡ie Reid, Anonymous, April C. & Dirty Bill, Arshad, Astra, Astrea, Barbara Shaurette, Benjamin Wester, Benjy Feen, Bent Haugland, Bix Warden, Blysse Burnerchic, Brandi Benton, Brenda Kahler, Brent, Brettt Roncelli, Brian Donovan, Brian O'Cuddle, Brian Shipwreck Escobar, Britt Selvitelle, Bruce Sanchez, Camtastic, Candace Locklear, Carla Riggi, Carlo Rizzante, Casey Ann Dilou, Catie Magee, Catyanna Amelie Pfeiffer, Charity, Charley & Kate, Charley Chaz, Chicken John, Chris Mays, Christian Volk, Christopher Gabbert, Christopher T Palmer, Claire, Clara Bella, Clay Graham, Coley Cheng <3, Colin Arbuthnot Fahrion, Courtney, D.A., Damien Gonzalez, Dan Ackerman, Dan Girellini, Dan Shick, Dan Sneddon, Dana Brecher, Dani Mayer, Daniel R. Sinderson, Darf Nader, Dave Ambrose, Dave Austin, Dave Kap, Dave-O, David Alexander Wilson, David Calkins, David Llewellyn Holcomb, David Wilson, Davor, Deb and Rob Reiter, Diane Gordon, Digger Keith, Dock Knowtorious,

Don MacAssdaddy, Donia love, Ed Hunsinger, Elizabeth
Coach, English Mike, Eric, Eric Lamothe, Eric Reid, Erling
Wold, Eve Killaby, Eve Minax, Eveline Darroch, Flambeau
the Klown, Frank Strona, Frog, Rabbit & Otter Lillypad,
Fudgie Frottage, Geoff, Geri Wittig, Ginger & Mitz,
Glen E. Ivey, Gregory Smith, HazMatt, Heather Alcaide,
Helen Hickman, Helena May, Hoobler!, Hot Turkey, Iain
McAusland, Ian Hannula, If-N'-Whendy, Ivy Red, Jake
von Slatt, James, James Carrington, Jamie Katz, Janine C,
Jared, Jason, Jason Grant Anderholm, Jason James, JCH
Ex-Pat-Texan, Jed!, Jeff Anderson, Jennifer Devine, Jes M
Rivet the "Little Tiger", Jesse Drew, John, John A. Hechim,
John Hawthorne, john law, John Pettitt, Jörg Mussgay, Josh
Murphy, Juan Cinco Rodriguez, Julie Danger, June St. Croix,
Katrina Maestra Voltage Fong, Kevin Bubbles Beals, Kevin
Mitchell, Kim Nolan, Kisser Of Sinners, kitten, Kitty, L.I.,
Larry, Laurence Skegg, Lawrence R. Jensen, Les Vogel,
Levi Weintraub, Lightning Clearwater III, Lisa Green, Lisa
Pimental, Lisa Sherman, Logan Mirto, Luna Xix, Lyla
Warren, Lynn Bryant, Magnus Schevene, Maika C. Hemphill,
Mancake, Marc Bejarano, Mark Everett, Mark Hogenson,
Mark Jerome Growden, Mark Pankratz, Marty Falatic, Matt
Ho, Matthew & Gabrielle Harbowy, Mcabra, Megan Rose,
Megs, Melanie Venus Rose, Mic Rawls, Micah Elizabeth
Scott, Michael Holland, Michael Michael, Michael Michael,
Michael Michael, Michael Vav, Michael Vavricek, Micelle
Novick, , Mike Marinacci, Mills, Mister Bill, Mistress Kara,
Moira, Monica Wan, Motorboat, Ms Ribena, Naarah R.
McDonald, Natasha Tchesnokova, Nayomi Munaweera, Neil
Martinson, Nelz, Nicolas Padfield, Nieves, Nija Mashruwala,

Niki Fallen, Nina Ramos Harrison, Nina Stavinga, North
Pitney, Ouchy the Clown, Paola, Patricia Miller, Patrick
Brooke McGilvray, Paul Spiegel, PaulVvanotti, Penis P.
Penis, Pete Harding, PK, Praveen!, Professor Patterson,
Psychokitty Ryan, Rafael Reynolds (Much Thump), Ramon
Yvarra (@hackmancoltaire), Rave'N Loves Mark, RCWSF,
Rebecca Holtzman, Reid Mihalko, Renee Kyrie, Rennie,
Rhys Cazenove, Rob Jellinghaus, Rod, Rodger & Petite,
Rose Marie Carlyle, Roxane Ambrose, Roy, Sabrina Veksler,
Saffery Durrant, Samantha Pope, Sawdust, Schuyler Erle,
Sebastian Hogarth Turnbull, Sex Culture Revolutionary,
Shameless Heather O'Brien, ShowerFun Karen, Sister
Mable Syrup, Skot Kuiper, SluttyDaphne, Soleil Marley,
Sophia Psaroudakis, Stanton McCandlish, Starchy, Steffanos
x, Stephanie Mufson, Stephen, Stephen Headley, Steven
LeMay, Su-Brat !!, Suzy Lanza, Tamara Li !!!, Team Jenkins,
The Crostons, The Double D's, The Greatest, The Indra
Lowenstein, The Juggernaut-Bitch, The KK Duo, Theresa
"Miss T" Schreiber, Tim Woodward, Timmy Hogan, Timothy,
Tony Jackson, Tony Rocha, Tracy & Aaron Stone, Tracy &
Don, Tracy Lakin, Uri, Vavriccini, Velo Raptor, Venus Simon
French, Vlad Katz, Wee Heavy, Wesley, Whit Missildine,
Whitney Moses, Wonderboy!, You are sooo hot!, Yoz, Zoltan
DiBartolo

About the Author

PHOTO BY TODD HARTMAN

POLLY WHITTAKER is a twenty-first-century sex culture revolutionary. She has dedicated her life to sexually progressive communities as a latex fashion designer, a creator of arty, sexy parties, and as a spokesperson for sex culture. Born in London, England, in 1974, she is the daughter of a hot air balloon pilot and a sex therapist. She relocated to San Francisco—home of the sexual revolution—in 1999. Her award-winning event, Kinky Salon, takes place in a dozen cities across Europe and North America. She recently joined forces with Christopher Ryan, author of NYT bestselling book *Sex at Dawn* to create Kotango.com—a social network for global sex culture.

www.sexculturerevolutionary.com
www.pollysuperstar.com

Lightning Source UK Ltd.
Milton Keynes UK
UKOW04f1029060315

247394UK00002B/29/P